# THE PARTIALLY EXAMINED LIFE

With over 50 million all-time podcast downloads to date, and an average of 350 thousand downloads per month, *The Partially Examined Life* has earned its place as one of the world's most popular philosophy podcasts.

Starting from modest beginnings in April 2009, the podcast celebrates its fifteenth anniversary in 2024. With an archive of over 300 episodes and counting, it has become the go-to resource for those looking for a fun, accessible, yet intellectually-substantive introduction to nearly any philosopher—including many from groups and traditions underrepresented in the mainstream English-language discourse.

"I'm a huge fan of *The Partially Examined Life*..."
- Dr. Drew Pinsky (*Loveline*)

"I've never before heard my work discussed like that, and rarely as intelligently... I enjoyed every minute."
- Arthur Danto

"I've been laughing at you for the last year... I thought that I would... go back to university and study philosophy... all because of you."
- Lucy Lawless (*Xena*)

**Wes Alwan**'s work has appeared in *3:AM Magazine* and on the *Partially Examined Life Blog*, for which he is also Executive Editor. He has appeared on *The Dr. Drew Podcast* and *Revolutionary Left Radio*, taught a seminar in psychoanalysis and literature at St. Lawrence University, and given talks at Harvard, The Brattle Theatre, and The Boston Graduate School of Psychoanalysis. He is a reviewer for the *Journal of the American Psychoanalytic Association*. He has a degree in Liberal Arts from St. John's College, Annapolis, and a Master's Degree in Philosophy from the University of Texas, Austin.

**Dylan Casey** spent the 1990s in high-energy experimental particle physics, studying proton-antiproton collisions at the Dzero experiment at Fermilab, and contributed to the discovery of the top quark. Following a post-doctorate posting, he joined the faculty of St. John's College in Annapolis. He currently leads a team of physicists developing and supporting cutting-edge radiation therapy devices for treating cancer. He has undergraduate degrees in Political Philosophy and Physics from Michigan State University and a PhD in Experimental High Energy Physics from the University of Rochester.

**Mark Linsenmayer** manages day-to-day operations of *The Partially Examined Life* and is also the host/creator of *Nakedly Examined Music* (for which he's interviewed 100+ songwriters), *Pretty Much Pop: A Culture Podcast* (featuring actors, comedians, critics, *etc.*) and *Philosophy vs. Improv* (exploring philosophical concepts "from the inside" using improv comedy). Mark is the author of *Philosophy for Teens: Core Concepts and Life's Biggest Questions Examined* (2022). He is also a prolific musician, having recorded over a dozen albums under the name "Mark Lint." He graduated from the Honors Program in Philosophy at the University of Michigan, Ann Arbor and attained a Master's Degree in Philosophy from the University of Texas, Austin.

**Seth Paskin** is a technology marketing executive, and advocate for the liberal arts in the commercial world. He is an accomplished public speaker, having presented to thousands of customers, at scores of industry conferences and to students around the country at institutions such as Reed College, St. John's College, The University of California at Riverside, The University of Texas at Austin, Tarrant County Community College and Houston Community College. Seth has an undergraduate degree in Philosophy from Reed College and a Master's Degree in Philosophy from the University of Texas at Austin.

# THE PARTIALLY EXAMINED LIFE
## 15 Years with Your Favorite Philosophy Podcasters

Wes Alwan, Dylan Casey, Mark Linsenmayer & Seth Paskin

*Edited by*
Christopher Sunami

*Illustrations by*
Genevieve Arnold & Chris Warr
with  Sterling Bartlett, Charles Valsechi & Shane Wood

PEL BOOKS

KITOBA
BOOKS

PEL Books / Kitoba Books
Nimbus, Inc.
Columbus, Ohio

Published in the United States.

Paperback ISBN: 978-0-9702438-4-3
Hardcover ISBN: 978-0-9702438-5-0

*kitobabooks.com*
*partiallyexaminedlife.com*
*marklint.com*

First Edition: April 2024

# CONTENTS

# Introduction

What is *The Partially Examined Life*? It's a podcast that was founded in 2009, by three friends who went to philosophy graduate school together at the University of Texas in the '90s. I initiated this after listening religiously to a couple of other podcasts: One was called *GeeksOn*, where four guys talked in surprising depth about pop culture topics, the other was called *Wasted Words,* which was a joking discussion of various topics by some smart folks whom I knew from hanging out at the humor magazine *The Gargoyle* during my undergrad years.

I had become burnt out on reading philosophy by the end of my graduate career in 2000 ("ABD PhD," as they call it: finishing all coursework for the doctorate without bothering to write the dissertation) but was missing that kind of reading and that kind of dialogue, and I thought it would work well in the podcast format: Not a reproduction of our philosophy seminars, but more like the "going to the bar after the seminar" vibe.

Wes Alwan had been my first-year roommate, and Seth Paskin was the cool older guy who was dating one of the professors. Both of these fellows had likewise dropped out of the doctoral program after finishing their coursework, but before finishing their dissertations. So we were all fully trained, but not fully certified, and not working in the academy. They were both interested in revisiting some of the texts we'd studied "back in the day," and made our first recording within just a couple of weeks after the idea was raised.

Wes had gotten his undergraduate degree at St. John's College, known for its "Great Books" approach (everyone takes the same classes) and its all-discussion format, where the professors are "tutors" who do not lecture, leaving undergrads to figure out how to sustain productive conversations with minimal guidance. One of our early fans was my brother-in-law Dylan Casey, who was one of those St. John's tutors (he actually got *his* PhD, though in physics, not philosophy). After he was a guest a couple of times, he joined as the fourth host. So, with the increased influx of the St. John's approach, our format became a bit more formally academic, but still free-wheeling and generally fun.

But what does the phrase "the partially examined life" mean? The original trio had all escaped academia, and so our lives were not full-time philosophy. Philosophical examination is fine and good, but making it your whole life may lead to some fundamental imbalance... or so my rhetoric went at the outset. Supposedly, our years spent in the "real world" of non-academic jobs gave us a sense of perspective that we wouldn't have had coming straight out of grad school into teaching positions. We weren't afraid to disrespect revered figures, to call bullshit where we saw it, even while admitting that these were, after all, just our honest opinions, not backed by a thorough knowledge of the relevant secondary literature. We were (skeptical) fans, inviting listeners to be fans with us, not telling them what to think, but acting as amateur tour guides through these strange realms, passing on what we could remember from our professors and our overall impressions through years of schooling, but also trying to take a fresh look.

Guests were strictly optional on the show, but the idea was that we could gain something valuable from the insight of any ordinary person; we invited on friends, people who said smart things on our website, and the occasional celebrity who took interest in the show and was likewise interested in learning philosophy. We generally don't want scholars of the figure we're reading who are just going to give us all the answers (and dominate the conversation!).

Eventually, we began to cover some contemporary philosophers, bringing them on to discuss their current book and typically also discussing the work that made them famous. But the focus was on the books that have changed the world, that have laid the foundations for modern thinking, and so we have been very selective about author-guests, largely restricting ourselves to those whose work was being actively taught in philosophy classes along with the canon of classics.

Another meaning of "the partially examined life" is perhaps more personal to me. It has to do with how self-analytically you live your everyday life. Even before my philosophy studies, I was overly reflective, preferring thought to action, but generally open to flaunting convention, at least in how much lip-service I would give it. *Religion was for idiots, "the canon" is overrated, all the current political positions on the mainstream menu are overly simplistic, if not actual nonsense, titles and ceremonies and various traditions (and most of all, jobs!) are all for suckers who haven't thought life through well enough.* But of course, however well-analyzed you think you are, there are always parts of yourself you can't see, different ways you're being a fool even as you point out and try to avoid foolishness, and limits to how well thinking helps you to cope with the business of living.

So... we present ourselves with all our flaws in these discussions, with our forever in-progress agendas and irritating quirks, hopefully letting listeners know that it's okay for them, too, to be wherever they are currently in their intellectual journey.

*- Mark*

# Notes on the Text

*This is your editor, here to give a few short notes on the text before you dive into this adventure. I'm sure you must have some questions.*

**Yeah. Like, why is "10" crossed out on the cover?**

*That's a funny story. You'll laugh. Working with philosophers is kind of like herding cats. Ask any two philosophers a question, and you'll get three different opinions.*

**So?**

*So that can make it hard to get a group project moving forward. Not that I'm complaining. If it wasn't for that, they wouldn't have needed a "cat herder" like yours truly.*

*At any rate, to make a long story short, when we first started talking about this project we were coming up on the end of ten years of the podcast. But now we're aiming to release in time to celebrate the podcast's fifteenth anniversary.*

**Speaking of that: After I waited 15 years for this book, it doesn't even include my favorite episode! What's up with that?**

*I see we're getting right into the tough questions. Well, as of this writing, there are 331 episodes to choose from, so I had to make some editorial decisions. I tried to include episodes the PEL team considered personal favorites. I also gravitated towards well-known guests, whether philosophers, or celebrities, admittedly in the hopes it would convince more people to pick up the book. For the remainder, I tried to get into some topics and figures who are less well-represented in mainstream philosophical literature—philosophers from non-European cultural backgrounds, for instance—because I saw an opportunity to fill an under-served need.*

### So you got all woke on us?

*Guilty. But don't worry, if you make this book a success, we'll put out others, maybe on specific themes. Write in and let us know what topics you'd like to see.*

### I feel cheated. I wanted full transcriptions.

*But did you, really? And a book over 400,000 words long?*

*Think of this as an appetizer-sampler. I wanted to give a sense of the range and diversity of the podcast. Sometimes that means we only get a taste of each episode. But hopefully that inspires you to go back and listen to the originals. So you can go second-guess my work if you really want to.*

### About that. It's not even word-for-word accurate.

*That's not a question, technically. But no, as an editor, I was guided by* Rule 3.

### Rule 3?

*Any real fan of the podcast should remember the famous "three rules," right?* Rule 3 *was "We shall be rigorous and exact in all that we say, except in cases where not doing so seems like it would be more entertaining." So, my version was "I will present an accurate and faithful representation of each episode, except when not doing so seems more entertaining."*

*In practice, that meant I was aggressive about editing these down into the highlights. Many conversations were two to three hours long, so a lot inevitably ended up on the cutting-room floor. And sometimes I got a little creative in the interest of making the conversations easy to understand and follow. Here's the main things I did:*

- *I removed "ums", "sort ofs," "kind ofs," and lots of other hedges, filter words, and modifiers.*
- *I removed bigger chunks of dialog when they were going into confusing tangents. (That was pretty frequent.)*
- *Every once in a blue moon, I inserted a word that was obvious from context, usually to make a reference more clear.*
- *Even more rarely, I would transpose a few words, again, to make the meaning more clear.*
- *I corrected quotes from external sources with exact quotations from authoritative texts, sometimes from a different translation. (Paraphrases were kept as is, but denoted with italics.)*

*In all cases, I was guided to the extent of my ability, by the intentions of the speaker as I perceived them. I never made changes that I thought were misleading.*

### What about the big bold headlines like this one?

*That's me talking. I inserted myself, as needed, into the original conversations to help the edited versions make more sense. You're welcome.*

### Who the hell are you to make those decisions, anyway?

*So kind of you to ask.*

*Well, like these guys, I'm someone who at one time was pursuing academic philosophy (BA at Swarthmore, unfinished MA at Ohio University) and then thought better of it. I still consider myself a philosopher, just one outside academia.*

*What else about me? I'm Black-American with Japanese ancestry, so I'm adding some much needed racial diversity to the core team here (the two-for-one special!). I first became part of the PEL family about six years ago, when Wes recruited me to do content-writing for the Partially Examined Life blog, and then...*

### That was a rhetorical question!

*Oh, sorry. I'm sure you just want to get right to the episodes. You won't hear much else from me, other than those big bold headlines. Oh, and a couple stray essays along the way.*

*Other than that, feel free to turn the page and...okay, you're doing it already, that's great.*

# THE PARTIALLY EXAMINED LIFE

*"The unexamined life is not worth living?"*

## Readings

Plato, "The Apology," *Essential Dialogs of Plato,* translated by Benjamin Jowett, 1871.

# Episode 1

*April 9, 2009*

Genevieve Arnold

# Plato (Socrates)

*This reading is all about how Socrates is on trial for acting like an ass, and proceeds to act like an ass, and so is convicted. Big surprise. On this, our inaugural discussion, Mark, Seth, and Wes talk about how philosophers are arrogant bastards who neglect their children, how people of all political stripes don't usually examine their fundamental beliefs (but probably should), why it might be better to know you know nothing than to only think that you know nothing, and how Plato was a super genius all of whose texts you should worship uncritically.*

*- Mark*

# 1 - Plato

**Mark**

You're listening to *The Partially Examined Life,* a philosophy podcast by some guys who were at one point set on doing philosophy for a living, but then thought better of it. This is *Episode Number One,* with the topic "The unexamined life is not worth living." My name is Mark Linsenmayer. I'm currently situated in Madison, Wisconsin.

**Seth**

I'm Seth Paskin. I'm currently in Austin, Texas.

**Wes**

This is Wes Alwan, from Boston, Massachusetts.

**Mark**

Let's do the ground rules—to be revised for future episodes, contingent upon our whims.

1.  The first rule is we do not assume that our audience knows anything about any of this. We're going to post links to the readings that we talked about, but we're not going to assume that you have read them before you listen. We're not gonna assume that you have any background in philosophy whatsoever.

2.  The second rule is there will be no gratuitous name-dropping. If one of us has a point to make, we should just make that point instead of saying, *You'll understand if you go read E. F. Stuckey's essay, "The Hyperbaric Chamber and Modern Stoicism."*

3.  The third and last rule: We shall be rigorous and exact in all that we say... except in cases we're not doing so seems like it would

be more entertaining.

**Seth**

Huzzah!

## What's the reading for today?

**Mark**

So, the reading for today contains the phrase "The unexamined life is not worth living." Supposedly a quote of Socrates.

**Wes**

This is Socrates' speech to his jury, which is basically about 500 people. (I think it's 399 BCE when this happens). He's been accused of corrupting the youth, and of making the lesser argument seem better (and the better argument seem worse), and of disbelief in the gods, and belief in a new spirituality.

There's actually a series of speeches. One is his defense, and interrogation of some of his accusers. And then there's the speech after sentencing.

**Mark**

And then they vote to kill him. So he talks about how excited he is about that prospect.

**Wes**

In the second speech, he can propose an alternative sentence, and says he would rather be sentenced to death than exiled. This is where we get "The unexamined life is not worth living" (38a). He would rather die than stop hanging around in public squares, irritating people by destroying their arguments.

**Mark**

For those that have never read any Platonic dialogs about Socrates. It's all Socrates going and asking rubes questions to prove his various points—trapping them into contradicting themselves, showing that they're all full of crap. And people eventually got fed up.

**Seth**

He's in his 70s. And he's been harassing Athenians for a long time. *What do you think you know? The truth is, you don't actually know what you think you know.* Eventually, he's brought up on these trumped-up charges. This is a show trial, just *pro forma*, accuse him of whatever he needs to be accused of, so that he can be put to death by the guys who don't like him.

But he's already in his 70s. And this is, in some sense, a day late and a dollar short.

**Wes**

Socrates himself mentioned he wouldn't have much longer left.

**Mark**

But he has two young kids. Three kids total, one of whom was an adult now, and two that are still children.

So... he's getting some right up toward the end.

**Seth**

Wasn't his sexual prowess supposed to be one of legend? He was supposed to be extremely well-endowed.

**Mark**

I don't know why he didn't use that in his defense.

**Wes**

It's interesting. He was well-known as a soldier, during the Peloponnesian War, for his stamina. He could drink a lot without getting drunk. He could march for days without getting tired. That's part of the legend as well.

He was celebrated in his youth, coming back from the war, but then he becomes sort of a bum. He's known to neglect his affairs, his wife is always berating him. He doesn't make any money. He doesn't provide for his children. And he's going around, walking up to the most powerful people in Athenian society, and demolishing their egos in front of a set of groupies—which is the whole corrupting-the-youth charge. (There's a pack of young people admiring him and imitating him—Plato is one of them. And there are some others mentioned at the trial.)

The other context here is that he's often thought of as a sophist, and there's a very anti-sophist climate at the time.

### Seth

Maybe we should explain what a "sophist" is. At one point it had an academic meaning, as a teacher of rhetoric. But it came to take on a negative meaning, because it was thought that rhetoricians would just use language and tricks of wordplay and reasoning to confuse people and confound them. So that's essentially what he's accused of—being a rhetorician, and not a speaker of truth.

### Wes

I always think of them as the self-help gurus of the ancient world, because they went around selling their services. And the interest in sending your kid to a sophist to study was to make him successful, someone who is going to become wealthy. Which was an idea that was offensive to Socrates. It was painful for him to be thought of as one of those hucksters going around selling spiritual snake oil.

### Seth

Another bit of context: He claims to be doing this all at the direction of "the God." (There was always a lot of controversy and debate about what deity was intended. But he's really referring to the Oracle.) But one of the things I noticed when I was reading through it again, is that he was never told what to do. He was told what *not* to do.

In my old-man guise, now—as opposed to my youthful philosophy-student guise—I thought, *Man, this guy's really obnoxious.* I thought he was a champion, back in the day. But now, it's like *What an obnoxious guy.*

### Mark

His central claim is "I don't know anything." Except that I know that I'm directed by the gods to do exactly what I'm doing. And so I'm entirely confident that I should be doing this stuff instead of supporting my family and being civil to people.

### Seth

"I don't know anything," except there seem to be a number of exceptions to that rule.

### How are the arguments?

**Mark**

There's one argument here I thought was particularly ridiculous. He's talking about the charge that he's been corrupting people intentionally.

> When you accuse me of corrupting and deteriorating the youth, do you allege that I corrupt them intentionally or unintentionally?
>
> Intentionally...
>
> But you have just admitted that the good do their neighbors good, and the evil do them evil... am I, at my age, in such darkness and ignorance as not to know that if a man with whom I have to live is corrupted by me, I am very likely to be harmed by him, and yet I corrupt him, and intentionally, too? ... Either I do not corrupt them, or I corrupt them unintentionally... on either view of the case you lie. (25c-26a)

**Mark**

So in other words, if you corrupt someone, you'll be part of a society with the corrupted, and there's a chance that they would hurt you. So therefore, nobody ever corrupts anybody intentionally, unless they're just not thinking clearly about it.

**Wes**

It's not unique to the Apology. It's one of those Platonic themes. *No man knowingly does evil.*

**Mark**

"A lesser man can do no harm to a greater man."

**Seth**

I didn't like that piece at all. When he talks about the artisans, he says *The artisans knew a lot of stuff about their craft. But they didn't know a lot of stuff about higher things, but they suppose that they did.* So, basically *If you know how to make a table, that's good. But making a table isn't a higher-order thing, it can't corrupt or influence or improve another person. But a lot of table-makers think they know about corrupting and improving people just because they make tables. And I showed them that they were wrong.* And I'm like, "At least they can make a table, what can *you* do?"

### Wes

I think most of us recoil at bumming around and not supporting your wife and kids as the highest kind of life to live.

And in a way, he's a notorious liar. Because he says things like I'm not a clever speaker. And I'm just gonna say things that randomly come into my head. But, of course, he is a very clever speaker.

### Mark

By the end, it's clear that he could have—by being a little nicer to the audience—had them vote him not guilty, or at least give him a sentence less than death. Clearly he's trying to make himself a martyr. He even says *If you kill me, then you'll have all my students* (who have been holding back until this point) *bugging you just as much, and I'm going to rule the world with my philosophy.* Do you think that's his aim there? Or am I looking too far into it?

### Seth

I guess there's a veiled threat, although I imagine the tone of the conversation to be more like, *If you get rid of me, you're just gonna open the floodgates. You should keep me around, because at least it's keeping all these other people quiet.* But the thing that's most interesting is not whether the arguments are good, or bad, or correct. It's that he's got this divine commitment to the state, and to the people, or the community, the leaders, the youth, whatever, to go around, and put everybody through these exercises, in order to either get to a truth that can't be refuted, or because he believes the process itself is virtuous.

And that's the thing that I find shocking and interesting. Imagine that today, somebody said *In order to make this a better place to live, I'm gonna attend all these city council meetings. And anytime*

*anybody talks about land development, or clean water, or light rail, or*
*anything like that, I'm just going to grill them until they're confused.*

### Is there anything you actually like about Socrates?

**Wes**

Now that we've reconvicted him... First of all, there's this idea
that he knows only that he knows nothing. Which is awesome,
something very foundational to philosophy.

One of the things he's accused of is delving into everything
under the earth, and in the heavens—being a natural philosopher
in the spirit of Anaxagoras. He says he has nothing to do with those
things. He's not interested in being a scientist and establishing facts
about the external world. So in a way, it's definitive of what it means
to be a philosopher, because it's a critical activity.

And the idea is that you can do all this stuff reflectively is a pretty
radical idea. In one sense, it's a very modest claim to say "I know
nothing." On the other hand, you can write volumes about what you
"don't know," in the sense that there's a rich, expansive world of the
subject, and what it means to be a subject, and identity, and the idea
of virtue.

**Seth**

It's a novel, new way of thinking, a new way of approaching
things where he's looking for truth someplace different than in the
gods, in natural philosophy, in poetry, in rhetoric, and so forth.
He's undertaking an activity, which is extremely unusual, creating a
space for this type of reflective philosophical thought.

### Let's talk about that "examined life" idea.

**Mark**

Maybe first deal with that in the narrow sense that he proposes
it. He thinks this specific sort of self-critique, and ripping down your
fundamental assumptions, is necessary. It's not even worth being
alive unless you do that.

So the hordes of people who have not heard him are leading
useless lives unless they've independently come up with the same

thing.

**Seth**

I think there's a little bit more meat than that:

> ...to discourse daily about virtue, and of those other things about which you hear me examining myself and others, is the greatest good of man... the unexamined life is not worth living... (38a)

So, to undertake this activity itself is the greatest good, but I don't think it's the only good nor that you do it to the exclusion of all other things, like he did.

**Mark**

I think it does imply that it's a necessary activity. Unless you know what the good is, you can't be doing the good consistently.

**Seth**

True. But what I'm hearing him say is *You need to undertake the activity of examining what you believe, or examining what other people tell you, and you need to do that regularly.* And people who don't do that, it's not worth them living. Which I'm not 100% sure I agree with.

**Mark**

That could be one of the exaggerations for dramatic effect.

**Seth**

Didn't the Athenians still have slaves at this time? So there were probably people who could afford to spend all day examining their lives if they wanted to, including Plato.

But, in today's day and age, we have a different kind of society. So if he just says *Every day, or at least every other day, you should meet with like-minded people, and discuss virtue, good action, politics, art, and so on, hopefully with the goal of getting to some sort of truth,* we can talk about that. If you don't take the time to do *that,* then you need to re-examine whether your life is worth living.

**Mark**

Even for someone like myself, who was into this enough to be in grad school, I've noticed the amount of philosophical questions involved in my talking has gone down a great deal. And it's not just because I'm not reading philosophy as much. It's because when they do come up it's like *Well, we've covered that ground before.* Unless there's a specific practical problem for us to deal with, there seems to be no point.

But you're saying this has to be a regular thing, where you renew yourself. I can certainly see the value of thinking about the state of your life on a regular basis, but I wouldn't call it a search for virtue.

## Speaking of virtue...

**Wes**

Interestingly enough, the youth that he's accused of corrupting haven't really gone down. Plato, of course, was interested in all this stuff. But he never became like Socrates. He didn't give up all his money and live in poverty.

**Mark**

Let's just make another clarification. For the completely uninitiated, the author of our reading is Plato. You don't think this is necessary?

**Seth**

It's absolutely necessary.

**Mark**

Somebody needs this.

He's writing about his teacher, Socrates. So these are supposedly things he overheard Socrates talk about. But it's clear with Plato's later writings that even though he uses the character of Socrates, he's not giving Socrates' philosophy anymore.

So in Plato scholarship, there's this whole division between the early dialogs, about what Socrates actually said, versus the later Plato things, which are probably just more Plato talking about himself.

**Wes**

Isn't it crazy for someone to say that the mere act of being contemplative is the best thing in life? Conan the Barbarian would say it's *crushing your enemies, seeing them driven before you,* and so on.

### Seth

You still have to cook dinner every night. There's a certain amount of practical action that's necessary every day to move the world forward, for people to continue to live. The tension I feel in this particular dialog is that it draws a stark line between the extreme of Socrates saying *I'm just going to wander around, neglect everything, and spend all my time thinking about how I can't come to a definitive truth* and the kind of the people who might be interested in doing that for half-an-hour, and then have to get back to work.

I think the activity has value. But saying "The unexamined life is not worth living" may be a bit extreme. In my life, I've been able to take the process that comes from examination and discourse, and apply it to all kinds of topics. At the end, what I'm going for is not absolute truth, but instead, some kind of pragmatic state, where you can impel action or move forward. Right? It doesn't really matter whether you're right or wrong about the thing you're discussing, as long as you get to a point where you can make an acceptable decision about what correct action to do—or what action to move forward with.

### Wes

I only want to do things that are useless, which seems like an odd thing to say. When we were together at the University of Texas, studying this stuff, I was tormented by the idea that this was all bullshit. And totally impractical. And completely pointless. I knew I was attracted to it. But I knew also that there was no prestige to be gained from it, no money. And that you weren't going to answer any of these questions. Socrates himself doesn't seem to think you're going to answer any of these questions, you're just going to go about confirming your own ignorance.

We could talk about all sorts of pragmatic consequences—the kinds of thing that they use to lure undergraduates into the liberal arts program.

**Mark**

You'll be able to write clearly.

**Wes**

You'll be able to go into a business program, you'll gain analytical skills...

**Mark**

Law schools will love you.

**Wes**

Logical, critical thinking skills, and writing, and the pure pleasure of the contemplative life.

The modern version of the examined life—which is something that a lot of people do—is going to therapy. It's reframed in terms of the idea of health, which is our modern idea of what it means to be virtuous.

**Seth**

I always wanted to do philosophy. At the time, I was an arrogant, obnoxious prick, and it seemed well suited for that kind of temperament... which turned out to be true. But I always thought that studying philosophy was valuable.

I had this idea that philosophy started off as everything, and they kept carving off small pieces of it, and turning them into sciences. You see natural sciences, and then the other kinds of sciences, and psychiatry and linguistics in the 19th and 20th century, and philosophy was the original, that still asked the critical questions.

But the problem was that you kept getting to the point where there was no way to resolve the decision. If you get down to a certain level, some people agree with one, some people will agree with the other, and you get stuck at an impasse. What I've found is that the judicious application of the process of reasoning to practical matters has made me extremely effective in my life, and in my professional role. The reason I tell everybody to not go to business school, and to get a liberal-arts education, is precisely because you learn how to discriminate arguments and facts from opinions and beliefs. As long as you're able to apply that to a wide variety of things, you'll be successful.

The thing about therapy is that it's very centered on the individual. You don't go into therapy to talk about the nature of truth. So there's still that gap. There isn't a public forum to have the examined life in this day and age.

### Mark

You guys both gave an origin story, so let me do the equivalent. I started in philosophy as a sort of religious quest for knowledge. The idea was very much like Plato has, that you can't do the right thing, unless you know what the right thing is. And you can't know what the right thing is, until you have a conception of what "the right thing" means. You have to do meta-ethics before you could do ethics. And before you do that, you have to know metaphysics. You have to know whether there's a God or not, or if there is no God, then is there any sense in which you should do anything or not?

I really thought we have to answer the basic metaphysical questions about the structure of the universe and stuff before we can even figure out what job to pick. And so I was convinced that every adult I had any contact with was fundamentally clueless, because surely they had not discovered these profound things. And so had chosen their shitty job at being a cafeteria lunch lady or business person without the requisite reflection.

Certainly in religious matters, you get to a point where you can't convince other people. I think that's what Seth was saying. But I got to a point where I could convince myself. I figured out how likely I thought the various things were, and so, by the middle of college I figured out my spiritual journey far enough, reached my endpoint.

At that point, doing philosophy and reading more about these things, and arguing these things is a kind of fun.

*Is it the content of our beliefs that matters?*

READINGS

Aristotle, *Metaphysics*, translated by C.D.C. Reeve, Hackett, 2016.

Kant, *Critique of Pure Reason*, translated by J.M.D. Meiklejohn, 1872.

Plato, *Five Dialogues*, translated by G.M.A. Grube, Hackett, 1981.

Plato, *Republic,* translated by John Llewelyn Davies and David James Vaughan. Wordsworth Classics of World Literature, 1997.

Plato, *Theaetetus,* translated by M. J. Levett, revised by Myles Burnyeat, edited by Bernard William, Hackett Classics, 1992.

# Free Speech & Socratic Ignorance

*2001*

*Chris Warr*

## Wes Alwan

*W*es never sent me a description for this essay. So instead, please enjoy this heartwarming "portrait of the philosopher as a young man."

*- Editor*

# Free Speech

Is it the content of our beliefs that matters? Perhaps our reasons for having them matter more. But then it is perhaps our willingness to remain uncertain that matters most. That willingness, after all, may have the most benevolent human consequences. Those who remain doubtful about moral and political truths, for example, are probably less likely to wish to impose them on others, including by violent force. Perhaps our best reasons for favoring a skeptical rather than dogmatic disposition are the historical costs of dogma: At the political level these costs include the tremendous human suffering caused by totalitarian regimes and tyranny in general.

Besides these practical considerations, there is no demonstration as to whether or not a skeptical disposition is better than a dogmatic disposition. Arguably a skeptical disposition is, in the beginning, just an inquisitive disposition, or an inclination for inquiry. In that sense skepticism must begin as a faith in reason and dialogue, despite the fact that dialogue will quickly reveal the problematic nature of things. It does so through a dialectical pruning away of possible truths as inadequate hypotheses.

Hence when the preeminent practitioner of dialectic, Plato's Socrates, concludes that he knows only that he knows nothing, it is worth noting that this knowledge begins with a significant sort of faith. Socrates' conclusion also implies that he has gained some comprehension of what it means to know, and that he has tested and discarded enough of his opinions to conclude that he has no other knowledge. But then again, Socrates' understanding of knowledge will be tied very closely to his faith in reason, and so will his dissatisfactions with various attempted explanations of the world. In fact, the failure of explanation is a way of describing a failure to encounter explanations that are both consistent and not subject to further questioning. Future tests, after all, are as inexhaustible as the world and the imagination. But these facts may have much to do with the nature of questioning. Hence knowledge of one's ignorance and the skeptical disposition flow very naturally out of faith in reason and dialogue, which may be described as a commitment to the *dialogic principle.*

The political manifestation of the dialogic principle is freedom of speech. Societies that embrace this principle may be called open or liberal societies, for they leave open to discussion the question of the best way to live. In such societies, for example, government does not promote one religious faith and ban others.

One might argue that liberal societies indeed have answered the question of the best way to live. Liberalism and "freedom of speech" may just be one sort of dogma. Members of open societies need not be skeptical or thoughtful to embrace the notion of freedom of speech. This observation leads me back to my original question concerning the irrelevance of the content of people's beliefs; it may be that even a commitment to the dialogic principle is in some sense not relevant. After all, many tyrannies have been instituted in the name of democratic principles. Theoretical fascist may be liberal in his practical life, and theoretical liberal quite intolerant, cavalierly (and ironically) discarding certain views as "fascist" without any reflection. Hence liberalism itself may represent just another sort of political imposition, and might even be construed as a kind of tyranny.

But all this is to say that a skeptical disposition and a commitment to the dialogic principle are not the same as their avowal. The commitment is better shown than avowed. Unlike its dogmatic alternatives, the dialogic principle is not a theory about the world but a critique of our engagement with the world. If I feel puzzled by things, I can know that I feel puzzled by them regardless of how things really are. In this sense the dialogic principle is akin to Descartes' privileged access to his cogitations, even when he has experimentally doubted everything else. If I believe that everything is uncertain, at least I know my own lack of certainty.

Similarly, the political manifestations of the dialogic principle are often critical, negative, and reflexive. For example, the Constitution of the United States reads more as a series of restrictions on the government itself rather than as a list of commandments for its citizens: *Congress shall not....* This is to say that liberal society strives to provide the minimum constraints required for political existence. Ideally liberal governments strive to make the fewest possible choices when it comes to concrete social alternatives and even allow for a maximization of the number of possible social forms. In this sense liberalism is more a negative critique of political engagement than a robust proposition. And after all, there is something perverse about claiming, for example, that a failure to enforce a uniformity of religious practice is itself a kind of imposition—as if a failure to bother people on the street was an imposition of a not-being-bothered upon them.

Hence societies that embrace the dialogic principle may become political containers for various social forms, including dogmatic alternatives. And adherents of various alternatives may indeed be dissatisfied with the failure of the law to reflect their alternative. They may advocate this alternative, and they may even advocate limits to competing advocacies or to advocacy itself. In that sense the dialogic principle can be dangerous to itself, depending on the political clout that dogmatic alternatives gain. (Socrates' death is itself one poignant example of how the dialogic principle may be self-terminating). Indeed, because the dialogic commitment is about behavior rather than avowal, it cannot survive even its own elevation to the level of dogma.

But beyond dissatisfaction with an absence of legal regulation of speech, many adherents of various dogmatic alternatives will be especially dissatisfied with the social impositions of an open society. For instance, the ubiquity of television and computers or certain kinds of popular culture have very real social consequences. People are not immune to their environments, and they are not immune to influences that in closed societies might be regulated. Further, even those with skeptical dispositions may come to see certain social forms as quite dangerous to liberalism and to freedom of expression even in the absence of their political triumph.

Open societies inevitably contain contradictory social orthodoxies with regard to freedom of expression. On the one hand a respect for speech may reflect a respect for truth—a willingness to talk about and hence seek out the truth. On the other hand, even the social glue of society often entails a cavalier treatment of facts in favor of an emotional attunement to others. I spend the bulk of my day using words whose import has nothing to do with their meaning: Small talk is all about tone, and the whole catalog of our politenesses and inquiries about each others' days carries the same translation, best represented by a large "plus sign." The nuances of the plus sign include "I care about you," "I like you," "I will help you," and so on, and they are testaments to the amount of effort it takes to smooth over the various and potentially dangerous irritations of daily life. They amount to the claim: "You are more important than *the way things actually are,* including the negative moments of my emotional flux and your actual weaknesses." It is a sacrifice we make for others if we care about them: We say things we don't quite mean, show our open palms, and generally make ourselves vulnerable so that they will not be threatened. In doing so, we often willingly sacrifice the truth, including threatening truths about our natural advantages over others and our negative reactions to them.

Without the constant flow of calming symbols, fears may surface and peace may be endangered. If we are socially well-adjusted, we are less in-tune to descriptive rather than emotional truths in our daily life; we instinctively try to make others around us feel good and know that we care, even during those lapsing moments when all we feel is irritation or apathy. Hence the calming flow is full of untruths—little white, noble lies. Perhaps, as Nietzsche claims, untruth is not merely a basic social need but a "condition of life."

But even this sacrifice of small truths grounds our ability, in other circumstances, to freely express thoughts about the truth. It means that we respect both humanity and the truth more than the feeling of certainty, and it is essentially a compassionate impulse that ultimately suggests to others that we will respect their expressions even when they disagree. Compassion is part of the foundation of the dialogic principle, because by tolerating and discussing incompatible views we increase our chances of getting closer to the truth.

But here again, even the social foundations of the dialogic principle can be dangerous to its realization. We may come to believe that reassuring others is more important than the truth even when it comes to intellectual rather than social activity. Social favors may become political favors, and political favors can become the trend in philosophical dialogue and even artistic expression. It may be asked of us that we overvalue one part of the dialogue based on its political or ethnic origins; or we may be told that the only way to evaluate pieces of the dialogue have to do with the extent to which it elevates certain favored classes of people. We may be asked to disregard the truth entirely. We may even be told that there is no truth.

Such views represent the self-immolation of the dialogic principle via the exaggeration of its compassionate, skeptical aspect. Our likely distance from the truth is not the same as the notion that the truth is unimportant, or does not exist. The danger here is the seepage of social obeisance and the habits of personal interaction into serious discourse. Its result is a willingness to ignore the blatant self-contradiction of relativism.

We can choose to ignore the law of non-contradiction. It is difficult to offer the required transcendental proof, although Aristotle may have succeeded in *Metaphysics Gamma*. What we can't ignore is the subtle Aristotelian implication that without a respect for consistency we cannot speak, *at least in any way where we have an established method for avoiding violence.* Without a respect for consistency and hence the existence of truth, there is no means for arbitrating that part of the dialogue which concerns the course we take collectively. We are left mute in our rejection of the law of contradiction—left to drums, left to marching, and left perhaps to force. Relativism offers no established way for avoiding violent resolutions to political questions, and at the political level it offers no hope of avoiding tyranny. Respect for reason and truth may constitute a faith, but they are also hypotheses that can be tested by the negative and very real political consequences of their rejection. A faith in the existence of the truth is part and parcel of the dialogic principle's entailment that we are ignorant of the truth.

Hence while the extension of social and political favors to serious dialogue and artistic expression often masquerades as a friend of the dialogic principle, it is actually quite hostile to it. As I noted above, there is reason to believe that the dialogic principle cannot survive its own elevation to the level of dogma. The compassionate aspect of the dialogic principle—including the willingness to hear the voices of groups of human beings who have traditionally been allowed no part in public discourse—may easily transform itself in the willingness to take some sort of vengeance on those thought to be part of traditionally more powerful groups. Likewise, the skeptical aspect of the principle may be transformed from humility concerning our relationship to truth to an open and dogmatic hostility to the very notion of truth, especially when the truth interferes with the image of a new favored class. In other words, the dialogic impulse is as susceptible to tyrannical overthrow as philosophical instincts are to sophistic ones.

Perhaps the self-immolating danger of the dialogic principle is best represented by the story of the goose that laid the golden egg. It is the attempt to overcome the limited nature of the fruits of openness that can destroy them; to guarantee freedom we would have to institute certain controls that do away with freedom. In reaching out for something unlimited, we destroy our limited good.

Kant describes a similar plight for philosophy: we may do serious damage to our philosophical endeavors, or alternately to faith, by supposing that our scientific endeavors are unlimited. We can, according to Kant, have access to the ultimate causal and hence epistemological boundaries of things only via faith and thought; there is no scientific knowledge to be had of God and Soul, and treating them as knowable objects of experience (which is to say, something like objects for empirical science) leads to various contradictory notions concerning their existence and nature. Human consciousness, for example, is not an object within sense experience. An eye may be an object of sensation, but a sensation cannot itself be such an object. My private consciousness is felt as the medium of objects, and other consciousnesses are merely inferred and extrapolated. They are not objects for science, and while they are invisible their existence is not subject to proof or disproof—neither, if Kant is right, is God's. Treating God as an object within experience evokes the biblical idolatry of the golden calf. It also evokes the Ark of the Covenant—that is, the temptation to put God in a box and ride him into battle. These are dogmatic and potentially tyrannical impulses.

In part, Kant is teaching a respect for the ineffability of *form*. The formal characteristics of things are not themselves "objects" in the typical sense; that is why talking about them becomes a philosophical, problematic enterprise. The corresponding problem in philosophical logic is recognized by Frege in his distinction between sense and reference. But the history of 20th century philosophy includes some hubristic attempts to overcome Kant's version of the dialogic principle with arbitrary fiat. For Bertrand Russell, it is enough to create a rule that because some formal objects are not scientific objects we ought not to talk about them at all. Such a rule allows us to escape corresponding problems in mathematical logic and set theory, including the paradox of the set of all sets being a member of itself. It also means we ought not to have philosophical discussions, except for those which show philosophy to be a foolish enterprise. Wittgenstein was more modest in his distinction between what we can show and what we can say, preserving the sense of what is mysterious and problematic in the inaccessibility of form.

This is to say, philosophical talk may, strictly speaking, be nonsense, insofar as it is not offering objective and empirical theories. But as I noted above, it is a privileged and useful sort of nonsense. Kant's *Critique of Pure Reason* is an involved description of the structure of human ignorance. An acknowledgment of our cognitive limitations, strictly speaking, involves us in talk about talk, rather than about the empirical world. But the alternative is dogmatic hubris and its political consequences—forgetfulness about the problematic nature of form, whether cognitive or political.

Plato is, of course, also concerned with our access to form. *Eidei*, after all, are said to be *invisible*; Plato is concerned with the same banishments from the empirical realm as Kant. Knowledge of one's ignorance includes the repeated experience—via dialogue—of producing accounts of things that are scientific in their aspirations but more like stories in their results. In other words, thinking is reproductive in character. In *Theaetetus*, Plato describes the failure of these reproductions—mere images, opinions, or perhaps idols—as stillborn children that fall short of what they are meant to represent, the *ontws ontos* (really real).

Hence the dialogic principle includes a respect for *form* and its ineffability, as well as a respect for the inevitable *artfulness* of our attempts to deal with formal truth. We end up, after all, writing books and metaphorical stories—we end up producing likenesses that fall short of the truth by being merely words about the truth and not the truth itself. One way of embracing this tragic fact is to write, as Plato does, *stories about philosophy*. And of course, Plato's protagonist Socrates is himself unabashed in his use of mythological stories to explain certain philosophical problems.

Ideally we would banish such artfulness because of its failings in relation to the *ontws ontos*. Similarly, in the ideal political order we might banish art, as does Plato with grand irony in *The Republic*. But Plato's republic is an otherworldly order, and tellingly it begins as an artful metaphor for the soul. It is an otherworldly order in the sense that the *ontws ontos* is not the possession of living human beings. Philosophy is like dying, according to Socrates in the *Phaedo*, because the dialogic principle and subsequent failed philosophical attempts lead us to believe that knowledge of anything but our own ignorance is not an experience of this world; at best, it is limited to afterlife and pre-life. (Nietzsche also skillfully describes the ascetic and nihilistic qualities of the search for truth, and it is worth mentioning again that so much of our daily life requires untruth). So while the *Republic* may represent the artless, truth-engaged horizon of political endeavor, it must be given to us in an artful and dialogic container free of political banishment or control. It is not surprising that as *eidei* are banished from the empirical realm, the political ideal banishes the mimetic. It is a way of recognizing a certain incompatibility. But arguably it lends itself to the more general notion that political orders of *this world* ought not to *possess* the artistic activities of its citizens any more than the empirical realm possesses Kantian *noumena* or the *ontws ontos*. Fascist governments do not get rid of art and speech, they control it.

But again, in an open society it is the social order's political aspirations, rather than legal regulation, that become dangerous to genuinely free expression. Art may come perniciously under the sway of various social and political pressures and trends. One way that the adherents of socially conscious art argue in favor of such pressure makes use of a historicizing, relativist theory to the effect that artists are never really free of those pressures anyway. Many adherents value art merely for its anthropological value—for the ways in which it reveals cultural influence. They seem less in tune to or excited by those parts of great works that seem to be free—that seem to break the bonds of the here and now to offer us some fundamental vision of our basic humanity. Some seem enamored with control, extrapolating from a pseudoscience of historical determinism to the consolation that while we may not be free in our artfulness, we can be powerful in our political control of that artfulness. The same people would balk at the notion that the government controls artistic expression, but they have no qualms about subjecting their own expressions and the expressions of others to political projects.

In the meantime, it is forgotten that it is the potential for freedom that is precisely the ennobling element of art. Ideally, mimesis is just as respectful of its various content, ugly and beautiful, as is the liberal political order; it also allows for the maximization of social forms. We need our villains as well as our heroes, just as for psychological health we need to have access to the full range of our emotions, negative and positive. One of the boons of art is the ability to express and observe even our worst instincts with some sort of detachment. We need in art to see the full range of human emotional life, unshackled by the instinct for political pamphleteering or the willingness to interpret characters as political statements dangerous or beneficial to one's cause. It is far better to empathize with Milton's Satan than feel outraged by some gratuitous literary martyrdom of an oppressed class. At least Satan isn't trying to manipulate us.

Political insertions fare no better in art than do objects of faith in the realm of scientific experience and natural law, or human beings in tyrannical societies. Artistic mimesis overcomes the ineffability of form by showing rather than referring to it. That includes the privileged access that literature gives us to other fictional minds, and its unique role, as Faulkner noted in his Nobel acceptance speech, in facilitating compassion.

Hence a respect for form implies a respect for human beings—that is, for their humanity and limitedness. It is something like a Kantian respect for formality and the experiential (and hence scientific) inaccessibility of the human soul, and for our only means of access to other souls, compassion. It is fundamentally an instinct for decency, and a willingness to say that no seeming truth or scientific consideration ought to be cherished at the expense of human beings. It is a transcendental argument of sorts: we are bound to love just as we are bound to faith, because, to say the least, this life may have nothing better to offer.

*The original trio: Wes, Mark & Seth*

*What effect should the* avant-garde *have on our understanding of what art is?*

## Readings

Danto, Arthur C., *The Philosophical Disenfranchisement of Art,* Columbia University Press, New York, 1986.

Danto, Arthur C., *Connections to the World: Basic Concepts of Philosophy,* University of California Press, Berkeley, 1989/1997.

Hegel, *The Phenomenology of Spirit,* translated by J.B. Baillie, 1910.

Kant, Immanuel, *Critique of Judgment,* translated by Werner Pluhar, Hackett, 1987.

Plato, *Republic,* translated by John Llewelyn Davies and David James Vaughan. Wordsworth Classics of World Literature, 1997.

# EPISODE 16

*March 17, 2010*

Chris Warr

# DANTO (KANT, HEGEL & PLATO)

*I understand you may not have heard of Danto, and you may think modern art is goofy, but you'll definitely enjoy this discussion and the reading anyway.*

*Note that Danto, himself, listened to this episode... and liked it!*

*- Mark*

# 16 - Danto

**Mark**

Hey, we're going to give a new introduction to a reissued episode, on Arthur Danto.

### Can you get some digs in at academic philosophy first?

**Seth**

Yeah. Some listener had said *You guys seem pretty angry and disgusted with philosophy. Like, why do you hate it so much?* And the net for me was that I don't hate philosophy. I just didn't want to do academic philosophy. I haven't even been connected to academic philosophy in any meaningful way for many years now. So maybe it's just blooming with creative thinkers who are not simply engaging articles full of jargon, and having disputes over minutiae with each other.

### Mark, what was it you said about your tendency to get lost in philosophy?

**Mark**

I just have kind of an addictive personality like that. I guess it's better vented on something like this, then say, smack.

### Smack?

**Mark**

Marcel Duchamp refers to art as an "addictive drug." There are many people that treat philosophy the same way. Wittgenstein described it as the fly trying to get out of the fly bottle.

## So then why are we doing this again?

**Seth**

This is still my favorite episode. Precisely because it restored my faith that a professional philosopher could write things that were consumable and interesting.

## And?

**Seth**

And then he, of course, did listen to us and made a comment about it, which was very nice, you know.

## Very nice. Let's get into the episode.

**Mark**

Hope you enjoy it. It was really energizing hearing something from when we were younger people with more energy.

**Younger, More Energetic Mark**

Our question for *Episode Number 16* is "What effect should the avant-garde have on our understanding of what art is?"

Actually, that's one of many questions raised in the reading, which is three essays by the current American philosopher Arthur Danto. He's a big-time aesthetics guy, but wrote a lot of other stuff as well. He also, just as recently as last year, came out with a book on Andy Warhol, which is going to be very relevant to what we're gonna talk about today.

**Wes**

Music critic for *The Nation* for a long time, right?

**Mark**

Yes. From 1984 to 2009. But now he's, like, 85 years old, so I guess he doesn't need to do that.

**Seth**

Let me say this to anybody who may be hearing this and going, Oh, okay. This is Andy Warhol and the *avant-garde.*

This guy is as much a philosopher as anybody. The fact that art is the milieu that he is using to discuss philosophy is simply... well, what I'm trying to say is "Don't run away just because you hear the words Andy Warhol."

Which I would have, myself.

**Mark**

He's in the analytic tradition, but has an appreciation for the continental figures. Even in these essays, he talks about Schopenhauer, he has a whole book on Nietzsche, brings up Sartre and Foucault and all these cool guys like that.

**Seth**

He's a true intellectual and a staunch Hegelian.

> So philosophy... is baffling to those without its walls because philosophers communicate with one another, typically, in dense, technical articles, often inaccessible to readers illiterate in the notations of symbolic logic, addressing issues whose larger human relevance is as obscure as the immediate purport of the articles themselves. But philosophers, able of course to say what limited achievement is being aimed at in these communications, themselves may be at some loss in explaining what ultimate human purpose is furthered through that limited achievement. (Danto, 1997, p. xiii)

**Mark**

In context, he's saying that the history of philosophy in the 20th century has been a history of self dissatisfaction, as its many internal critiques testify.

**Wes**

It's always a crisis.

**Let's talk about the *avant-garde* project.**

**Mark**

Warhol, Jasper Johns, Robert Rauschenberg, John Cage (a musician). To some degree, they were all trying to get past the distinction between art and life. The senior of these was Marcel Duchamp because he did most of his work in the '20s. Pretty early, he would do these "readymades," which are: He would go buy a urinal at a plumbing supply store. And he submitted it to this museum showing, specifically because the museum had said *We're not going to be judgmental about what you guys are doing. So he's challenging that.*

He submitted the urinal as is, signed a name on it that wasn't even his name, and submitted that and called it *Fountain.* Which seems like just a joke. But eventually, these things did get displayed. And they're a part of the thing that Duchamp is most remembered for. So there's a lot of interpretations of "how is this art?"

It's conceptual art, it's not the thing itself. It's not like he went and built it with his own two hands, and you can admire his handiwork. You could say, "Oh, what a beautiful urinal." But Danto argues against that. Duchamp was trying to pick things that were aesthetically neutral. He was challenging this whole notion that art is about beauty. Art is something more than that.

The question Danto gets out of this is *If you accept that this is an artwork, it looks exactly like a regular urinal. It's just posted into a museum, and it's called "art." So what is it that makes one "art" and one "not art"? Is it really just being in the museum?*

**Why not?**

**Mark**

So maybe the guys who were shoveling the snow outside the museum went in and left their shovels against the wall. Those wouldn't suddenly become exhibits, because they were in the museum. So there must be something else.

**Wes**

What if the snow shovel has the weighty title *In Advance of a*

*Broken Arm?*

**Mark**

Do you find that a challenge to your notion of art, or just a stupid conceptual joke?

**Seth**

I have always had problems with 20th-century art and understanding it. I took a class in college about art that focused on the Middle Ages and the Renaissance. So my conception of what art was and the value of art was wrapped up in that. And I got caught up in the ideas of viewing artworks in their political context and their social context and their economic context. There's lots of different ways to do art history, just like there's lots of different ways to do history, where you look at the material conditions that produce the art, you look at the social conditions around the artist, and so forth. And 20th-century art—I never really understood it. It never really appealed to me. And it wasn't until I read this book that I had any sense of why that was a problem for me.

**Mark**

Not just this wacky postmodern stuff that we're talking about, but modern art itself, Picasso and those guys?

**Seth**

I'd say yes, with increasingly difficult degree as you get through the 20th century. So, for example, there's Picasso and Matisse and Klimt, guys that I can appreciate, or at least I have my own way of judging and appreciating. But when you talk about Kandinsky and Miro and Pollock—the more abstract it gets, the less I was able to get ahold of it. And I didn't understand why. Now I have a much better understanding of why that was so difficult for me and why I didn't have a grip on it.

**Is it a matter of context? Seth, you were struck by what Danto said about** *Guernica.*

**Seth**

*Guernica* was made by Picasso and it was intended to illustrate an act of terrorism or violence. Danto's claim is that anybody who lived at that time would have recognized that it was a kind of protest, or at least a statement about the violence of Germans against this Spanish villager. But to an audience even 20 or 30 years later, the historical context of what happened at that village is completely lost. And if you don't know that this was originally intended to point out this atrocity that happened here, then how does the artwork have meaning to you?

### Wes, what was the anecdote Danto told about Picasso talking to the German officer?

**Wes**

Picasso responded to the German officer's question, having handed him a postcard of the painting, *Did you do that?* The response: *No, you did!*

It reminds me of my own experiences with museums. Visual arts—for me—aren't as powerful as, say, literature. I need the historical context. When I was in Venice, my favorite parts were the armory and the dungeons. I'm really a Philistine when it comes to the visual. I'm that typical American that William James writes about, who just sort of "glances blank." I need the handheld audio thing, or I need to be able to look at some description, and then I can appreciate it. Otherwise, it's difficult for me to go in and look at 14th-century iconic stuff of the Virgin Mary and, and appreciate it at all, because I am not a Christian.

And I think even for Christians today—because they're not Christians in the way that 14th century Italians were—is it any longer a work of art to them? It certainly is not going to have the same power. It's certainly not going to be the communication that it was at the time.

**Seth**

We should start with his central philosophical thesis that he lays out in "The Disenfranchisement of Art." Danto's claim is that philosophy has disenfranchised art, that Plato is ultimately responsible for this, and that everything in the last 2500 years, or whatever, is just echoing Plato. Plato says that the purpose of art is to represent things—to mimic or represent the image of something. Philosophy is responsible for trying to get at the things themselves, but focusing on the representation or the image of something is one step removed from that. So art is, by definition, less central and less useful than philosophy, because it's one step removed from the object.

And in general, art has no utility, because you can't do anything with art. It doesn't serve any purpose. A work of art doesn't shoot a horse or create a building or define a vehicle.

**Mark**

All it can do is fool people. You'd say, "Look at all of these grapes I have here."

"Oh, that's just a picture of grapes, you bastard."

That's all you can do.

**Wes**

It also can corrupt them.

**Seth**

It's dangerous, even though it's completely impotent, which is the central paradox that Danto brings up. His key point is that the definition of art from a philosophical perspective, from way back when, all the way through Kant, is that it tries to mimic or represent reality, and it does so poorly, at least at the beginning. And so the history of art is the history of getting successively better and better at representing.

**Mark**

Which for Plato was especially bad, because the objects of our experience are themselves pale imitations of the real things, the *True Forms* of the world. But you don't have to be a Platonist to feel art is epiphenomenal, right? It sits on the surface of things. It has no causal power. It has no utility, it's just a surface-level phenomenon.

**Seth**

And in modern times, if a huge part of philosophy is trying to get through perception, or sensory data, to the things themselves, or to actual objects, or to monads, or whatever, then art is doubly useless because it's just creating a barrier between you and your sense perceptions.

**Mark**

In high school, I read *Brave New World*. And I really saw it as just poorly written philosophy. *If you throw away the art part of it, and just tell me your philosophical thesis, then I would be able to evaluate it much more easily.* I thought, at the time, that putting it in the story form, and dressing it up, could only serve to obscure the alleged truths contained therein.

**Wes**

The "Ayn Rand effect," where you have some thesis and you hit it too hard, and the message overwhelms the aesthetic.

### Let's get back to Danto

**Mark**

Let me clarify. *The Transfiguration of the Commonplace* was the book that he wrote before this one. The "transfiguration" is like the snow shovels, or the urinal. This is a commonplace object, and somehow we can interpret it aesthetically or present it aesthetically or as something transformed into a work of art.

**Wes**

The question is how that transformation takes place. Is it merely by giving it some sort of aesthetic features?

**Mark**

Let's get more of this history: Plato slams art as a copy of a copy. Kant presented aesthetic appreciation as something that has to be disinterested, right? It can't be something that you're actually excited about, it's "purposiveness without a purpose." (Kant, I.I.I.3§10, 220/65)

**Wes**

I don't see disinterest as a lack of interest, I see disinterest as a lack of personal interests unrelated to the aesthetic value. This is related to his idea of freedom, where it's a difference between being subjected to the laws that emanate from yourself, versus to some whimsical pleasure. So if you say, *Oh, I love this book, I connect with it so much, it's entirely about me and my personal circumstance. And what happened to the main character is just what happened to me,* and if you can only connect to works like that, that's the non-disinterested connection.

Part of what art is doing is to take things that are ordinarily ugly and painful and make them beautiful. Shakespeare doesn't present the villains in his plays as merely cardboard cutout characters that you're supposed to hate. He creates empathy for those villains, and he creates a sense of beauty for those villains. And that's the aesthetic standpoint.

If you hate George W. Bush, let's say, and you go to a play about him, it's not really an aesthetic experience. The play bashes him and you're supposed to reinforce your own hatred. That's a specific political or personal-animosity type of interest. But if you can empathize with him as a character, then you've reached the aesthetic. That's what I would say about disinterest.

### Can we make this a bit sexier, please?

**Mark**

The obvious one is nudes. Are you appreciating the nude aesthetically? Or because you want to have sex with the statue?

### Thanks.

**Wes**

The other thing I'll say about Kant, which is connected to his moral philosophy: When you see something beautiful, the idea that anything is beautiful to us in nature is an odd thing, right? It has to be functional for us, it has to sustain us, it has to lead to our survival. But the idea for Kant that anything is beautiful, it gives us hope. Even though he's still a skeptic. It's not evidence of God, or it's not evidence of a world in which natural law coincides with moral law. But it's sort of a hint of that. And so there's always this moral dimension to the aesthetic. I don't know whether or not Danto thinks that.

**Mark**

This vision of artistic contemplation as something that is divorced from practical action, Danto thinks that that's disenfranchising—saying art is impotent to influence anybody's point of view in a way that would make them take political action.

**Wes**

That's not the way I read Plato and Kant. Danto himself points to this paradox. Plato thinks art is very powerful, and he has to ban it from the city. But he doesn't ban it entirely. He has the guardians of the city listen to, like, rock-and-roll so they can get revved up for the fight. Different types of music affect you in different ways emotionally. Philosophy is trying to keep art under wraps *because* of its dangerousness,

**Mark**

Right. This is an ongoing fight between philosophy and art. It seems like, *Oh, we're creating a special place in philosophy. And we're going to think hard about these things.* But by divorcing it from the rest of philosophy, and creating aesthetics, he compares it to putting women on a pedestal. Ooh, they're so lofty and noble. Let's put them up here so that they can't actually have any effect on society and get involved with serious matters. So again, it's sort of making it ineffectual.

**Seth**

He says that it's interesting that philosophy is afraid of art. And at the same time, the history of philosophy is the history of saying that art has no use. And when you say "no use" it means it has no causal force, and it has no utility, it can't improve the human condition.

But then he says aesthetics was invented in the 18th century, a bold final stroke, to set artists to creating aesthetic distance, which is to say that perhaps they finally got to the point where there was enough of a realization (particularly after Hegel, who gives art a very critical place in *The Phenomenology of Spirit*) to say that, *Oh, well, we need to give it some purpose, but it needs to be still disenfranchised.* And the purpose given is to create beauty. So the job of art goes from representing the world to representing beauty. The job of the artist is to create beauty. And if you don't create beauty, you're not a good artist, or you're not an artist at all. This is the final stroke in the strategy to completely disenfranchise art.

### Mark

And we still have that strain very strong now, which is just to dismiss art as entertainment. Right? If it's not entertaining, there's no art for art's sake, it's just subservient to these human needs.

### Wes

But there's always that tension between mere entertainment and high arts and lower arts.

## Can we talk more about Hegel?

### Mark

Well, this was the hardest part, how he has this Hegelian view of art history. We talked last time about Hegel's view of history as distinguishing history—like the narrative of what's really going on with the spirit of a culture—from the actual events. There are many events that are not historical. Because they don't contribute to the movement of the ideas of the culture forward to the next kind of culture. There are whole cultures he thinks are historically irrelevant, which seems pretty frickin' obnoxious.

But Danto wants to at least use that setup and say you could conceive of artworks in the same way. We've had these historical movements in art history, and in a certain point, where you have Duchamp making his readymades, you've now broken the machine of progress.

You can look at art-history as this movement, becoming better and better at representing things. But then, when photography comes along, visual art can't be about that anymore. So it changed to expressing things. But Duchamp is not even trying to express anything, he's picking something that somebody else made, something that his own emotions are not going into— which is what modern art, Picasso and those folks, were trying to do. Something that a camera couldn't show you, the events how I see them.

And they got more and more abstract. You have these guys

just splashing paint all over things, in a very expressive way. That's modern art, and postmodern art is supposed to be the step beyond that, where museum curators don't even know what to call "art" and what not to call "art." *Everything is permitted.* And since then, there haven't really been artistic movements. There's just lots of individual artists doing their own thing. Maybe something will look like a movement here and there, but it really doesn't contribute to overall progress. You have to judge each of them by their own standards.

So he's got that picture of art history, and that's what he calls the "end of art." In other words, the end of art as a progressive discipline, as we've seen it before. But how is this supposed to work with the disenfranchisement? What Duchamp is doing is no longer about the work anymore. You're not supposed to gaze on the urinal, he wants to make art not about the retina anymore. Not about seeing things. You want to make it about the mind, he wanted to bring it back to thinking about stuff. So in other words, it becomes philosophy. It's totally descriptive. It's entirely intellectual.

## Seth

As long as the purpose of art is to be representational, it's tied to an object, and how well or poorly the representation occurs. The development of the representational is really a development of technology. He talks a lot about the invention of perspective, for example, and then the advent of photography, and the moving picture, and so forth and so on. But as soon as you divorce it from representation, and it becomes expression, so that it's supposed to express some kind of emotion or feeling, then the object becomes irrelevant.

And that's when you get the abstract expressionists who are trying to represent something without any object whatsoever. And once you're divorced from the object, then there is no construct to guide the refinement of art as an expressive form. It just merely is. Each individual artist becomes expressive of their own individual experience. And you can't even necessarily relate the vocabulary or the grammar of an artist's work with any other artist's work, unless they have some sort of real-world experience that's shared that they're speaking out of. So the end of art just means the end of art as representation, and then it just starts to spin its wheels.

...at the end is theory, art having finally become vaporized in a dazzle of pure thought about itself, and remaining as it were, solely as the object of its own theoretical consciousness. (Danto, 1984, p. 111)

### Seth

At the end, he says that, essentially, art becomes philosophy. It's kind of like taking a stick and poking philosophers and saying, "Okay, well, now I can explain what happened." What happened is that art became completely self-reflective, and became completely theoretical, and not about the object, and all about its theoretical construct in its historical context. And hence, it's just basically philosophy. And now philosophy is going to have to deal with it. After 2500 years of making artists second-class citizens, it has to realize that art is itself philosophy.

# Outline of a Science of Art

*September 2006 - February 2024*

*based on an image by Chris Warr*

## Christopher Sunami

*I first encountered Danto (via his work, that is) during an abortive attempt at pursuing a higher degree in Philosophy at Ohio University (they could not appreciate my genius, and so forth...). My aesthetics professor was Jack Bender (Harvard '78), a doughty and mustachioed gent whose art survey course touched on the problems raised by figures such as Kant, Beardsley, and Margolis, and culminated with Danto's challenges to traditional conceptions of art. To conclude my own work in the class, I worked my way through the chief problems posed across the history of aesthetics, brought them to a resolution, and announced that, in so doing, I had created a new "Science of Art." Suffice it to say, Bender remained unmoved. Nor, in the subsequent years, has the theory (as yet!) revolutionized the world. Given the happy occasion of this book, however, I've taken the opportunity to polish it up for this surely more discerning and appreciative audience.*

*- Kitoba*

# What is the purpose of art?

## READINGS

Beardsley, Monroe, "The Aesthetic Point of View", *Contemporary Philosophic Thought*, 3, 1970.

Danto, Arthur, *The Transfiguration of the Commonplace: A Philosophy of Art*, Harvard University Press, 1983.

Dickie, George, *Art and the Aesthetic: An Institutional Analysis,* Cornell University Press, 1974.

Kant, Immanuel, *Critique of Judgment*, translated by Werner Pluhar, Hackett, 1987.

Kennick, William, "Does Traditional Aesthetics Rest on a Mistake?" *Mind, 67,* 1958.

# Science of Art

## Art Problem #1: "Purposiveness without a Purpose" (Kant)

One of the most famous definitions of "the beautiful" in the philosophical literature is Kant's "Purposiveness without a Purpose" (*Zweckmäßigkeit ohne Zweck*) from the *Critique of Judgment*. A phrase that has baffled, amused, and dazzled generations of philosophy students, it expresses the idea that the beautiful object appears to have been crafted with intention, and towards larger aims, but cannot be put to utilitarian ends, as can a vase or a knife (except incidentally, as when the utilitarian object is gratuitously made beautiful).

As discussed in the preceding podcast, Danto finds this problematic, part of an ongoing attempt—by the discipline of philosophy, as a whole—to "disenfranchise" art by reducing it to the purely ornamental, or, in other words, by making "lack of purpose" one of its defining characteristics.

However, there is a simple way to both honor Kant's intuition of "purposiveness without a purpose" and Danto's intuition that art *qua* art does have utility. To do so, we can adapt two concepts (used often in psychology, computer science, and many other fields), "algorithms" and "heuristics."

An algorithm is a detailed, step-by-step way of solving a problem, suitable for programming a conventional computer. If all steps are followed exactly and accurately, the goal is reached. A heuristic is a general approach to solving a problem. It can be translated into algorithms, but it gives neither detailed steps, nor guaranteed results. It cannot be used by a conventional computer, and might baffle an untrained or unskilled person, but it communicates well to a human expert (or possibly a sophisticated AI). In contrast to an algorithm, which is optimized only for a single, well-defined problem, a good heuristic can be helpful in innumerable situations, some of which may be quite different from each other.

A lot of folk wisdom can be thought of as heuristics. "The early bird gets the worm," is not an algorithm for worm-hunting by birds. It's a general piece of advice that can be applied in many disparate situations where a limited resource can be exhausted by its earliest exploiters. Similarly, while the modern, analytic tradition of philosophy seeks an algorithmic-like approach to problem-solving, many of the famous dicta of classical philosophy are more like heuristics. "The unexamined life is not worth living," is not an algorithm for a worthwhile life, but it might arguably be a heuristic for one.

If, as Danto claims, art and philosophy are rivals, then—if we take philosophy as analogous to algorithms—art might be thought of as analogous to heuristics. Both present general strategies for approaching widely different aspects of the world, but where the philosophical approach can be articulated, the artistic approach is apprehended at a subconscious level.

In other words, when the artist solves a difficult artistic problem—for instance, how to render a recognizable image of a person using paint and canvas—the record of that solution (the painting) becomes useful for the audience in solving a wide, perhaps unlimited, set of superficially dissimilar problems—for instance, how to present yourself to your best advantage in a business meeting. The art provides no algorithmic step-by-step set of instructions, and the audience member is unlikely to have any conscious apprehension of how the exposure to art has been helpful to them, but familiarity with art gives the connoisseur access to a library of subconscious strategies for dealing productively with a wide range of goals and obstacles.

**Testable Prediction 1:** Exposure to (good) art should allow people to perform better on problem-solving activities. (Note: Some studies along these lines have already been performed.) In particular, there should be consistent, reproducible correlations between certain specific pieces of art and certain specific problem-solving tasks.

## Art Problem #2: "No Accounting for Tastes" (Kennick)

One of the most characteristic problems of art is that different people like different things. You like Michelangelo, and I like Basquiat. You like Bach, and I prefer Beyonce. In his 1958 essay, "Does Traditional Aesthetics Rest on a Mistake?" William Kennick argues this is because there is no ultimate fact of the matter. *You like vanilla, and I like chocolate.* Art is solely a matter of subjective personal preferences, and to search any deeper is an error.

This is consonant with contention that art, by definition, has no utility, but since we have rejected that conclusion, we must likewise reject this one. Just as different flavors of food can give us valid information about what is in them (even if the flavors we gravitate to are not always the ones that are best for us) so too does our quest for a science of art demand we go beyond beyond the banal commonplace "there's no accounting for tastes."

The problem is that art objects vary widely. A painting is not like a song, and a song is not like a movie. They are made of different materials, they are structured differently, they function in different realms. There seems to be little we can point to that unites them.

Conversely, even two art objects that are almost identical in many ways can be judged very differently. We prefer Mozart to Salieri, even though both are writing music that's superficially similar, in the same musical genre, using similar instruments, songs of similar length, and even similar elements such as rhythmic patterns and chord progressions.

Monroe Beardsley, in his 1970 essay, "The Aesthetic Point of View," offers at least a partial solution to this problem. He contends that we should not focus on the art object itself—in pursuit of an analysis of its physical composition, as we might with a chemical substance—but rather on the art experience, which is a subjective phenomenon internal to the audience.

This, of course, poses challenges for scientific study. The difficulties posed by internality, although not insignificant, are not unique to the artistic realm. They can, therefore, be addressed by the same kinds of techniques developed for other topics of psychological study, from surveys to brain scans. The problem of subjectivity, however, must be addressed directly: True, it may not be possible for an individual to be fully objective about any given work of art. But in the aggregate, there may be dispositions that affect people's reactions to art objects in predictable ways.

Intuitively, one such disposition may be a sense of identification with the artist. To paraphrase an infamous quote from Van Halen rocker David Lee Roth, *Critics like Elvis Costello, because he looks like them.* To the extent that the audience members resemble the artist in ways both superficial and profound, they may overrate the experience they receive from the art. To put it in crudely demographic terms, *The White male audience member might have a tendency to overrate Bach and underrate Beyonce; the Black female audience member might have the same tendency in reverse.* Similarly, all other things being equal, we would expect a teenager to gravitate to teenaged singers, or a cowboy to music sung by someone in a Western-style hat.

Another, related-but-distinct disposition is artistic education and/or familiarity. We might expect that audience-members who are familiar with similar works of art, and perhaps even their history and their theory, will judge an artwork more accurately than someone not familiar with this type of art. In other words, their art experience is a more valid reflection of the actual underlying quality of the art object than is the experience of a less well-educated critic.

A final reason for difference in tastes may be the fact that different people face different problems in life, and therefore that different pieces of art may be more or less relevant to specific individuals in particular situations. For instance, the highly abstract music of Bach might be more useful for mathematicians. Electronic music might be helpful to computer programmers, and country music to farmers. Hip-hop, with its focus on sampled beats, might address the problem of asserting your own identity in a context created by others. Pachelbel's *Canon*, which harmonizes different parts of a single melody line with itself, might help people seeking more psychological unity, and so forth.

**Testable Prediction 2A:** It should be possible to identify, and ultimately control for, demographic similarity with the artist, and familiarity with similar works of art as factors that cause predictable variability in the valence and the accuracy (respectively) of evaluations of art objects.

**Testable Prediction 2B:** Building on *Predicition 1,* that we should be able to find correlations between specific pieces of art and specific problem-solving tasks, we should then be able to control for variation among people's perception of a piece of art on the basis of its personal relevance to them and the characteristic problems of their own lives.

## Art Problem #3 - Concept and Context

Modernist and post-modernist works of art pose a particular challenge to theories of art, often by deliberate design. For instance one of the most famous postmodern works of art, *Fountain,* an ordinary restroom urinal submitted to a gallery show by Marcel Duchamp (but attributed contemporaneously, by him, as a work by an anonymous "female friend") challenges all notions of what qualifies as an art object, as do later works by "conceptual" artists (such as John Cage's *4'33",* a piano composition in which the pianist sits silently at the piano for four minutes and thirty-three seconds, or Robert Rauschenberg's *Erased De Kooning Drawing* which is a blank piece of paper from which a work of art by Willem de Kooning has been removed) where the art object itself is secondary to the concepts behind it.

George Dickie, in his 1974 book *Art and Aesthetics: An Institutional Analysis,* suggests that art must inevitably be considered in the context of a "artworld," which provides the necessary framing to allow the audience to consider the aesthetic qualities of the art object. Conversely, Danto, in his 1981 book *The Transfiguration of the Commonplace,* goes further than this to challenge the notion that the art object must have any aesthetic qualities at all. But our previous move, from the art object to the art experience, provides a solution to both of these difficulties. Since the experience, not the object, is primary, it's not problematic to assume that concepts and context might make up essential pieces of some artworks, and that other artworks might not need any physical component at all. A piece like *Fountain,* might indeed, in accordance with Dickie's intuition, require the context and concept of an "artworld" to be framed and appreciated, whereas a less conceptual piece, like a classical sculpture, might be capable of producing an art experience without any unusual conceptual context.

**Testable Prediction 3:** Conceptual works of art will be shown to have similar impacts as other works of art for, and only for, an audience with the necessary conceptual context.

## Positive Thesis:

Art is notoriously difficult to judge accurately, and with consistency. Towards the development of an objective science of art, and in accordance with the above, I propose the following:

### Definition of terms:

- *Art object:* The physical portion of the artwork (including elements such as sound and light).
- *Artwork:* The full range of contributing elements of the art experience, exclusive of purely personal elements, but inclusive of conceptual content and context.
- *Art experience:* The experience of the audience stimulated by the artwork.
- *Artistic value:* The ability of a given artwork to stimulate an art experience across a wide range of audiences.
- *Perceived artistic value:* The perceived ability of a given artwork to stimulate an art experience, from the viewpoint of a given audience member.
- *Derived artistic value:* A value theoretically equivalent to the actual artistic value, derived from perceived artistic value, as corrected by consistent modifications.

### Thesis:
*By properly measuring and analyzing perceived artistic value, and then accounting for predictable misperceptions, it will be possible to determine a stable, objective artistic value for a given artwork, suitable for meaningful comparisons. Furthermore, it will be possible to use that knowledge so gained to create better, more impactful works of art.*

### Methodology:
In order to gain better starting measurements of artistic value,

evaluators will be asked to judge work on three independent qualities: Craft, originality, and depth. These can then be plotted in a three-dimensional, perpendicular vector space, to produce a rectangular solid. The area of this solid (perceived craft x perceived originality x perceived depth) will be used as the perceived artistic value.

By applying modifiers with experimentally derived values to the constituent vectors, we can obtain the derived artistic value, which will theoretically approximate an actual artistic value.

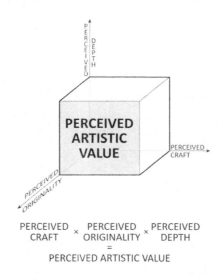

PERCEIVED CRAFT $\times$ PERCEIVED ORIGINALITY $\times$ PERCEIVED DEPTH

=

PERCEIVED ARTISTIC VALUE

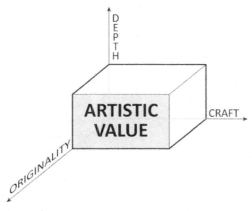

CRAFT $\times$ ORIGINALITY $\times$ DEPTH

=

ARTISTIC VALUE

# *What does the physiology of the brain have to do with ethics?*

## READINGS

Churchland, Patricia S., *Braintrust: What Neuroscience Tells Us about Morality*, Princeton University Press, 2010.

Hume, David, *A Treatise of Human Nature,* edited by Ernest Rhys, Everyman's Library, 1740/1911.

Hume, David, *Enquiry Concerning the Principles of Morals*, Prometheus, 1751/2004.

# EPISODE 41

*June 26, 2011*

*Charles Valsechi*

## CHURCHLAND ᴏɴ CHURCHLAND & HUME

*P*atricia Churchland *on her book* Braintrust: What Neuroscience Tells Us About Morality. *We also discussed David Hume's ethics as foundational to her work.*

*- Mark*

Note: *This episode marks an early appearance of Dylan Casey, but is missing Seth, as well as Wes (who had an unexplained emergency five minutes before the episode taped!).*

# 41 - Churchland

**Mark**

Pat will be on with us in a few minutes. We thought we'd chat a little first.

**Dylan**

She seems to be interested in scientific grounding, and a kind of pragmatic attitude with respect to it. She's skeptical of overexcited reduction of neurological research into a deterministic formulation of how morals work.

The big problem, to me, with overly scientific accounts of morality (as rooted in our emotions, our hormones, or whatever) is this kind of "one-to-one correspondence." Once you sort out what gene was that "morality gene," then you'd understand exactly what moral decisions ought to be made. So you displace the universalism of Kant into a biological universalism.

But she embraces this notion of biology and mind of the "many-to-many," the organized-network mode that involves multiple solutions to multiple problems. The notion of "what judgment is" ends up playing a great role in it. There's social effects, there's biological effects, but I'm interested in what the notion of judgment is on her part, and how that comes into morality.

### Enough intro, let's welcome Pat.

**Mark**

Hello, Pat. I'm here with Dylan Casey. Dylan has done a number of these with us—he's my brother-in-law.

I edit these pretty heavily after the fact. So it can be really rude about your colleagues.

**Pat Churchland**

I take that as encouragement.

## Enough pleasantries.

**Mark**

Your work does not seem combative. But certainly the discussions of scientism that it engenders are heated.

**Pat**

It's quite interesting, in reading Hume in the *Treatise,* how combative he is. He takes on the people that he regards as the opposition, and it's really slash-and-burn.

**Mark**

Just "commit them to the flames."

**Pat**

Yes, exactly. Anyway, he's so wonderful to read.

**Mark**

You mentioned Hume a number of times in here, as both a foundation of your work, and as a figure that is sometimes brought up to argue that the entire point is just wrongheaded. The *is-ought* distinction is so sharp, as Hume described it, that talking about brain physiology in the context of morality is useless.

**Pat**

I was introduced to Hume as an undergraduate. And it seemed very reasonable and very sensible. But then of course, as you take other classes, Hume comes in for a lot of criticism. Over the years, I looked at many other points of view so far as the origin and the nature of morality was concerned. And I kept finding myself coming back to Hume. I still do, even though I have looked hard and long at many others, including Kant, Rawls and Nozick.

Metcalf's article on Nozick was thoughtful and well-researched. He opened up some important issues. When I went back to look at Hume, the discussion that's most relevant to Nozick is the discussion in *Book Three* on justice. He makes it plain that it's in our interest to live together in groups and to cooperate. We all know that there's these enormous benefits that accrue to you if you live in groups, and have a division of labor, and take advantage of other people's knowledge and skills, and so forth.

He goes on to say, as you grow older, and as you leave childhood behind, you recognize that it's in your interest to sometimes make sacrifices for the good of the group, because of the benefits of group living. I started thinking about Nozick in that context, and how he evaluates liberty so highly.

Of course, Hume evaluates liberty highly as well. But Hume would say if it is to the detriment of the group, as a whole, that nobody ever pays taxes, you may want to rethink that, because the stability of the group is extremely important. Hume, like Hobbes, was very sensitive to issues of stability, because the English Civil War was still very much on their minds. And it had been truly, truly horrifying. And they realized—which we sometimes don't—that our social institutions can be very fragile. And that instabilities that undermine social institutions can be very, very destructive.

### Mark

That addresses very specifically what the first chapter of your book focuses on, and what seems to be one of Hume's focuses: Arguing against the claim from Hobbes that everybody is primarily selfish. That's something that we just have to deal with, in considering the foundations of morality, that maybe morality is something that does not come from human nature itself. Human nature is selfish. So we need morality to protect us against our own nature.

But you've claimed that in fact, self-interest itself is an evolutionary leap, a system of internal balance.

### Pat

Yes, that's right. In all organisms, there is a well-organized and well-protected circuitry for self-survival and self-wellbeing, and what changed with mammals was an extension of that circuitry to the care and wellbeing of the offspring. And then, over evolutionary time, as mammals spread out and found new ways of living, other small changes took place to alter the sociality in various ways. You could think of that in terms of the expansion of the circle of people within your group,

**Mark**

The Libertarian camp seems to act as if self-interest is self-evident. If anybody says, "You're doing something altruistic," then that's just because it makes them feel good, or something like that. And in a sense, they're right, it's the same brain circuitry that makes you care for yourself, just tweaked here to expand that circle. It's almost a redefinition of what self is. Self is not just this organism.

**Pat**

You can see in nonhuman primates, such as monkeys, for example, that individuals in the group will come to the aid of a baby who has been captured by a python. They mob the python, and hit him and bite him, and extract the baby. This is behavior that's not imposed on them by an external force. It's an expression of their nature. We see a very similar thing in the case of humans, and not just their own offspring, but also the offspring of others.

Hume is great on this too. He has a passage in the section on justice, where he addresses the question *Aren't we really just selfish, and the rest is imposed and alien to us?*

> Consult common experience: Do you not see, that though the whole expense of the family be generally under the direction of the master of it, yet there are few that do not bestow the largest part of their fortunes on the pleasures of their wives, and the education of their children, reserving the smallest portion for their own proper use and entertainment? (*Treatise*, 3.2.2¶6)

Of course, we know that that doesn't always happen. But it's very interesting that in order to make the case for saying that cooperation and social life is very natural, and not contrary to our nature, Hume starts by making that case with regard to the family. And then, he says, you can see that it's in your interest to belong to a group. Slowly, over time, these responses become automatic, these responses to cooperate, and to engage in group living, and to sacrifice, to take a cost, sometimes, to yourself in order that the group as a whole may thrive.

### Dylan

How would you contrast that kind of claim by Hume with Aristotle's *The human being's a political animal, in the primacy of family*?

### Pat

They're very close. I think Aristotle understood much the same thing. By "political animal," I think he meant political in the broadest sense, what Hume would mean by a "social animal." They're very similar. Ethics is fundamentally a practical business, about solving practical problems of social life. How can we do things in such a way as to preserve wellbeing? Hume makes those remarks throughout the book *Of Morals* in the *Treatise,* but also in the *Enquiry*. But of course, it's all there in Aristotle.

They're similar in this other respect, which I find to be really quite interesting: They both realize that social institutions of criminal justice, of enforcing contracts, of defense, are not just throwaway political things, but the essence of taking morality from the province of a very small group to what you need to prosper in a large group. And so much of contemporary moral philosophy missed all that.

### Dylan

The conventional way of thinking about these problems is "What is a moral choice for an individual?" without paying attention to the notion that we are embedded creatures, that part of being human is being a part of a community, and that those aren't exclusive things.

### Pat

The European philosophers understood that in a way in which the American philosophers did not. Part of who you are, and what makes you the person that you are, and gives you the kind of quality of life that you can have, is being a member of the group, and having a role in the group, and learning the group conventions and practices, and then learning to improve upon those conventions and practices.

The problem was that when the Europeans talked about those things, they made it sound so weird, and woolly and difficult and obscure, that people would just throw the book down and say "To hell with it!"

**Mark**

I think of Nietzsche, who has, I think, a very similar ethical view in terms of *Let's look at what human nature actually is*. There's no normativity, other than what comes from our own impulses, or how we deal with other people's. Yet he never made that leap to explicitly being systematic about the political. The political is big and scary, and the essence of the moral situation is "I," right now, as an individual. I'm in some situation, maybe in chains, maybe in a concentration camp, it doesn't matter how unfree. What is my duty to do in that situation? As opposed to this state-building. Even back to Plato's *Republic*, those problems go hand-in-hand, you can't even really talk about the virtues of the individual without talking about the virtues of the state.

**Pat**

Hume certainly understood the importance of institutions, but so did Aristotle. They thought that a good deal of our moral efforts ought to go into what kinds of institutions would promote prosperity and stability and what kinds of institutions would undermine them, and that is an important part of the contemporary public conversation about morality. The case in point has to do with the drug laws that have been a source of horrendous grief and misery. As this new report has shown, this war on drugs has been a colossal failure. So what we have to do now is figure out *Well, then what should we do?* This is a huge moral consequence.

**Dylan**

I agree. But it's interesting that you pick that example, because I think it crystallizes the conflict about what morality is. On the other side of that you have people saying *Taking drugs is just wrong*. It's a kind of universalism, a notion that kind of moral distinction is written in stone—you appeal to something outside of a pragmatic, beneficial compromise or solution.

**Pat**

I don't want to suggest that the only important moral domain has to do with public institutions that affect us all. On a day-by-day basis, each of us does make decisions, and often they are consequential in terms of the prosperity and misery and wellbeing of others. But when you think about something like the drug laws, you want to take many, many things into account. That includes the consequences of having a "war on drugs" that causes a lot of misery, and is inefficacious and expensive. So you ask, *Are there better ways of doing things?*

And I think that's as moral a question as some of the questions that arise for an individual. *Should I blow the whistle on Mrs. X?* for example. They're all part of our moral life, it's just that if you're living 200,000 years ago, in a small group, you have a very different set of moral questions than you do if you live in a hugely complex society as ours is.

### Mark

We had a discussion of Kant's ethics. He insisted that morality has to be a "categorical imperative"—it has to apply in all circumstances, regardless of what your individual desires are. Hume's position, on the other hand, was that it's all based on consistency with what you already find yourself believing, right?

### Pat

Well, up to a point for Hume. And this is also how I see it, now that we know something about the neurobiology. For Hume, there is the moral sentiment. That provides a disposition, so that you find certain options unacceptable, and others okay. But the moral sentiment in-and-of-itself doesn't provide answers to moral questions. It puts you into the space of moral reasons. Once you're there, then facts are important, memories, what other people think, history—all this comes together in a certain way to help you make a decision about what you ought to do.

He was sometimes read, quite wrongly, as a simple *If your gut's telling you do "x," do "x."* Yet he goes on in many places to talk about how reason can actually provoke a moral response, or stimulate a particular moral passion to do this or to do that. So he knows that the story is going to be very complex.

I fancy the very vague account that I have of "constraint-satisfaction," as a process whereby nervous systems light on a solution, would have appealed to him. Constraint-satisfaction is something that we can roughly understand in all animals' decision making, even rats, where the variables are very well-controlled. But it also seems to be something about the way humans make decisions as well, whether those decisions are made very quickly and automatically, or whether they are made over many days, as one struggles to find a good resolution. But I think constraint-satisfaction is what's going on. And that means it's not just reason in the sense of deduction, there's all kinds of perceptions and emotions and memories and so forth.

### Dylan

I understood judgment as not merely "satisfying the outputs," for lack of a better term, but as being the weighing of all kinds of unspeakable things. Would that be congruent with what you're talking about?

### Pat

I think it is. "Judgment" is the outcome of the constraint-satisfaction process. In all animals, when they need to make a decision, there is some process that goes on where their immediate perception, and what they've learned, and various other factors come to bear. The brain goes into a local minimum, the decision is made, and the rat makes its choice—or the monkey, or the person, or what have you.

Hume, when expressing skepticism about the role of reason in morality, means by "reason," deduction, the kind of certainty that you get with algebra and geometry. But he knows that there is this other thing that we also sometimes call "reason" (which Peirce would have called "abduction"), whereby you make an inference to the best decision. And that's judgment.

### Dylan

I had a question about that. Judgment allows for predictive behavior, so when you make a judgment, you have implicit assumptions about what's going to happen. Some of that is going to be from habit, and experience: You dropped the ball, it goes down, that kind of thing. Others are going to have to do with the kind of social things that you speak about in your book, that you learn. However this works, it allows for refinement of that predictive power, so that you come up with different conclusions, a new conclusion that wasn't there before.

### Pat

Absolutely. And we don't understand that process well.

It's probably got analogs in reasoning about the physical world, where somebody is using a tool, and then it occurs to them that if they made a slight adjustment, it would work better this way. It's the same kind of process. You started off with just a sharp rock. And then after a few modifications, you have it tied to a stick, and now you've got a spear that you can use to catch fish. And we do that in the moral domain as well.

### Dylan

In a moral context, you might acknowledge, back in 500 BC, as part of their social structure, slaves were an intrinsic part of it. We can say, "Look, we know slavery is wrong, and that they could have known that then. And they just made a mistake." Another way of saying it would be "Based upon their social structure, the question of its wrongness across time could be more complicated."

And I would contrast that with something like our disposition with respect to sunburns. Now, the convention is that you go out in the sun, and you wear sunscreen. There's a sense that getting a tan is not necessarily healthy. And that was not true 30 years ago. Smoking would be another example, where it's not quite so clearly moral in the way slavery is, even if people can have a kind of moralism about it. But there's a different set of standards and judgments that have developed and we wouldn't be uncomfortable in the case of smoking, or in the case of sun-tanning, to say *People just thought differently back then*. And we think differently now. And there's no big whoop about that.

Slavery, we would feel differently about. The universalism would come out in the argument. So I was wondering about the notion that morals change based upon social circumstances over time, because that's where a lot of the fist-pumping and table-banging comes in.

**Pat**

You're right, there has been a surge of scapegoating the notion of relativism in a way that has masked important things about social behavior. Obviously, we don't want to say "Something is right, if someone thinks it's right," we can't go that direction. Philip Kitcher's very good on this point. He said, don't use the word "relativism," use the word "pluralism" as a way of acknowledging *relative to certain ecological conditions* and *relative to certain needs, and the traditions that people have, in the history of where they are.* A certain practice may be one that, from our particular vantage point and level of prosperity, we think is wrong. We can still say that "their practice is wrong," but without condemning it in a way that makes us look arrogant, smug and foolish.

But there are other kinds of cases that are different. If you think about the practice of infanticide, which was practiced very widely in all cultures, until very recently, and actually still, in some cultures, is practiced quite a lot. Amongst the Inuit, to take the easiest example, where they always lived on the knife-edge of survival, every year was a fight against starvation. It was not unreasonable if they had too many mouths to feed, and yet another girl was born, to feel sad and regretful, but to let it go.

Now, if the only alternative is that everybody starves, you can understand why there was such a practice. But it's also important to realize the practice was not one that people took joy and delight in. They didn't toss the baby into the ocean and laugh about it or anything.

**Dylan**

It wasn't based on desirability, it was based upon judgment.

**Pat**

The case of slavery in Greece was a very different institution from slavery, as we knew it, let's say, in Alabama, or Mississippi. Often Greek slaves were freed, they were often educated, they were treated with quite a lot of respect. So you can look at Aristotle with his slaves, and think, "Oh, how dreadful." But if you actually take the time to put it in the context of what life was like, for those slaves, and their expectations and the style of life that people led, then you back off condemning it as something that is just horrendous. It wasn't.

And I am betting that every table-stomping abolitionist who lived in Athens at that time, with that set of social practices, would have had slaves. We like to think that our knowledge is so deep, and that we are so good that we never would have. I'm betting you would have. At least I'm betting I would have.

### Dylan

Every time people think about living in the past, they imagine themselves as being part of royalty... rather than one of the serfs!

**Amen, brother!**

### Pat

Even in the recent past, when one thinks about attitudes that men had towards women, you think, "Wow." I had a wonderful mathematics teacher in high school, and he did this very generous thing of holding calculus classes after school for the few of us going on to college. Except that he wouldn't let any of the girls take the class, on grounds that we wouldn't be able to do calculus.

Now, I still love the guy. He was a wonderful teacher. He was mixed-up about that. I'm sure he changed his mind after he had five daughters. I can't bring myself to condemn him. I think he was wrong about that.

Okay, fine. Enough said.

### Mark

This pluralism makes more sense to me when you're taking the approach that Hume's taking, which I guess I call a bottom-up approach, rather than a top-down approach. We're not looking for universal rules. Even when moral philosophers turned away from what the *Scriptures* say should be the rules for everybody, and when they made the turn to (like Locke, say) *Let's justify these things through reason,* they still had the top-down paradigm, the divine-command paradigm.

A lot of what you're saying, in terms of how reason can inform moral judgments and how the complexities enter, turns into arguments about facts. I want to make sure we hit that.

You can say you can't get values strictly from facts. Folks' brains can be working perfectly well, in terms of the way that they understand facts. But if the part of their brain that drives the valuing is not working correctly, they can be psychopathic.

I don't want to oversimplify this. You were warning against saying *Well, whatever desires you have, that's what morality is.* That's clearly wrong. But that's the foundation right? You have to start with what purposes people actually find themselves having? And then it's just a matter that they have to live in a society. So if their purposes are antisocial, and at cross-purposes with each other, what sort of laws are we going to come up with? Unless I'm the absolute tyrant, I can't have it reflect solely my selfish desire.

**Pat**

Although Hume makes a claim that everybody has a moral sentiment, he was wrong. Normally, if an infant is loved and reared in a loving environment, and is not abused, and so forth, they grow up with very normal social responses. They are disposed to cooperate, to help, to be generous, to care about other people. But there is evidence that psychopathy is linked to abuse as a child—if the child doesn't get cuddling and nurturing and love when it's an infant, or if it's beaten up, and so forth later.

Sociality is so strong that it takes quite a lot in order to change the wiring, to make the person different.

**Mark**

It's not possible to have the experimental documentation of "Let's have a control group that treats their kids normally, and why don't you twelve people abuse your kids from their birth, and then we'll measure."

**Pat**

What we know, from studies, is if you take pups when they're born away from the mother so that she doesn't do the usual things (which involves a lot of licking, and there's her warm body and so forth), even if you feed them and keep them warm, they do grow up with a different neural chemistry. Their oxytocin and vasopressin organization is different. And socially, their behavior is different, they don't carry on properly, they don't meet properly, they don't take care of their own pups properly.

And this has provoked research on humans to see whether or not there is anything comparable. There's not much data so far. But for what it's worth, there was quite a large study done on two groups of women. One group had a very normal upbringing, got the usual cuddling and nurturing as infants, and had a loving family. The other group consisted of women who were routinely neglected as infants and who were abused.

Of course, the behavioral differences you can easily understand. But when they did the oxytocin levels, they found a significant difference. Biochemistry is going to be affected by environment. And when the environment is typical, in the sense that it's social in the normal way, you'll get one effect. But if it's very atypical, you're gonna get a different social behavior.

### Dylan

It's not just the biochemistry, but the biochemical development. The infrastructure that gets developed, that results in hormone dispersion, is socially affected. So that's an interesting hard piece of evidence regarding the significance of nurture.

### Pat

That nurturing in the very first days turns out to be really important. At least we know this in rats, we don't know this in humans. But it turns out to be very important for the density of oxytocin receptors in particular places. Genes don't express oxytocin receptors, unless the environment has a certain feature, namely this touching and licking and so forth.

### Dylan

Broadly speaking, there's a way in which we say, well, human beings are all somehow fundamentally alike. And that's one reason why we apply laws. And then we come up against this problem that some people, while they are human beings, have diminished capacities that require us to treat them differently. And there are easy examples of that.

But these examples that you just talked about, where you might be able to point to quantitative differences between individual human beings, and you could with some reliability, say "Look, you know, they're just hard-wired differently." How should we deal with that growing amount of information that allows us to make these micro-distinctions between people that are more than "Oh, your skin's different," "You're taller," "You're shorter," and stuff like that.

These are more substantive changes. You see these questions in criminal justice: "He's got real brain chemistry issues."

### Pat

These are difficult questions. In part, my response is that the most important part of the information that's coming out—about the bad effects of hitting and spanking and abusing kids—has to do with prevention, and making it broadly known to people that there are ways of teaching self-discipline to kids that don't involve beating them up.

But suppose we have a population of people, and for the sake of argument call them "psychopaths." Let's say that they don't feel remorse, they don't feel social pain, they are manipulative, and exploitative, and very dangerous. But it's not their fault.

I do go back to Aristotle. The law is there for a practical reason. The law, the criminal justice system, is there to serve social safety, civility and stability. If people have done something horrendous, and they can't be treated, then we have to be protected from them, regardless of whether or not it's their fault.

If someone likes to torture children, and is a psychopath, and gets a certain amount of pleasure out of this? We're interested in three things: *Did he do it? Can he be treated? And will he do it again?* If he can't be treated, and we are pretty sure he's going to do it again, then you have to put him in a place where he can't harm others. Considerations like "But it's not his fault," are not relevant.

### Dylan

That makes complete practical sense to me. I don't have any issue with it. But those extreme examples are, in some ways, a lot easier.

**Mark**

I want to dispel the specter of Hume here before we continue. So let me read the quote, the notorious quote, that's at the end of *Treatise: Book Three,* "Section One," the *Is-Ought distinction:*

> In every system of morality, which I have hitherto met with, I have always remarked, that the author proceeds for some time in the ordinary way of reasoning, and establishes the being of a God, or makes observations concerning human affairs; when of a sudden I am surprised to find, that instead of the usual copulations of propositions, *is,* and *is not,* I meet with no proposition that is not connected with an *ought,* or an *ought not.* This change is imperceptible; but is, however, of the last consequence. For as this *ought,* or *ought not,* expresses some new relation or affirmation, it is necessary that it should be observed and explained; and at the same time that a reason should be given, for what seems altogether inconceivable, how this new relation can be a deduction from others, which are entirely different from it. (*Treatise* 3.1.1¶29)

**Pat**

The critical word is deduction. And what he thinks and he's absolutely right, is that they imagine that they have a deduction, a logically valid argument. And it's obvious to him that they don't have a deduction. He's right to say you can never get a logically valid argument that takes you from what *is* to what *ought to be.* On the other hand, the rest of the *Treatise,* and indeed, earlier parts of that section, make it clear that we do come to draw inferences about what we ought to do on the basis of this moral sentiment that we have, and our assessment of the consequences of an action.

*Patricia Churchland is an analytic philosopher noted for her contributions to neurophilosophy and the philosophy of mind. She is UC President's Professor of Philosophy Emerita at the University of California, San Diego, where she has taught since 1984. She has also held an adjunct professorship at the Salk Institute for Biological Studies since 1989. She is a member of the Board of Trustees Moscow Center for Consciousness Studies of Philosophy Department, Moscow State University. In 2015, she was elected a Fellow of the American Academy of Arts & Sciences. Educated at the University of British Columbia, the University of Pittsburgh, and Somerville College, Oxford, she taught philosophy at the University of Manitoba from 1969 to 1984 and is married to the philosopher Paul Churchland.*
(Wikipedia)

*Brothers-in-law: Mark & Dylan*

# What's the deal with our f'ed up relationship with celebrities?

## READINGS

Burkert, Walter, and Peter Bing, *Homo Necans*, University of California Press, 1986.

Payne, Tom, *Fame, What the Classics Tell Us About Celebrities*, Picador, 2010.

Plato, *The Republic*, translated by Francis MacDonald Cornford, Oxford University Press, 1941.

Plato, *Symposium*, translated by Robin Waterfield, Oxford University Press, 1994.

Nietzsche, Friedrich, *On the Genealogy of Morals, Ecce Homo*, translated by Walter Kaufmann and RJ Hollingdale, Vintage Books, 1989.

# EPISODE 64

*September 12, 2012*

Genevieve Arnold

## LAWLESS ON PAYNE

*P̳ayne says that celebrities serve a social need that's equal parts religion and aggression. TV's Lucy Lawless (Xena, Spartacus, Battlestar Galactica) joins us to discuss the accuracy of this thesis, along with her obsession with philosophy (and our podcast), the relation between fandom and mental illness, the drive for fame, sacrificial heroes, celebrity encounters, fame for fame's sake, infamy, celebrity philosophers, mentally ill philosophers, and what Nietzsche's will to power has to do with all of this.*

*- Mark*

# 64 - Lucy Lawless

**Wes**

Thanks for coming in.

**Lucy Lawless**

Excited to hear you guys live. I've been laughing at you for the last year.

**Mark**

Now how do we prove you're not a Lucy Lawless impersonator?

**Lucy**

We don't. We're just going to embrace ignorance.

### What's Lucy working on right now?

**Mark**

We're not going to talk about what Lucy's working on right now. This is not an interview, this is her participating in a discussion. And if she talks less than half of the time, that's because there are five people on the damn call.

**Wes**

No, that's because one of us is dominating the conversation.

**Lucy**

It'll be Seth again. As usual.

**Wes**

Seth never stops.

**Lucy**

I want you guys to have an intellectual punch-up. I love it when Wes swears, and when Mark goes into Jack Black mode, and Dylan gets really cross with him. And Seth says "I'm really glad you brought that up," and then proceeds to devastate you with his quiet insight.

**Wes**

You've summed up the whole show.

### How'd you get into philosophy, Lucy?

**Lucy**

I went to the UN Summit on Sustainable Development after getting involved in the whole *Fuck you, don't destroy the Arctic, we need it to cool our planet* protest (which I'm getting sentenced for, day after tomorrow, by the way). I saw all these people working very hard, but at cross-purposes, about how do we create a just society, and environmental justice, and I wanted to know what makes a just society.

I've been listening to you guys for a while, so I thought that I would take up my little baton and go back to university and study philosophy. So it's all because of you.

It's really calming me down, going to school because I realize there's nothing new under the sun.

### And who's your favorite philosopher?

**Lucy**

The thing that surprises me the most is the Confucians. I'm really digging Daoism, and the Confucians lead into that. Sometimes I feel I'm that little praying mantis that Zhuangzi talked about, who's waving his arms in front of the wagon wheel, with the Mack Truck coming on.

**Dylan**

Zhuangzi talked about a Mack Truck I guess.

**Lucy**

He was so prescient. He knew everything.

So that's what I'm loving at the moment, and I'm struggling with other things. It's really confronted my ideas of God. It's all good stuff!

**What about today's book,** *Fame, What the Classics Tell Us About Celebrities,* **by Tom Payne?**

### Mark

The point was that even though you might think that the celebrity culture of today is a product of the media, there's at least something that can be compared fruitfully to your own experience. He managed to plunge into Homer, James Frazer's *The Golden Bough*, Faust, Ancient Greece, the Roman emperors...

### Lucy

Don't you think it's the drive for prestige –the need to stand out in a group? It's a human need to stand apart from your peers, and yet be one of them. It's so entrenched in us that it doesn't surprise me that people sought celebrity way back then. I thought about people like Elizabeth Taylor, and Richard Burton, who remained actors their entire lives. You could take those people out of Hollywood, and put them back in a Welsh mining town. They're still going to be celebrities, they're still going to be stars, because they have crazy charisma and wouldn't accept being normal.

So celebrity is a desire for prestige and to have the admiration of our peers. Because you don't really want the admiration of people you don't respect.

### Wes

I wondered about that with the emperors, if that was one of the distinguishing features with the kind of fame that Payne was talking about. He seems to be pointing to people who were famous amongst everybody, and in many cases they *didn't* respect them. They didn't seem like they were their peers.

Also, for most people, there's a need to have famous people that they can identify with, or they have some relationship with. They may not be driven to become famous themselves, but there's a cultural, societal need that goes back to some very primitive needs. Which Payne is giving us—he's recounting Frazer's *Golden*

*Bough* and, and then Walter Burkert, who wrote this book called *Homo Necans*. The idea is that we have this relationship to a sacred sacrificial animal, or to the gods, which helps us form a community. We can't even form a community without this sort of relationship.

And fame takes that over. Once we get to a stage where religion is no longer as significant as it used to be, fame and celebrities fulfill that function.

### Lucy

I remember you saying something about human sacrifice—that we need to project all our aggression or desires onto some other person, and then sacrifice them at some point when they displease us. So it helps us excise some of our own aggression as a society.

### Wes

And we need to sublimate that aggression. To form a community, we have to have these sorts of friendly bonds to one another. And to do that, we have to find a way to get rid of aggression, to turn it outwards.

One way of doing that is to direct it towards a sacrificial animal. Payne recounts this sacrifice he sees as the foundational moment for community, and even for the development of language. The sacrificial animal is the first symbol.

That's important because Burkart talks about a hunting community, where you need to kill things in order to live, and there's a fundamental conflict there. When human beings become conscious that they're going to die, they strongly identify with these animals they're killing. They're driven by this conflict between having to kill things to live, and their own desire to live. So, part of the atonement for that guilt of killing, and for the anxiety that to kill one living thing is to kill life itself and to deplete the cosmos of life-giving qualities, is to engage in the sacrificial ritual. Which, in a way, is undoing the idea that you're killing off life itself. So you elevate this animal. You make this animal important. At the same time as you're dealing with anxiety about mortality, you're also channeling these aggressive impulses to something outside of the community.

### And we love these sacrificial animals?

**Lucy**

Yeah, we love seeing those wounded animals in the magazines. I was looking at Demi Moore in the Chinese food store last night, and she was on the front looking really thin—but smiling!—and she had her hands on the shoulders of a little African boy saying, "I want to adopt."

And, you're just like "Yeah, okay. That's going to make you complete." But it's that wounded creature struggling to get up and do something that's really good. We just want to watch that and be snooty about it.

Well, maybe that's just me, I don't know! But I do recognize what you're talking about.

**Dylan**

I have this image of Lucy Lawless reading all the celebrity tabloids.

**Wes**

You're not only a celebrity, but you're into celebrities.

**Lucy**

Look, I'm just explaining to you.

**Dylan**

She was researching for the episode. That's all.

**Lucy**

I bloody sacrificed myself last week, because I went and watched the *True Hollywood Story of Britney Spears*.

**Dylan**

Wow.

**Wes**

That's legitimate.

**Lucy**

What was fascinating is how those stalkerazzi really did make her life a hell—and it's we consumers of these shitty magazines. We buy them, but we abrogate ourselves of any of the responsibility for the way those images are collected, like our hands are clean. *I just paid $2.30. I'm not stalking her.* Oh yeah, we are. It's horrifying how we turn these people into animals that we're hunting down. It's like, *Get a wicker man and stuff that kid in it, so we can laugh while she burns.*

**Wes**

That's part of what Payne is trying to understand, why we have this desire to idealize and worship and then suddenly turn that into demonization. There's a *Huffington Post* article on the slut-shaming of Kristen Stewart.

**Lucy**

Having an affair with the director?

**Wes**

That's a perfect example. She was a child actress, so there's a little-girl quality, and there's a reticence to her. She's the perfect object for these sorts of fantasies...

**Lucy**

Because we all loved her when she was an awkward teenager who looked like she might cut herself in her spare time. She looks so on the edge. We're going to love her and support her because she's bloody talented.  But she goes and makes an adult mistake, and we're going to punish her for growing up.

**Wes**

Right. The first sign of sexuality and it's this hysterical reaction, and of course the media loves it. They glom on to that, and that creates headlines for weeks.

**Seth**

The assumption of Payne's book is that we are violent creatures. It endorses a particular view of the state of nature—the "nasty, brutish and short" point of view. We're violent creatures, and somehow in forming communities, in order to be civilized, we have to have an outlet for that violent aggression. Fame is somehow this relationship between individuals in the community whereby we are able to live out certain kinds of violence. So our celebrities are set up specifically to fail or to be caught in these traps.

**Lucy**

The book explores all the different ways and reasons that people court fame.

It's interesting to see kids who didn't ask for fame. You know, let's see what happens to Tom Cruise's child. Don't you find it so disgusting that we don't know our neighbor's kids, but we know Suri Cruise and what the hell she's wearing on her feet this week. It's really perverse.

**Mark**

As you were saying, we are to blame as well.

**Wes**

I don't think any of us has escaped celebrity worship.

**Lucy**

Whether it's sports stars or whatever, right? Doesn't it go back to that thing about Zeus splitting us, with the double people? We sense some lack of wholeness, so we're trying to fill it with all kinds of stuff that can't possibly nourish you, and this is just another one of those addictions.

> It was their very essence that had been split in two, so each half missed its other half and tried to be with it. (*Symposium* 191b)

**Mark**

That's exactly what religion jumps in to take advantage of. From Payne's point of view, that is the appropriate role of religion, and he considers this celebrity worship as a religious phenomena. It's not that different even if you're completely secular, and you say *Oh I don't want to make these crazy metaphysical claims about God.* The role psychologically that these things had historically is very much the same role that celebrities have now.

**Lucy**

That's interesting. Sometimes I think that the God belief is almost like replicating that inner sense. If I get up, *a la* Descartes, and I'm going to doubt everything I ever was told about God, and I look around and I see so much chaos, and people are doing bad things, I want to think that there is some big Mack Daddy out here that is going to take revenge, and they'll get what's coming to them. Then my God is like a means of revenge for me.

**Mark**

The Furies.

**Lucy**

The Furies will come down on you. I know them personally. I did a few episodes with them.

### So, is it time for a fresh virgin?

**Mark**

Payne says normally we have this cycle of celebration, consecration and sacrifice. But that's not inevitable. It's just that when the celebrities displease us, we're so willing to turn against the ones that we've worshiped.

**Lucy**

When the beauty fades, you want to get a fresh virgin. In the book it goes on about Britney cutting her hair off, very publicly—that's the sort of thing women do when they're wanting to get a divorce. It's about taking back your power. You take on a male role. Cutting your hair off is a very significant thing for a woman.

**Dylan**

Being happy that people who have success get brought down to our level—the phenomenon of wanting to cut all the strands of wheat that stick out—it seems to be related.

Part of the deal with fame is that people want it. So the virgins who are being sacrificed fought over the privilege to do that, and the athletes who are going to be tossed out, after they lose a fraction of their batting average, fight tooth-and-nail to get there, and the politicians—they're all trying to get there and enjoy that fame, whatever that is.

## Lucy

In the book, he talked about glory over death. We're going to die anyway, I might as well die sooner with a whole lot of glory, go out and do something spectacular with my life.

## Wes

It's not just there are celebrities—demigods—and we worship them. There's the idea that if we get lucky, or if we work hard enough, we could become one of them. And that's part of the identification that's going on. Is that what you're getting at, Dylan?

## Dylan

I'm not even thinking about identification. I'm thinking about distinguishing yourself from other people. If you really want to be famous, you don't want to be like everybody else. If you crave being famous, you want to make sure that you are different and distinguished from everybody else.

If you want to be famous by being the one chosen to be sacrificed, you're fighting for that and you don't want somebody to cut in line ahead of you for that. If you want to be the most famous band in the world, yeah, you want other people to be successful, but you really want your band to be the most famous. You're craving notoriety, you're craving success, and it gets all smudged together. You may want to be successful for the right reasons. But fame doesn't distinguish between those things.

## Mark

I think resentment is a pretty key part of that. I know from my own experience that I will feel like *Why is that band getting press? My band isn't getting any.* You feel that at least some portion of the celebrity crowd does not deserve it. It's supposed to be meritocratic, they're supposed to be so charismatic or so talented, and of course people's opinions are always going to be different. No matter how honestly talented and charismatic some particular celebrity is, there's going to be a significant portion of the people that person's image is thrust upon that are going to disagree, and are going to be cheering if they go down.

**Wes**

These days, it's not even a meritocracy. People are famous just for being famous. That's the common complaint.

**Dylan**

They've always been famous for just being famous.

### But enough about the Kardashians...

**Lucy**

Here's the thing though. The only reason I log into Twitter—ever!—is you've got to feed that monster a little bit. You've got to be recognized in order to be cast in certain shows. It's not a meritocracy. It's not enough to be talented to get cast in a certain movie. You have to be on a list of actors who are considered hot right now, whether they're good or not. There's this bizarre little list in Hollywood of young up-and-comers. You have to have some profile, some worth in the media in order to get cast.

**Seth**

It's not just about the individual's desire to be famous, it's about the fact that who is famous is determined by the people in the community. You can create fame, but at the same time you also have to satisfy a certain set of needs or desires that people have for the famous.

**Lucy**

Unless you're good, unless you're talented, you won't keep a career past that honeymoon period, when your beauty fades, or they have rubbished you enough and you just fade into the distance. You better be something other than just beautiful, or a good sport, or whatever to keep working. But you do have to service it.

**Seth**

In the book he talks about how the animal sacrifice was an occasion to eat meat, and that there's this transference through the blood. Maybe people feel like if you are holding something transcendent or unique, or some spiritual power...

**Lucy**

...they can consume that.

**Wes**

Love and hate are intimately related. Idealization leads to demonization because the idealized object of your affections can't really live up to them.

**Lucy**

Because you've been made to look bigger, taller, shinier than you are, and let's face it, there's six people who are doing your wigs and your make-up and sewing you into a corset and making you look a certain way and lighting you in a certain way and putting words in your mouth, so you do seem like an elevated creature but really you're just a composite of so many people's hard work.

**Dylan**

You can't have a Julius Caesar unless you have all of the centurions, or Napoleon without his dedicated soldiers who were willing to throw themselves on a pike.

**Lucy**

You're right. That's why you have to give them a little bit of something all the time. You have to nourish that bloody fan base a bit. They're the ones who are getting really mad if they get rejected. The ones who want to be associated with that for the sheer sake of touching fame up close and personal.

### What about the fans at home?

**Lucy**

I think people like having that one-way relationship, where they have all the power—Nietzsche bringing down the aristocracy.

**Mark**

The resentment of the weak.

> Born of weakness, *ressentiment* is most harmful for the
> weak themselves. (Nietzsche, 6¶6 / 231)

**Lucy**

We don't want to see them as real people because then we might have to feel something.

**Mark**

And yet we want them to be our best friends in some sense.

**Lucy**

Only on your terms. You'd be friends with me when I want you, and when you say, "Well, sorry I've got a life, I've got children or I've been too busy," you broke the fourth wall. You ruined the fantasy.

**Dylan**

Fame would not be compatible with friendship, in the sense that you would have to have a different relationship with that person.

I've experienced this in the relationships with students. Just because I was their teacher, or because they had seen me give a lecture, they would have to work up the courage to come and talk to me. I would say in class, "Well, you know, if you want to go get a cup of coffee, and talk about something, come and get ahold of me."

So they will, and then they won't have anything to say. I have to run the whole conversation.

**Lucy**

Friends don't want you to be a celebrity. My friends and I never watched each other's shows. We don't even know when they're on. Nobody cares.

If you're a smart celebrity, you are also going to have a very normal life. You can go off and be famous in order to service your work, as a tool, but it's a terrible folly to think that all those images are real.

*continued on page 332*

*What is the relationship between one thing and many things?*

READINGS

Brann, Eva, *The Logos of Heraclitus,* Paul Dry Books, 2011.

Heraclitus, *Fragments: The Collective Wisdom of Heraclitus,* translated by Brooks Haxton, Viking, 2001.

# EPISODE 79

*June 22, 2013*

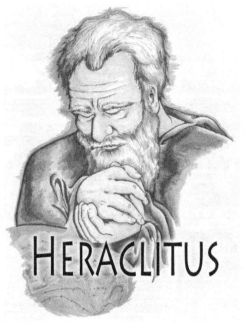

HERACLITUS

*Genevieve Arnold*

## EVA BRANN ON HERACLITUS

*Eva Brann discusses her book* The Logos of Heraclitus *(2011). What is the world like, and how can we understand it? Heraclitus thinks that the answer to both questions is found in "the Logos."*

*- Mark*

# 79 - Brann on Heraclitus

**How did YOU jokers manage to get Eva on your podcast?**

**Dylan**

I tutor at St. John's College, starting in 2001. And Eve has been a tutor at St. John's since 1957! I had the great fortune in my very first year as a tutor here to have Eva as my seminar partner. And for me, who had not studied philosophy and came in as a physicist, it was a real pleasant experience.

**Eva Brann**

I knew right away, he belonged to us. So it was a happy year.

**Dylan**

So you should know that, within the first month, there'll be 50,000 downloads of the conversation, that people listen to, all over the world.

**Mark**

And maybe some of them will buy your book.

**Eva**

You guys out there should know that I don't have a computer.

**Dylan**

I told them that.

**Mark**

Yes, that you write your books on papyrus.

**Eva**

Stone tablets if I can get them.

**So why didn't you read a book by Heraclitus for today?**

**Mark**

Because there is no book by Heraclitus. It has not survived.

**Eva**

It isn't that it didn't survive. We don't even know if there was a book. It may have been some sort of collection. And it's not clear just how much of it there was. I'm convinced that we have the most important parts of some aspects of what he wrote.

**Wes**

He has a dense aphoristic style. If it were a book, it'd be hard to sustain that as a longer narrative.

**Eva**

It would look like a book by Nietzsche, you know.

**Wes**

Exactly.

**Let's get started.**

**Dylan**

One place to start with is pointing out Heraclitus' reputation as the "fire and flux" guy. "Everything is fire," "Everything is flux." "You can't step into the same river twice." All those are Heraclitus.

**Eva**

Fire is true. And flux is false.

**Wes**

Most of us get to know Heraclitus through Plato and Aristotle, right? That's really our first encounter with them. And each of them has an agenda—that's part of where the flux thing comes from.

**Eva**

That's where the flux comes from, and sayings that he never said, like "You can't step into the same river twice."

I have huge respect for Aristotle. But as far as Heraclitus was concerned, he just didn't get it.

He's not the only one. These people reported on him a generation or two after he died. They thought that he had something to do with making harmony out of opposites. But he had no interest in harmony whatsoever. He was for head-on contradiction, and strife, stress, and war. He thinks that's what makes the world alive. Not reconciliation.

**Wes**

He used the metaphor of two wrestlers who are in stasis, but they're pushing against each other. Despite that antagonism, there's also something synthetic going on, right? The world is, in some sense, being unified through this process?

**Eva**

It's a synthesis, which is not a melding into each other, or a reconciliation with each other. It's the synthesis of two opposites that abut on each other, and in doing so prop each other up. That's when the wrestlers are a really good picture. They stand up because they're falling into each other.

**Mark**

Could we give a Darwinist picture of all the parts of nature struggling against each other? And that's what makes it a unified system? Would that even make sense, if you're talking about physics?

**Eva**

There are some partial answers to that. For instance, Heraclitus is interested in the force of tension, what it means to be in tension with each other. Where is the tension located? Is it in the ends, or is it in the middle somewhere? That's a way of being held together by opposition.

What is it, that goes through everything, that's present everywhere, in such a way as to make all things comparable? He thinks that's fire. He thinks that there's a kind of fundamental matter, but it's not a material matter, that underlies all physical being and makes it possible. That's the reason why physical beings have number-relationships to each other. It's why they are measurable. Things like that make him a philosopher of opposition.

### Wes

A lot of listeners will come to this confused and say, *Well, what is Heraclitus doing? What kind of question is he trying to answer? Is it metaphysical? Is it epistemological? Is it physics?* In a way, it's all of those things, right? He's looking for some fundamental unified theory of the cosmos, this fundamental cosmological principle, but it will have all kinds of explanatory power, that transcends these distinctions between metaphysics and physics and epistemology.

### Eva

He's interested in whether rationality, the ability to answer to mathematical formulas, is immanent, or comes from the outside. That is to say, whether the *Logos*, the ratio-relation that obtains between kinds of matter, between times, and powers, whether those are inbuilt and right in the matter itself, or whether they come from the outside, and beyond it. My ability to give a mathematical account of the world, does that come from some extraphysical character that the world has? Or is it right in the natural being of the world? And if it isn't, then where can I find it? Because by looking at it, you certainly can't find it.

### Mark

I always thought that was a place where the physicist-as-pure-physicist would stop. Scientific laws just describe regularities. You don't ask, "Where does the scientific law come from?" You might ask, "Is there some underlying feature that's causing this particular regularity?" But in terms of what makes things lawlike in general? That's just taken as a methodological given. If they were chaotic, then there'd be no point in doing science to analyze them. And, while we found that mathematical models seem to represent all these complicated physical phenomena, that's just one of the paradigmatic assumptions that the scientist is proceeding on, and not inquiring into itself.

**Wes**

But they are looking for mechanisms, right? Part of what particle physics is doing is trying to explain regularities in terms of lower-level forces, including (interestingly, because of its relevance here to Heraclitus) forces of attraction and repulsion. So it's not that you just established a regularity, and then you can't go any further. There's some mechanism that you can find beneath that. And often that depends on these kinds of part-whole relations.

**Eva**

And what does "beneath" mean, in that case? In some way governing the phenomena you're observing, from the outside? Or arising from within the phenomena that you're looking at?

**Dylan**

This makes me think of someone like Leibniz, where his whole world is turned, but in the end, it's turned from the outside. Deterministic physicists end up having to have some starting point. Even Aristotle. You have the prime mover that somehow manages to have one foot in and one foot out all the time. It's never from within, it's a crank that's turned on the outside.

**Mark**

The modern take is more that we will always look for an immanent structure. The "lower level" means the next smallest particles composing what you're talking about.

**Wes**

You're looking within, in the sense of one particle breaking down into other particles, with properties that determine the overall property of the larger particle.

**Eva**

That means you're always dealing with emergent properties going upwards, and then it's "turtles all the way down," as far as the elements are concerned.

**Wes**

Is he saying that we need the *Logos* to save us from that?

**Eva**

He would ask, "Look, I'm at a level in which physical substances, physical beings, have number-relations to each other. And those are transformational relations. And others, they turn into each other according to certain numerical values. Where exactly in the pieces I'm looking at, do I find the numbers? Do I impose them on nature, as nature contains them? Or does some principle of rationality impose them from beyond?"

I think he had his own opinion. He thought that what he called the *Logos* was a principle that imposed, from beyond, the capability for things in nature to have mathematical relations to each other. But I think he'd understand the argument that's not right, that there isn't a principle beyond that imposes relations, but that it's somehow internal. *What it is internally that makes that possible?*

He actually has an answer to that, he thinks every part of nature, whether those are substances, or time relations, has a fiery basis. And fire is an analytical element, which allows natures, and which is analyzed to be numerically understood.

The Pythagoreans faced the same question. They thought that the answer was simply that nature was numbers-and-geometry, was numerical. Heraclitus understood the problem. But he had an answer.

**Seth**

Don't you ultimately conclude, in the book, that his answer is to say that the Logos is transcendent and immanent?

**Eva**

It's the transcendent Logos, and it's the immanent fire. And the logs on the fire have similar characteristics. Fire is analytic. It breaks things up. The etymology of the word "analysis" is breaking things up. Fire does that, and it's transformative, so that the world is one through transformations, one through many.

**Seth**

So would his response to the argument that the organizing principle is immanent be something like "In order for that immanence to have force or be impactful, there has to be that transcendent element and we're just not seeing it"? Or is he making a sly move here and saying, "My transcendence is immanent."

### Eva

I don't think he waffles. He means to be ambivalent here. There is a visible element, namely fire. But there is an invisible element, that is not specific, but that is absolutely universal, that has fiery characteristics, and has the characteristic of imposing a rational character on different parts of nature.

I think he'd say *The question you ask is one on which I mean to be paradoxical. I mean to be ambivalent. And the reason is because that's the way the world actually is.*

He wants to put the Logos behind everything, or above everything, and then allow the *logoi*—that is to say, the individual ratios—because it's important to him that Logos means "ratio" and "speech" and "principle." So this *super-Logos,* that's a principle, a philosophical basis. And then there are the *logoi,* which are the ratios of mathematical relations that he thinks govern all of nature. So there's Logos outside, and there's Logos inside.

### Mark

In this book, you've made the case that we shouldn't translate "Logos," because *Logos* has some important ambiguities that we should just preserve. We already are familiar with the term from all the kinds of "ologies," pretty much any kind of science—it has to do with knowledge, right? It has to do with "I'm giving an account of something." *Ratio* is the Latin word for it. So all rationality, all that stuff having to do with the human mind is all Logos.

Folks might know that it also just stands for "word." And it's used in the Christian tradition, as *The Word,* capital "W," which is the meaning behind things. And the way Heraclitus is using it is not just the meaning of what somebody says, but the meaning in the world, the force that drives it to be the way it is, the underlying pattern.

### Wes

It seems to be something like a divine presence, or something someone might want to call "God." His language is suggestive of that.

**Eva**

I sometimes call it the "Super Logos," although Heraclitus wants to prevent us from giving you a specific god's name. He does think not only that it is at work, but it's wisely at work. And he blames Homer—of all people, Homer who wrote epic, gory fighting for pages and pages—for being too conciliatory. He wants the world to be antagonistic. There was something about antagonism that appealed to him—he mentioned that he was personally hard to get along with. But he really thought vitality was a battle. He says "If you harmonize everything, then everything goes away." It becomes flat. There's no real world anymore. So there's a sense that antagonisms, antitheses and oppositions keep the world vital. And there's a certain truth in that, it seems to me.

**Wes**

Think of modern physics. If there were only attractive forces in the universe, everything would just collapse. There needs to be a certain amount of repulsive forces for things to maintain some sort of articulation. It can't just be one big indiscriminate soup, things have to stand out from each other.

**Seth**

What echoed for me was classical Greek poetry and histories, and talking about strife and Eros as being motivating forces. Without war, strife or tension, you end up with something that's static.

**Eva**

Yes, something blankly unified.

It's not possible that these two people ever met each other. But imagine if they did, what Heraclitus would have said to Parmenides.

*Look, we both care about the same thing, how the world, on the one hand, has a certain unity, and on the other hand, has infinite variety. You say that only what is unqualified being could be said to 'be,' and that everything else is simply appearance.*

*Well, appearance is also something. It's in appearance that the world becomes a world, and being is just a great blank. What is this being that I'm not allowed to say anything about? It doesn't move. It doesn't have coloration. It doesn't smell like anything.*

Heraclitus had great faith in what you see and hear.

**Wes**

Parmenides and Heraclitus would have been, not good friends necessarily, but they would have been very good frenemies.

**Eva**

It's not clear to me that Heraclitus was friends with anybody. This is one of the things that attracts me to him. There's something so personal about him. He's hard to get along with, pessimistic, harsh. He says all the Ephesians should go hang themselves and let the kids take over!

> As for the Ephesians, I would have them, youths, elders, and all those between, go hang themselves, leaving the city in the abler hands of children. With banishment of Heromodoros they say No man should be worthier than average. Thus, my fellow citizens declare, whoever would seek excellence can find it elsewhere among others. (114/121)

## Back to this idea of stability

**Mark**

Is it even coherent to say there's a stable ambiguity in nature itself?

**Eva**

One way to understand the notion of a stable ambivalence is as a perspectival notion. Look at it from one point of view, and this is how it is, look at it from another point of view, the opposite is the case. Then, have the kind of intellect that is capable of holding both of these perspectives in view at once, and not only living with it, but finding some meaning behind that. If you allow yourself to take two perspectives, you often get direct antitheses. Such truth as we can reach consists of allowing both of these to be alive in your intellect. So you might argue that it is more of a prescription for being human than it is a way of saying, "What is the truth?"

The sea is both pure and tainted, healthy and good haven
to fish, to men impotable and deadly. (52/61)

**Mark**

This is taken to say that Heraclitus is a relativist of some sort. But
the way that you had talked about perspectivism is that it's not a
matter of relativism. There is one unitary fact of the matter here. But
the fact of the matter implies different things about fish and about
people. You have to have a fixed point, in order to have different
perspectives on it.

**Eva**

You may have to give up. Or you may have to declare the answer
a mystery. What is that stable background which allows you to have
different viewpoints? But he would have said that he does have a
name for the answer, even if it isn't an absolutely clear one. And that
the name for that answer is Logos.

# Brann

*Genevieve Arnold*

*Why should some things not be for sale?*

### READINGS

Sandel, Michael J., *What Money Can't Buy: The Moral Limits of Markets*, Farrar, Straus & Giroux, 2012.

Smith, Adam, *Theory of Moral Sentiments*, Penguin Classics, 2010.

# EPISODE 98

*July 10, 2014*

*Genevieve Arnold*

## MICHAEL J. SANDEL

*I*nterviewing *Michael Sandel on his book* What Money Can't Buy: The Moral Limits of Markets *and continuing the discussion of his first book,* Liberalism and the Limits of Justice. *Free economic transactions are supposed to benefit both the buyer and the seller, so why not allow prostitution, vote buying, pay-to-immigrate, selling ad space on your house or body, and premium versions of everything for those willing to pay more? Sandel thinks that these practices are degrading even if uncoerced, and argues that classical liberalism–by trying to maintain neutrality on philosophical questions like "what is the good?"–doesn't have the resources to prevent rampant and undesirable commodification.*

*- Mark*

# 98 - Sandel

## Can you introduce the book, Mark?

**Mark**

This book is made for popular consumption. It's all concrete. It's all current events. It's related to a specific point in time. This book is being driven by the financial crisis, and what our reaction should have been to it, which is to reevaluate completely the encroachment of economics on our lives.

**Michael**

I did write this book in the hopes that it would address questions in a way that is accessible not only to scholars, but to citizens generally, and to interested readers. And so, as you mentioned, I use a lot of examples and illustrations and ethical dilemmas, with an eye to bringing out some of the big philosophical questions that lie just beneath the surface of the debates we have.

**Mark**

This book is a political act. It's a push to say, "There are conversations that should be driving our political decision making, but aren't—our political rhetoric is too empty." You'd like a public discourse on values.

**Michael**

I think the great missing debate in our public life is what should be the role of money and markets in a good society.

Today, there are very few things money can't buy. Economic thinking and market reasoning have reached into spheres of life far beyond the domain of material goods. So the question is whether we want to live in a society where (almost) everything is up for sale, where market values and market thinking dominate family life, community life, health, education, civic life, politics and law? How can we think about where markets serve the public good, and where they don't belong?

### Seth

I've seen quite a few videos on *YouTube*, where you've gone and done lectures. Did you want to insert yourself into the public discourse, maybe even in the political realm? To make this more activist?

### Michael

I was drawn to philosophy in the first place through an interest in politics. Growing up, I was always a political junkie, I love to follow elections and campaigns and debates from a practical point of view. And it wasn't until graduate school that I became interested in philosophy. I wanted always to connect philosophy to the world, to show that the debates we have every day in our public life, and in our personal lives, rest on big philosophical questions, competing principles of justice and ethics, even though we may not reflect directly or systematically on those questions. And so, with this book, I wanted to take an issue that has always interested me as a philosophical matter: *Does market thinking miss important values? And does it undermine certain important social practices?* I wanted to connect that debate to our contemporary public life, because in recent decades, we've drifted, almost without realizing it, from having a *market economy* to becoming a *market society*. The market economy is a tool for organizing productive activity, but a market society is the place where everything is for sale. And the question I'm hoping to generate discussion about is *Do we want to live this way?* And if not, how should we conceive the social goods and practices that we prize?

### Mark

You're saying it's not just corruption that we've had this drift, it's a lot of individual things. An airline says *Instead of making everybody wait in line*, which is a very democratic thing, *let's offer premium seats, so folks can jump the line if they pay an extra amount.* And there are lots of other different cases like that. Even if you're okay with those on an individual basis, they build up to this idea that everything is for sale.

We think immigration is something based on merit, or on whether you're a refugee from somewhere. But if you invest this much money in US companies, to create so many jobs, you get a loophole. You've said that for many mainstream economists this is built-in. They think that, in a pluralistic society, the best that we can hope for in terms of maximizing the good for people, maximizing justice, is market thinking. Any market exchange benefits the seller, it benefits the buyer. If it didn't benefit both, they wouldn't do it. It's the ultimate form of distributed power. Instead of some central agency saying *You can or can't make this kind of exchange,* just let people make the exchanges they want. It's an argument that's supposedly egalitarian.

### Michael

Freedom of choice, that's the rationale. Markets embody freedom, because they consist of voluntary choices among consenting adults, to trade goods, and sell services of whatever kind, on terms they find agreeable. That's theory.

And that works pretty well, if we're talking about material goods: Cars, toasters, flat-screen televisions. It doesn't work so well—it raises hard moral questions—when that logic is extended to the kinds of questions you were raising: *Should we put immigration, the right to live in the US up for sale, as a way of resolving the messy disputes we have about immigration?* Gary Becker, who recently passed away, a Nobel-Prize-winning economist at the University of Chicago, proposed exactly that. He said, *Let's solve the immigration debate by simply putting a price on the right to emigrate, $50,000 or $100,000. And let the market decide.*

It comes up in debates about commercial surrogacy. *Should paid pregnancy be a practice that is permitted or encouraged by law?* What about voting? If you take the principle of mutually advantageous voluntary exchanges, why not have a free market in votes? After all, there are many people who don't care enough to vote, half the people don't even use their votes in presidential elections, we know there are people who would like to buy them. So why not allow the same logic of mutually advantageous voluntary exchanges to play out with regard to buying and selling votes? Or babies for that matter, up for adoption? We don't allow explicit, outright markets in votes. But maybe that's because we haven't extended that logic consistently enough.

I say the reason we don't allow explicit markets in votes—or in children!—has to do with certain limits to that logic of market choice. Limits that should also apply to many practices where we don't interrogate the role of market thinking.

### Mark

Can you say a little more about the point of view that you are opposing, that this is not only good for freedom, it does also end up fulfilling the utilitarian calculus.

### And also, can you make this sexier?

### Michael

What about prostitution?

### Perfect.

### Michael

Now, there are two familiar objections, ethical objections to prostitution, putting sex up for sale. One of them is that typically the prostitutes are not really choosing freely. They're under the burden of economic necessity, poverty, drug addiction, the threat of violence. So the choice is typically not truly free. That's one objection, the *implicit coercion* in poverty or drug addiction.

But there's a further objection that many people raise against prostitution, which is quite apart from the question of whether it's coerced. Some say it's degrading, it's contrary to human dignity to sell one's body for sex, independent of the question of consent. So there's two different arguments. Is the transaction really free or implicitly coerced? That's the *freedom question*. And even if it is free, does this amount to a degradation or a violation of human dignity in some way? I call this the *argument from corruption or degradation of a good.* These are the two main objections to putting everything up for sale. And while the first is the most familiar in our public discourse, it's the second that is the most far-reaching. Though some would say it's philosophically controversial, because to speak of corruption or degradation is to presuppose a certain conception of "the Good"—in this case, the good of human sexuality and of human dignity—and people disagree about those judgments.

### Dylan

Isn't it also true that the first one is addressable with market thinking? The reply from a market-based approach would be it's a fine-tuning problem of leveling the playing field.

### Michael

That's right. You could address that problem by saying "All right, let's establish fair background conditions in the society, such that no one is so desperately poor that he or she is forced to sell sex, or to sell a kidney, or a cornea in order to feed his or her family."

So you're exactly right. You could address what we might call the coercion objection, or the poverty objection, without in any way calling into question the market logic itself, which is why I put the emphasis on the second kind of question, because in some ways, it's the hardest. And it's philosophically the most challenging, because it requires us to reason, case-by-case, about *What exactly is the good being corrupted?*

Take an institutional example: Should private, selective, elite universities, auction off a handful of seats in the freshman class, admitting students who may not be so academically strong, but whose parents will give $10 million to the school or build a new library? Some would say it's unfair to those kids who don't have the good judgment to be born to wealthy parents. That's the fairness objection. But you might also ask "Does this corrupt the mission of the university?" So this corruption argument requires that we analyze and debate the goods, the missions, and the purposes that give meaning to social practices and human goods.

### Seth

If you see a lot of economic discourse around the financial crisis, it's *Oh, well, we set up the wrong incentives*. It's not that the system itself was structured in such a way that this was the inevitable conclusion. It's that the government did something wrong. And that seems to be the common response.

I wonder whether they even have the context or the framework to address the second of your criticisms. I don't think the advocates of the market approach have the language to address the notion of degradation. It takes somebody coming from outside to say the system itself has that built into it.

### Mark

I came at this more as an individual. If you're making choices, do you make choices explicitly, with an economic evaluation in mind? For instance, as a freshman taking sociology, I was informed that entering into college was "an investment in my future." I never thought about it in that way before, and quickly thought, well, that must just be my own lack of reflection; If you're a reasonable person you evaluate everything, looking in terms of the long-term and short-term practical advantages and lining it up with what you really value, *etcetera, etcetera.*

It ends up in the existentialist challenge of Ayn Rand: *If you're idling away your time, you're committing a sin against yourself, because you should be looking at every single thing you do from a pseudo-economic perspective.* Even if you can't put a number on how much you value time with your spouse, or any other things like that, they're all potentially quantifiable. It's no accident that individualist attitude is tied to Ayn Rand's advocation of laissez-faire capitalism.

### Michael

It's very interesting that it had never occurred to you, until they gave you this bromide about college being "an investment in your future." This goes along with the language we often hear about investing in one's human capital. So even the language of individual and personal self-development and education becomes assimilated to the language of building capital.

But this is an impoverished and potentially pernicious way of describing the purpose of education. I don't think we should be encouraging incoming freshmen to think of a college education primarily in those terms. Of course, the hope is that a college education will equip students to get good jobs, to be effective participants in economic life. But that's not the only, or even the main purpose. And the language implies that's the main purpose, rather than to become more effective citizens, to more fully explore one's own human capacities and to develop them.

So the economistic way of looking at life insinuates itself into individual life, into the way our aspirations are described. How many economists speak in mystic terms, yet are not alive to the questions of goods, of corruption, of degradation? One of the reasons for this, at least within the academy, is that economics today is presented and taught as if it were a value-neutral science of human behavior and social choice.

Economics has not always been conceived this way. If you go back to the classical economists—from Adam Smith to John Stuart Mill, and Karl Marx—despite their ideological differences, they all agreed that economics is a branch of moral-and-political philosophy. But in the 20th century, economics reconceived itself as a value-neutral science, which therefore, by definition, could take no account of questions of the meaning of goods or the way in which market relations and market thinking might corrupt or degrade the meaning of social practices.

So part of my aim in writing the book is to argue for a new way of doing economics, which is to reconnect economics with moral-and-political philosophy. And then, beyond that, to work out the implications of this for the way we do our politics and the way we conduct our public life.

### Seth

That's a really interesting point. It's well-documented how important the*ory of Moral Sentiments* was to Smith's development of economic theory, but even Hayek, the champion of the Chicago School, was very politically motivated. His conception about the free society and the free market was formed as a response to totalitarianism and fascism.

### Michael

Right. Agree or disagree with Hayek, he was connecting economic questions with philosophical and political questions.

### Dylan

That makes it more clear why, in response to totalitarianism, the subtext of the importance of freedom would ring loud and true. The further trajectory is to make it into a value-neutral science that, by its own structure, gives you the answers to all these questions that were previously moral and political questions.

But you say, *Now I have a value-neutral approach, I can backtrack and address all the questions that I originally used values for.* It becomes overextended.

### Michael

The temptation of this way of thinking goes beyond the academic. Economists desire to quantify everything, and to measure everything, and to enjoy the prestige of science. We need to ask, *Why does this way of thinking have a public resonance beyond the domain of academia?*

There is something powerfully appealing in the idea that we can avoid debating questions about the good life, questions about the right way of valuing goods and social practices. It's appealing, because we know that in pluralist societies, we disagree about competing conceptions of the good life, we disagree about the best way to live, we disagree about how properly to value sex, or child rearing, or family life, or education or health. And so, in the face of those disagreements, there's a powerful tendency to say *Let's try to conduct our public debate without reference to them. Let's set aside controversial conceptions of the good life, and decide our public policy and our laws without reference to them.*

The idea of economics as a value-neutral system—the idea that markets are mechanisms that don't require that we engage with these questions—is powerfully appealing. I think it's a mistaken impulse. But until we confront that impulse directly, we're not going to make headway.

### Dylan

One place you see this is the attempts to come up with ways of evaluating schools, or teachers, or students, in progressively more quantified ways, in which the measurements trump any other kind of judgment about whether the teaching process is working. Education becomes more and more naturally viewed as a commodity, and the students are fundamentally only customers that ought to be getting value for their investment. And then the fact that the student didn't get an A, and didn't get a great job, becomes the fault of their education, because they paid a lot of money for it.

Where that fails is in trying to think about the way we raise children. And even though we have that commodified, market-based discussion about public and private education, it doesn't seem like we think that that's the way parents ought to be judging their children.

### Mark

Michael, you've been putting forward thesis that everything is becoming commercialized. One could easily say, homelife is central, and is for the most part, not commercialized, unless we're talking about life-insurance, or there's a lawsuit involved. But for the most part, these are fringe elements upon a solid foundation that involves us not looking at our private lives as commercial. We have a sharp distinction between the private life and the public life.

### Michael

It's a fair point. And I do think there are important pockets and resources of non-market thinking in family life and civil society. And those pockets and resources provide the moral intuitions and understandings that I'm trying to appeal to. But at the same time, I agree there is a tendency to commodify education. The drive to assessment, and what is often called "accountability" (which are powerful movements in public policy towards education) can easily slip into a commodifying view of education and its purpose, that can crowd out the more intrinsic aspects of education—self-development, the love of learning, the capacity to become citizens.

And as for life-insurance—I have a chapter in the book on life-insurance, which may seem an arcane topic, but I found it fascinating morally, and philosophically. We think of it as a way of protecting families against the untimely death of the provider, that's a traditional view. But most insurance these days is not of that kind. As a result of the commodification of life-insurance and the financialization of it over the last 30 years, there's an enormous secondary market in life-insurance policies, where investors and brokers are engaged in the activity of betting on the lives of strangers and how long people will live.

So even in this domain, if you actually look at it, what begins as an instrument of security and protection for one's family becomes just another financial instrument. They now even have death bonds on Wall Street, where they securitize portfolios of life-insurance—slice-and-dice them as they did with the home-mortgage market and sell them off. These deaths bonds, of course, have nothing whatsoever to do with protecting the security of a family.

### Mark

The whole issue of betting brings the intuitions into stark display. If you accept that gambling in general is okay, then there seems to be no specific reason available to the economic point of view for why you should restrict what they can gamble about.

### Michael

The starkest example of this is that the *Wall Street Journal* reported about 10 years ago that Walmart and other big companies were taking out life-insurance policies on their workers. Not their CEOs, who might be expensive to replace if they suddenly die, but on their maintenance workers, on their cashiers, on their janitors. This was unbeknownst to the employee. And so, when an employee would die, Walmart would get the proceeds. From the standpoint of market logic, it's hard to object, because it was Walmart who entered into the contract with the life-insurance company. They paid the premiums, so that they, not the family, should get the benefit when the person dies.

The moral objection is that Walmart is placing a wager on when its maintenance workers will die, and reaping the benefit when they do. When it came to light, some state said, "We can't allow this without the consent of the worker." Although, strictly speaking, if someone's placing a side bet on when you will die, and if they don't put a banana-peel in your way to hasten your death, have they really harmed you?

It's not clear that they have, unless you accept a certain idea about the proper relation between an employer and the employee. *Is something contrary to the appropriate relation between Walmart and its employees embodied in this practice?* I think it's hard to explain what's objectionable about it, and why it shouldn't be permitted, without engaging in a moral discourse. People will disagree. But that's not a reason to avoid having the debate,

### Dylan

Part of the concern in your book is not just the degradation of the value of human life, but the effect that it has on the community as a whole, the harm that market-based thinking does to democracy as a whole. Eventually, the very things that are valued in our democracy get undermined.

### Michael

When I was a kid growing up, I was a baseball fan, and we'd go see the Minnesota Twins play. Back then, mid '60s, there were always box seats that were more expensive and bleacher seats that were cheaper. But the difference in price between the most expensive seat in the stadium and the cheapest was about $2.50. The experience of going to a baseball game was a kind of class-mixing experience. It was a place where CEOs sat side-by-side with mailroom clerks.

That's not why people went. They went to see Sandy Koufax, but that was the effect, and everyone rooted for the home team. Everyone had to wait in the same long line for the restroom. Everyone had to drink the same stale beer and eat the same soggy hotdogs, and when it rained, everyone got wet. That was just part of the experience. But during the last 35 years, almost every major league baseball stadium, and most football and basketball stadiums and arenas, have created skyboxes for those who can afford it. And corporate CEOs and their guests watch in air-conditioned comfort high above the field, and cut off from the common folk in the stands below.

The effect is that it's no longer true that everyone stands in the same long line for the restroom. It's no longer true that when it rains, everyone gets wet. I call that "skybox suffocation," and it wouldn't matter very much if it only happened in sports stadia. But something similar has been happening throughout American society during the last three decades, against a background of rising inequality. Putting a price on everything, commodifying every aspect of life, has the effect of driving people apart, of leading the affluent and those who have modest means to live increasingly separate lives. And so we look up and we find that we live and work and shop and play in different places, we send our children to different schools.

This isn't good for democracy, it's a corrosive effect. This relentless commodification and inequality together are corrosive of the sense that we are all in this together. And this brings me back to your question about the effect on democracy. Democracy doesn't require perfect equality. But it does require  that people from different social backgrounds, different walks of life, encounter one another, and bump up against one another in the public spaces of everyday life. Because this is what teaches us to negotiate, and to abide our differences. And this is how we come to care for the common good, to feel that we're all in this together. And so in this subtle but cumulative way, the relentless commodification of life, together with rising inequality, have undermined social solidarity— that commonality that democracy requires.

*Dylan through the ages*

*Nothing short of a scandal?*

## Readings

Nietzsche, Friedrich, *The Gay Science: With a Prelude in Rhymes and an Appendix of Songs,* translated by Walter Kaufmann, Vintage, 1974.

Rawls, John, *A Theory of Justice, 2nd Edition,* Belknap Press, 1999.

Sandel, Michael J., *Liberalism and the Limits of Justice,* Cambridge University Press, 1998.

# The Limits of "The Limits of Justice"

*October 21, 2015*

*based on an image by Genevieve Arnold*

## Wes Alwan

*M*ichael Sandel is one of America's best-known political philosophers, *and helped establish his reputation with a widely respected and widely taught book,* Liberalism and the Limits of Justice. *He was also kind enough to make an appearance on* The Partially Examined Life. *So I don't relish saying that I think that the esteemed reputation of* Liberalism and the Limits of Justice *is nothing short of a scandal. That is not because I dispute the plausibility of the claim that community is fundamentally important to human well-being, and that the ethos of liberalism is in tension with it. Rather it's because Sandel makes the stronger claim that a certain kind of liberalism "stands opposed ... to the possibility of community in the constitutive sense," and his central argument for this claim is based on fundamental errors in reasoning.*

*- Wes*

# The Limits of "The Limits"

**Michael, as much as we've all enjoyed** *What Money Can't Buy,* **I know your previous book** *Liberalism and the Limits of Justice,* **sent Wes into what I can best describe as "a rage." Since this is our book, we're going to allow him some uninterrupted time to attack your position. But would you like to set that up for us a little first?**

## Michael

My argument is against the version of liberalism that was worked out brilliantly by John Rawls, and which harks back to the philosophy of Kant, the version that says, *In defining justice, in defining the basic structure of society, in defining people's fundamental rights and liberties, we should set aside our disagreements about the good life or about virtue, or about the best way to live.* We should, as Rawls and Kant put it, assert the priority of the "right" over the "good." And that's the question, is it possible? And if it's possible, is it desirable to define justice and rights without taking sides on debates about the good?

My argument was, "No, it's often not possible to do that," and even where it may be possible, it's not necessarily desirable to set aside substantive moral conceptions in thinking about justice.

Contemporary liberalism has, in large part, been unable to raise serious questions or engage in serious debate about the proper role and reach of markets, because it draws on an assumption that derives from Rawls and Kant, namely, that in at least deciding the basic structure of society, and in shaping the essentials of public discourse, we should not get into messy debates about the good life. But to rule all that out is to disempower us from questioning the market logic that we've been discussing.

## Wes, your rebuttal?

### Wes

You're claiming this sort of deontological liberalism is inconsistent with the existence of real communities, because it's grounded in this Kantian conception of an unencumbered, transcendental ego that can't be constituted by its ends. But Kant's conception of the self is actually much larger than that. There's the empirical self, and the self that's constituted by its ends, and that has communal attachments, and so on, and so forth. I'm not sure, by the way, that Rawls is even depending on the Kantian conception of the self so strongly, but even if we assume that for the sake of argument, when I say for the purposes of setting up a state, I'm going to think about only this minimal conception of the good, the thin theory of the good, and I'm going to treat only one very thin slice of the self, let's call it "the transcendental ego," that doesn't imply to me that all there is to the self is the transcendental ego. It's just for the purposes of setting up the state, because we know the society is going to be pluralistic.

That's what we're going to think about. And so we're going to avoid legislating some conception of the good. We're not going to have an Islamic state, or a Christian state, or however you want to put it. And a liberal society, in that sense, is entirely consistent with real communities in which people have not just transcendental egos, but empirical selves that are strongly constituted by their communal attachments.

That's one objection. The other is a question. If we're not going to bracket out specific conceptions of the good for the purposes of setting up a state, how exactly does that change the way the state is set up? What are the practical implications of that? I don't think any of us want to see the state enforce religion, or enforce some other specific theory of the good life. So if the state's not going to enforce that, what is the practical upshot?

### Michael

Let me start with the first point. One way of putting this is to ask what is the connection between liberal neutrality toward the good—toward moral and religious and spiritual conceptions—and the idea of the unencumbered or the freely choosing independent self—a self conceived independent of its purposes, aims and attachments? In Rawls' work *A Theory of Justice*, neutrality toward the good would be to say *We are, above all, freely choosing independent selves.* To respect persons as free and independent selves is to create a framework of rights that allows each of us to pursue our own ends, however we may choose them, consistent with respecting a similar liberty for others. That's the standard view.

But is it possible to define a basic structure or framework of fundamental rights without passing any judgment on substantive moral or religious conceptions? I don't think so. Take the example of abortion. *What is the neutral position on abortion,* in the sense that it doesn't take sides in a theological dispute about the moral status of the fetus? Some would say some policies such as *Roe v. Wade,* where you leave to each woman the right to decide for herself without imposing any particular answer.

Now, *I* think something like *Roe v. Wade* is the best policy. But I don't think that I can defend that policy, or that anyone can, while claiming that I'm being neutral with regard to the moral and theological convictions of people who believe that, from the moment of conception, we have a human person worthy of respect. If they're right, I'm wrong.

There's something disingenuous for those who favor relatively permissive abortion laws to claim that they're not presupposing any particular answer to this theological or moral question about the status of the fetus. We should own up to it and articulate it and defend it and consider the counter-arguments from those who disagree.

Something similar is true in the debate about same-sex marriage. Now, you might say, *It's simply a matter of non-discrimination.* We don't have to pass any judgment about the moral worth of unions between members of the same sex, as compared to unions between a man and a woman. I disagree. I think that the argument for same-sex marriage—which I'm very much in favor of—requires that we engage with questions about what the purpose of marriage is. There are those who claim, for moral or religious reasons, that the purpose of marriage is to provide a framework for procreation and to encourage and honor procreation, and that therefore, same-sex marriage is at odds with the purposes of marriage. And there are other views that say that the purpose of marriage is not only the raising of children and the honoring of childbearing and procreation, but also a lifelong loving commitment between two dedicated partners regardless of their sex.

Now, choosing between these two accounts of the moral purpose of marriage-as-a-social-institution takes us to contested moral terrain, that implicates, in some cases, religious views, in other cases, strongly held moral views. I don't think we can decide the same-sex marriage question or even make a convincing case for same-sex marriage without engaging with those arguments.

So my main argument against the Rawlsian claim to neutrality is that even to define our rights, even to design the basic structure of society in a constitution, requires that we engage with, rather than ignore or set aside certain—sometimes controversial and contentious—moral, spiritual, or even theological questions.

**Thanks. There's a lot more discussion of this in the full podcast, but for the purposes of our book, we're going to turn this over now to Wes.**

## Part I: A Sketch of My Critique

Suppose I told you the following fairy tale, one that for some reason didn't make it into the compilations of the Brothers Grimm: A shepherd goes into a shop to buy some shears. The available shears are all very attractive for different reasons, and the shepherd cannot choose between them. The shopkeeper suggests that he close his eyes and pick blindly, and that's what the shepherd does. With his nice new shears in hand, the shepherd returns to his flock. But there is a problem: The shepherd finds that every time he uses these shears on one of his sheep, the sheep goes blind. So the shepherd returns to the shopkeeper to complain. The shopkeeper identifies the problem: It's not that the shears are poisoned, and it's not that the shepherd is using them incorrectly by applying them directly to the eyes. The problem can be explained, says the shopkeeper, by the following maxim: *Shears chosen blindly produce blind sheep.*

Now consider the similar logic at work in Michael Sandel's *Liberalism and the Limits of Justice*: Principles of justice derived without a view to identity tend to produce societies with identity-blind citizens. Here's a less awkward way of putting it: *Principles of justice derived from an abstract conception of the self produce societies that stand opposed to fully realized selves.*

By the same logic, citizens in political orders founded without regard to pudding, can't ever have any pudding. Not even after they've eaten their meat.

In case you doubt the accuracy and charity of this general sketch, let's dig a little deeper.

## Part II: Sandel's Central Argument

Sandel argues that liberalism—or at least a version of "deontological liberalism" he associates with the philosophers Kant and Rawls—"stands opposed ... to the possibility of community in the constitutive sense." This is Sandel's central thesis, and in what follows I'm going to describe the central argument he makes in support of it, while for the most part leaving aside the book's subsidiary theses. Along the way I'll be explaining some of the philosophical concepts at issue with my own examples.

What Sandel means by "community in the constitutive sense," is community insofar as it has a role in shaping who I am. If I belong to a certain religious community, then my identity is constituted in part by membership in this community. The primary mechanism here consists of the values I share with other community members, and that I have been bequeathed by the community: for example, the importance of going to church, or of virtues like chastity, or of certain religious rituals, or of the community itself. Sandel uses the word "ends" instead of "values," because values might be construed as something extraneous to our identities that we can adopt or discard as we desire—a view he erroneously associates with Kant (see *Part V*). "Ends" leaves us more explicitly open to the view—one sometimes associated with Aristotelian teleology and final causation—that what is good for a living being is part of its nature, and so is objectively grounded outside of desire.

It's worth noting that the way that Sandel uses the word "ends" is a significant extension of Aristotelian virtue ethics. Aristotelian ends are underwritten by human nature, and are applicable to all human beings. They define a set of virtues, dispositions grounded in character, that include such universally desirable qualities as courage and temperance. Courage is a virtue for human beings because it is the actualization of an end that is grounded in human biology and psychology. It is good to be courageous because we are so constituted that acting courageously enhances our well-being (*eudaimonia*, variously translated as "happiness" and "flourishing"). By analogy, I might think of a set of virtues and ends that are defined not by nature but by culture, including the specific communities to which I belong. In shaping my identity, these communities define for me goods that are more specific than courage and other Aristotelian virtues. If I am raised as a Muslim, then my identity is shaped in such a way as to define for me certain Muslim-related ends, in the same way that biology defines for me certain human-related ends.

Consequently, community-related ends are no more arbitrarily defined than those shaped by nature. If being a Muslim has shaped my identity, then ends related to being a Muslim—including certain religious beliefs and practices—are fundamental to my well-being. It is a matter of chance—and so arbitrary in a sense—that I grew up a Muslim rather than a Christian. But the ends defined by my being a Muslim or Christian—and the relationship of my well-being to them—are not at all arbitrary, and not merely a matter of choice based on desire: they actualize a set of dispositions that have been ingrained in me from early on. This is not to say that I might not find some other community, with formative powers that define new ends and new criteria for my well-being (as in a conversion from Christianity to Islam). And it's not to say that communities might define ends for me that are bad for me, insofar as the conflict with ends defined by my humanity; for example, communities in which violence and sexual abuse are norms. But what's relevant here is that my identity and my ends are shaped by membership in multiple communities, some of which are presumably important to my well-being. These may be national, religious, ethnic, professional, educational, and familial, and I assume this list goes on to any level of specificity we like.

Each of my examples—for example, being courageous, or a Muslim—

is an account of what is good for me based on my identity as determined by certain formative influences. Following Rawls, Sandel calls this a "thick" conception of the good, to distinguish it from a minimal conception that is less aspirational and focused instead on "primary goods," including basic rights and liberties. This "thin" conception of the good is indirectly the basis for Rawls of a derivation (via a set of actors in the "original position") of liberal principles of justice that are meant to be broad enough to allow varying thick conceptions of the good to flourish under their umbrella: in this sense, "the right is prior to the good." For instance, liberal societies prohibit murder but not certain religious practices (except to the extent that those practices violate other fundamental prohibitions). We call this "pluralism," and one of its goals is to allow the peaceful coexistence of people who want to live fundamentally different kinds of lives, in communities with ends that are different and in some cases opposed. Justice is meant to serve as the most general moral framework in which various more robust conceptions of the good may thrive to the extent that they do not contradict this framework.

According to Sandel, in deriving its principles of justice from a thin conception of the good, deontological liberalism derives them from a thin conception of the self. The thick version of the good includes the ends that are formative of a "thickly constituted self." By abstracting from these ends, we abstract from this richer version of the self. The ground of a liberal society is an "unencumbered self" that, instead of being individuated by its ends, is "antecedently individuated prior to its experience," and so individuated prior to its ends. This means that what distinguishes you from me under this conception of the self is not the richer differences in our identities that we often associate with our character, ends, and the social forces that go into shaping these things, including group affiliations such as race and religion. Instead, we are distinguished by the mere fact of being two numerically separate consciousnesses with differing desires—desires that are the result not of character or social forces but our own free choices. We are in this sense thinly constituted selves, not constituted by our ends, or "attachments that go to the core of identity." Instead we are in possession of desires that we can freely abandon as we will.

According to Sandel, this unencumbered self is not just theoretical ground for a liberal society, but its product. Basing principles of justice on such theoretical, unencumbered self leads to these principles being inconsistent with communities in which our ends and identities are at stake (I will treat Sandel's vague "stands opposed to" as "inconsistent with," since this is clearly the way he talks in the rest of the book: for example, a derivation of principles of justice from the unencumbered self "rules out the possibility of a public life in which ... the identity ... of the participants could be at stake"). Consequently, the pluralism of liberalism—the extent to which it provides a framework for differing conceptions of the good, for instance, different religious communities— is incomplete, and the principles of justice involved in liberalism are not neutral with regard to the varying conceptions of the good for which it is meant to serve as an umbrella, but hostile to them. This is not to say that we cannot form communities within liberal societies. It's just that these communities cannot be communities in the fullest sense, which is to say "constitutive." As a consequence, we are forced in liberal societies to live lives as something like the unencumbered selves that we theoretically posit for the sake of deriving our principles of justice.

## Part III: A Critique of Sandel's Central Argument

Let's assume for the sake of argument that Sandel is right that both Kantian and Rawlsian theories of justice require that liberal principles be derived from some minimal conception of the self. The question is, in what sense is the "unencumbered self" from which these principles are derived inconsistent with the existence of genuine communities in societies ruled by such principles? It's not, of course, that these hypothetical, non-existent, unencumbered selves of theory simply migrate into reality, becoming the actual real-world human beings who live in a state whose political order they were used to justify. Imagine here Rawls's actors in the original position: not quite as blind as the shepherd, but choosing principles of justice without being fully cognizant of their identities and ends. What's the mechanism via which they transfer this lack of encumbrance to the citizen-herd? Why do shears chosen blindly produce blind sheep?

Sandel's central argument in *Liberalism and the Limits of Justice* does not answer this question. (A preface and new closing chapter for the second edition of the book seem to be afterthoughts meant to remedy this problem—I address these below and in *Part IV*). Sandel seems to assume

a.  that a derivation of principles of justice from theoretical unencumbered selves imply that there is no more to one's "theory of the person" than these unencumbered selves, and

b.  that the negation of encumbered selves in any theory used to justify principles of justice means that these principles must be actually opposed, or causally negating, to the actual existence of thickly constituted selves and communities.

None of this follows. Consider the following analogous logical example: My derivation of some theorem from a certain minimal set of axioms doesn't make this theorem inconsistent with all the additional axioms that I might have—but didn't—include from the beginning in my system. I have to demonstrate separately that theorem itself is inconsistent with those other axioms. Pointing out that liberalism nowhere grounds itself in thickly constituted selves does absolutely no work when it comes to the task of demonstrating that its consequences are inconsistent with thickly constituted selves.

But suppose we concede for the sake of argument that the set of assumptions from which we derive our principles of justice includes or implies the impossibility of thickly constituted selves. This still doesn't get Sandel where he wants to go. We can derive true theorems from false axioms, and we can derive principles of justice conciliatory to thickly constituted selves from assumptions that deny their existence. Similarly, it is entirely possible that an eccentric potter who develops a strange method of potting based on the bizarre belief that there is no such thing as wine, nevertheless produces pots that are capable of holding wine. Sandel has somehow to make the transition from this logical inconsistency between a theoretical justification of liberal societies and thickly constituted selves, to a necessary causal relationship between liberal societies and thickly constituted selves. He has to identify some causal mechanism that explains why liberal principles of justice would be necessarily hostile, in practice, to identity and community.

Now suppose that liberal principles do in fact turn out to be opposed to thickly constituted selves, and that the assumptions we used to derive our liberal principles are also opposed to thickly constituted selves. Could these two facts have anything to do with each other? They couldn't. Rawlsian or Kantian justifications of liberalism can't tell us anything about the nature of liberalism. If it turned out that principles derived from premises opposed to thickly constituted selves abandoned some conception of human rights, then what we have derived is no longer liberalism. We know from the beginning the nature of liberalism, and our justifications cannot alter it, whether they involve accurate theories of personhood or absurd theories of personhood. Again, what we need is for Sandel to identify some causal mechanism that is necessarily associated with liberalism.

Despite Sandel's avoidance of talk about possible causal mechanisms in his central argument, there is one possibility that will immediately occur to most readers. It's clear that liberal regimes will not endorse more robust conceptions of the good (I use "endorsement" here to include some level of enforcement of such conceptions of the good, and perhaps prohibition of competing conceptions). So one method of establishing a causal mechanism linking liberalism to a lack of constitutive community would be to show that for ends to properly constitute us, they require such state endorsement. But Sandel does not make this argument, and I think we can assume he would see the necessity of state endorsement in this strong sense as a result whose perniciousness trumps the value of constitutive communities. Nevertheless, it is truly strange that Sandel fails to address this possibility: the whole *raison d'etre* of liberalism is to avoid the terrible consequences of endorsement (including, for example, of religion). Most readers will be wondering, and will expect Sandel to address, the following questions: Is he suggesting minor modifications to liberalism, or some alternative political scheme? In either case, how do we make sure to avoid the terrible consequences that liberalism is meant to solve, including the curtailment of liberty and the persecution of certain communities? Or does the value of constitutive community trump the possibility of such consequences? Anyway, what is the proposed political scheme even called, if it is not either some form of authoritarianism or some minor modification of liberalism? Sandel never addresses these questions, and it gives one the impression that he is avoiding the most difficult—and relevant—challenges to his thesis.

Sandel comes closest to explaining why liberalism is causally opposed to constitutive communities in his preface to the second edition of *Liberalism and the Limits of Justice*. Here he gives two examples. In the case of religious liberty, he argues that while religious pluralism ought to be preserved, it ought to be preserved for the right—that is, non-liberal—reasons. This means that we ought to ground religious liberty—including a "special respect" shown to religions and religious practices—not in human rights and respect for individuals, but in respect for religions themselves. This respect is to be grounded in the fact that the content of a specific religion is actually valuable, and as such "essential" to the good of members of religious communities, and "indispensable to their identity." A grounding of religious pluralism in liberalism implies that religion is just like any other preference of the unencumbered self, and so is deprived of its power to constitute encumbered selves. In his second example, Sandel makes a case for establishing limits to freedom of speech: "hate speech ... can inflict a harm as real and as damaging as some physical harms" and reaches "the core of ... identities and life stories." The remedy here is curtailment of such speech based not on liberal principles (which already imply numerous limits to free speech), but on the content of the speech itself. Specifically, we must balance "the moral importance of the speech in relation to the moral status of the settled identities the speech would disrupt or offend."

These examples seem to imply the following explanation for the inconsistency of liberalism and constitutive community: it's not that state endorsement is necessary in the strong sense (of outright enforcement and prohibition) to constitutive communities, but that state endorsement is necessary in some weaker sense. This causal principle focuses on the content of people's beliefs and their expression of these beliefs. So while the Sandelian state wouldn't be in the business of affirming one religion and outlawing other religions, it would be in the business of affirming religion-in-general and outlawing "harmful" speech.

Now, all of this ought to make you scratch your head, for two reasons. The first is that Sandel's focus on "content" is not actually consistent with the pluralism he seems to wish to preserve. Not all communities have laudable ends conducive to our well-being, however much they are "constitutive." And presumably not everything that calls itself a religion is good for us, either. If the state is to really endorse religion based on content rather than freedom of conscience, it must distinguish good content from bad. And the making of these distinctions is in no way consistent with the affirmation of religion in general. If all religions have valuable content deserving state endorsement, that's a curious result given that the content of religions is often contradictory. One, of course, might take the view that anything constitutive is good, as long as it doesn't meet some definition of harm. But this means that it was never the content of religious ends that was at issue, but their property of being constitutive. In this case then, even by his own account, Sandel only differs from liberals in that he thinks it's important that the justification for religious pluralism be the property of being *objectively-valuable-because-constitutive,* whereas liberalism relies on the property of being *subjectively-valuable-because-desired.* Special respect is due not because certain communal ends are objectively better than those of a community with diametrically opposite ends; but because these ends are beside the point, except to the extent that they do no harm and play their constitutive role. Are these ends then really all that different from what it is that I desire? Isn't desire arguably—as a matter of psychology—determined in part by communal ties, and inherently constitutive? Isn't the distinction Sandel is making here the product of analytic scholasticism, and ultimately bogus?

Here's the second head-scratcher when it comes to the implied causal role of weak endorsement: it's very clear that while liberal societies will do their best to avoid endorsement, strong or weak, it's not at all clear that constitutive communities can't survive without it. If Sandel wants to make this his causal principle, he must argue for it. And thesis he needs to argue is a cultural thesis, to the effect that the liberal ethos is corrosive to the cultural forces that make communities constitutive. It's entirely possible that the value of religious tolerance, for example, leads to a weakening of religious faith, and so nudges us closer to the imaginary horizon of the unencumbered self.

While this is a plausible cultural thesis, it is not one that Sandel ever argues. It is, after all, a complicated thesis that would benefit from some empirical data, and forays into anthropology, psychology, sociology, and history. Most of us intuitively accept the idea that the liberal ethos is in tension with community to some degree: this is a truism. But most of us would be surprised to find that it rises to Sandelian levels of inconsistency, and most of us would be surprised that this inconsistency could be derived a priori from theoretical justifications of liberalism.

In any case, the real questions are now many, and include: to what extent does the liberal ethos weaken constitutive community? How do we distinguish the effects of the ethos of liberalism with other possible causal mechanisms, such as technology?

Whatever Sandel might have established in defending such a cultural thesis, it would be a far cry from showing that liberal societies lead to the unencumbered selves he describes. It is not possible for a liberal society—through cultural mechanisms—to turn us into free-floating transcendental subjects, devoid of our empirical selves, including our bodies and our personalities. And however liberalism weakens communal attachments and ends, it could not deprive us entirely of our thickly constituted selves, with personalities and human relationships and ends that go far beyond "thou shalt not kill" and other minimal moral limits. The many forces that shape our identities—biological, psychological, social, and cultural—do not simply vanish in a liberal society. So Sandel cannot really argue that liberal societies are actually inconsistent with thickly constituted selves and constitutive communities. At worst, they have an attenuating effect.

Finally, even for this cultural thesis, Sandel's causal mechanism of weak endorsement won't get him very far. Is the death of God really to be explained not by the advent of science, technology, industrialization, and so on, but by lack of legislation that ensures that communities feel respected and shields them from offense? Are communities really so fragile as to be made non-constitutive by the lack of such protections? Are communities—these powerful, identity-constituting entities—really such shrinking wallflowers that offense and lack of just the right kind of "special respect" is the key to their downfall?

In any case, in his central argument Sandel fails to identify any workable causal mechanism for liberal hostility to constitutive communities, and rather harps on the *non sequitur* that the entirely theoretical, unencumbered selves used to derive principles of justice will necessarily lead to actual unencumbered selves that presumably get flattened out by actual liberal societies. He gives us a long account of the plight of the unencumbered self—its lack of identity, its arbitrary desire, and its inability to know itself. And he gives a bizarre account of Kant's transcendental subject, as if Kant thought there were no such things as bodies and psyches. Kant's transcendental subject is not his complete "theory of the person," which actually includes an empirical subject that is entirely capable of being constituted by its ends, including its communal attachments, in just the way that Sandel requires. That's why, as we saw above, an actual psychology of desire is not as distinct from the function of ends as Sandel would like. Sandel might rightly argue that such ends wouldn't, by Kant's standards, fall within the domain of moral obligation. But this is just to complain that Kant's ethics is not a virtue ethics, and that liberalism is not a virtue politics. And a virtue politics is decisively, as we shall see in Part IV, not something that any sane person should want out of a state.

## Part IV: A Critique of Sandel's Supplementary Arguments

Sandel's later addition to *Liberalism and the Limits of Justice*, "A Response to Rawls' *Political Liberalism*," departs entirely from the central argument I have critiqued above. Where the argument of the bulk of the book is that liberal principles of justice are hostile to community in the constitutive sense, its amended argument is that questions of justice cannot be settled without reference to some conception of the good that is stronger than the thin conception upon which liberalism rests. This is a movement from the radical claim that liberal principles of justice are inconsistent with more robust conceptions of the good, to the much weaker claim that liberal principles of justice are incomplete until we take into account more robust conceptions of the good. Specifically, Sandel claims that:

1.  It is not always reasonable to exclude particular conceptions of the good when thinking about what is just, especially when thinking about grave moral questions. Particular moral and religious doctrines might, after all, be true, outweighing the values of toleration and fairness. Since Catholics might be right in claiming that abortion is murder, we cannot simply bracket out this question. When courts abstain from ruling on the question of where life begins, they are issuing a *de facto* judgment against the claim that life begins at conception.

2.  Pluralism about morality and religion also apply to questions of justice: people can reasonably disagree about what is just, and often do (as with, for example, gay rights and affirmative action).

The liberal would reply here that what we reasonably disagree about in such cases is not the fundamental principles of justice, but their application. Sandel's rejoinder is that this is not the case with distributive justice: If Rawls can reason his way to preferring the difference principle over libertarianism, why shouldn't a society be able to reason its way to the permissibility of homosexuality (rather than merely remain neutral on this issue of permissibility and merely tolerate it)? In general, why can't we reason about moral and religious controversies in the way that Rawls reasons about distributive justice?

3. Despite its emphasis on free speech, liberalism places unduly severe restrictions on the content of our debates. It precludes incorporating our moral and religious ideals into our discussion of fundamental political and constitutional questions, and "leaves little room for the kind of public deliberation necessary to test the plausibility of contending comprehensive moralities—to persuade others of the merits of our moral ideals, to be persuaded by others of the merits of theirs." A politics that precludes such discussions in turn "generates disenchantment" and cedes the debate to intolerant fundamentalists.

Do any of these arguments work? I don't think so.

Let's begin with (1): Consider what a debate between interlocutors who disagree about abortion would look like, and how they might incorporate their particular conceptions of the good into that debate. The mere fact of having such a conception, and the identity associated with it, cannot itself form the basis for a justification of my belief, no matter how important a role it played in causing me to have the belief. If I were an anti-abortion Catholic, my justification for opposing abortion could never be, "because I'm a Catholic," even if my Catholicism is the primary causal force historically for my holding this position. In general, my justification on questions of justice could never be "because of my identity," or "because that's my faith," or "because that's my particular conception of the good" or "because I belong to such-and-such a community." These are causes, not justifications. If these were to count as justifications, then debates would consist of a crossfire of assertions between irreconcilable communities barred forever from genuine communication with each other by the event-horizons of their differing thickly constituted identities (and specifically, by that impossibly versatile tool that is taking offense).

In a real debate, interlocutors meet on common ground where it's at least conceivable that agreement could be reached. In a real debate about abortion, the central question is whether we think of a fetus as a person and if so, how we balance its well-being against that of the woman who carries it. What's common between the interlocutors here is the same principle of justice and morality: that we ought not to kill human beings indiscriminately. And if we can't agree on that, we have a disagreement not about whether morality can be deontologically justified, but whether there is such a thing as morality at all. Consequently, what interlocutors must differ on in the case of abortion is the application of a principle of justice, not the principle itself.

Disagreements about application of principles of justice will indeed rest on interlocutors' more robust conceptions of the good. But settling their disagreements about application does not amount to appealing to those conceptions as such, and seeing which one overpowers the other. To persuade someone that a fetus is a person, you must persuade them that their position is actually inconsistent with their own more basic moral intuitions, by analyzing the concept of personhood in the direction of these intuitions. You can combine this approach, if you like, with empirical evidence (for example, by linking studies of the nature of fetal consciousness to intuitions about the relationship between consciousness and personhood). This debate looks precisely the same, whatever your intuitions, whatever your ends, and whatever communal association provided you with such ends. Your Catholicism might have provided you, as a matter of influence, with a valuable way of thinking about the world, and it might provide you with motives for your beliefs. But your Catholicism would never be a form of evidence in a debate, never a justification for some position. It might be good enough for you, but it will never be good enough for others who do not already share your convictions. Consequently, there is no genuine version of debate that is anchored—at the level of justification—in identity. If liberal debates rule out the justificatory force of my identity, so does every genuine debate.

Further, it is not the case that when the justice system takes a neutral position on the question of when personhood begins, it is issuing a *de facto* ruling against the metaphysical claims of abortion opponents. Laws are often pragmatic compromises, not rulings on fundamental philosophical questions. We cannot abstain from making laws on the grounds that we have not settled such questions, which often show no signs of ever being settled. When we make a law prohibiting sex between adults and someone under the age of 16, we are not making a metaphysical claim that the age of 16 is a magical dividing line between sexual immaturity and sexual adulthood, when we know that such maturity—physical and psychological—varies greatly between individuals. Similarly, *Roe vs. Wade* is a pragmatic compromise. It says, essentially: people disagree about whether fetuses are persons. But almost everyone agrees that at the very least, sperm and unfertilized eggs are not persons, while newborn babies are. Therefore, as a matter of compromise, we can suppose at the very least that over the course of nine months, a fetus is gradually becoming a person, and we can accordingly allow laws regulating abortion to become increasingly restrictive over the course of that development.

Systems of justice can and do abstract from particular conceptions of the good. This sort of neutrality is not a claim to absolute neutrality, as Sandel suggests, since liberalism is indeed based on a minimal conception of the good. But there is an argument for the minimal conception: and the argument is that it is the most politically agnostic. It is the least presumptuous in what it claims to know about the world, the closest to being an admission of Socratic ignorance. It makes the fewest possible moral claims—drawing the line, for example, at "thou shall not kill" rather than at "thou shalt believe in Christ." Sandel's suggestion that such agnosticism amounts to a competing dogmatism is unworkable. If he is right, then any position we might take is dogma, and then the question becomes which position is least dogmatic. My claim to not knowing could never be more presumptuous than your claim to know something else, for example your claim to be a provider of good news concerning God or community or something else. But here's a simpler and more historically relevant way of putting it: I can never know enough to justify killing you for not agreeing with me.

In his second critique, Sandel seems initially to accede to the liberal rebuttal: that what we reasonably disagree about with regard to justice is not its fundamental principles, but their application. But Sandel points to an exception when it comes to the question of distributive justice, about which we can reasonably agree. And oddly, he wants to conclude that if we can disagree about distributive justice, then we can disagree about justice-as-fairness. But is this really the case? Does the fact that there is a debate to be had about the way resources are distributed in a society really mean that there is a debate to be had about fundamental human rights?

For example, Sandel is confident that he can ground the permissibility of homosexuality not in human rights, but in virtue ethics. To do this, he asks us to make a transition from the principle that all human beings ought to be able to live as they wish, providing this way of life causes no harm to others, to the principle that the permissibility of any way of life depends upon our reasoning about whether it constitutes the "highest end" in some domain. In doing so, we are to talk in the language of ends, and argue that the "highest end of human procreation" is not "the good of reproduction" but the goods of "love and responsibility."

What could possibly go wrong here? For a preliminary empirical investigation, I recommend picking up a book of history and reminding yourself of the millennia of human mass-murder and oppression in the name of upholding a strict equation between the permissible and the good. This is the glaring fact of conflict created by pluralism, the real motive for liberalism that Sandel tries to sidestep with his adventures into the a priori. "Goodness" and "highest ends" are not sound criteria for whether you get to prohibit gay people from living happy lives, or more generally, for what ought to be permissible within a society.

If you find this empirical investigation unsatisfying, remind yourself what is good in this strong sense—and what the highest human ends are—are bones of contention, not just a matter of historical circumstance, but of philosophical recalcitrance. "The good" in the strongest sense amounts to a difficult philosophical question that—like the mind-body problem—cannot in principle be settled, however much insight we gain into it. In the face of such difficulties, there is actually a moral imperative to admit our ignorance.

Such admissions of ignorance—or more broadly, states of moral agnosticism and open-mindedness—are not simply retreats into the psychical desert of the unencumbered self, and need not deprive us of our passions and ends, identity and faith. Consider Pyrrhonian skepticism, for which suspension of theoretical judgment is thought to be in no way inconsistent with ordinary belief and life. Consider the long theological tradition, in which wrestling with doubt is not inconsistent with faith. Consider Nietzschean irony and psychoanalytic integration, in which thought and passion need not remain mutually opposed, irreconcilable primal forces. Sandel may disagree with the possibility of such reconciliation; but since his theme is an irreconcilable conflict between liberty and identity, he ought not simply pretend he has never heard of accounts that reconcile theoretical agnosticism with personal commitment.

And such tension—psychological and political—between moral agnosticism and one's most deeply held commitments is a good thing: it is the ground for open-mindedness, curiosity, and even joy. It is of fundamental importance to good lives and good states. You cannot say the same about any random "end" that you have unthinkingly adopted as part of some community, however "constitutive" it is. Liberalism— and a more minimal conception of the good on which there is broader agreement—is not a perverse scheme depriving us of every other end we might have. It is a way of acknowledging our human frailty in the face of certain profound questions. It is an act of humility, in which we institutionalize the fact of our shortcomings. And finally, it is a matter of empathy toward those who would like to live lives with ends different from our own.

Meanwhile, any invitation to an analysis of permissibility in terms of "the good" is an invitation to abuse: it means that between the fact of our ignorance and our aspiration to something higher, anyone can insert the verbiage required to rationalize the oppression of a minority based on their supposed deviation from this good. The inherently flawed nature of human beings means that the elitist standards of state-mandated virtue ethics can be used as ammunition to condemn any group we like. By some ideal standard our relationships are always imperfect, and to some degree destructive and perverse. Consequently, traditional philosophical arguments concerning the unnaturalness of homosexuality are actually critiques of the imperfectness of all human sexuality, disguised to make them seem applicable only to a subset of humanity. The equation of the permissible with the good really just gives us license to arbitrarily decide which group we are going to hold to such standards.

Arguments against homosexuality have historically been framed in just such a way. Anyone can assert any end they like for sexuality, because the question of what leads finally to human flourishing—and whether it is the same for all—is actually so complex as to make the answer indeterminate. Sandel's assertion that the end of sex is love will only convince someone who already agrees with him; it is an *ad hoc* rationalization by someone who already assumes the permissibility of homosexuality, not something that might persuade anyone with a different idea of the good. By contrast, the concept of equality—insofar as it appeals to fundamental, shared conceptions of fairness—can be enormously persuasive to those who are willing to think something through, even if they start from the standpoint of bigotry. So I don't think it is a good idea to abandon the notion of human equality, so that a Sandel—or any other philosopher—can help us argue our way back to the dignity and humanity of some group within a society. We are better off taking a more cautious approach. The attempt to escape the limited nature of our moral knowledge—into the certitude of "ends"—is not something on which we can ground the well-being of others.

This leaves us with Sandel's third critique, to the effect that liberalism places unduly severe restrictions on the content of our debates, precluding the discussion of moral and political ideals. I think my arguments above show that this is not at all the case in principle. But does the ethos of liberalism nevertheless restrict our debates in practice? Presumably Sandel means either that interlocutors are

a. less likely to advance arguments motivated by religious beliefs or moral ideals or

b. unwilling to make use of the fact of their religious belief—or their identity or ends in general—as a reason for their beliefs.

If Sandel means (b), it bears reiterating that while identity can provide a causal basis for our beliefs, it can't actually be a reason for our beliefs, in the sense of a justification that is potentially appealing to someone who doesn't already share our ends. Arguments by their very nature abstract from these things. That means that it would be difficult for Sandel to empirically verify his claim in (a). Sophisticated arguments will tend toward offering reasons, not reiterating the fact of identity or religious belief. So when an author offers a religion-free argument in a magazine, it is not safe to assume that the author is not religious, or not motivated by religious beliefs (it is entirely possible, for instance, that my well-reasoned critique of Sandel is motivated by a deep commitment to Islam). It is safer to assume that the religion-eschewing author actually wants to communicate with human beings who don't already share the same opinions, and doesn't believe that "I'm a Catholic, so you should be too" is a persuasive form of argument. Meanwhile, there is plenty of public and academic debate premised on the notion that identity is a justification. This is the most degraded, least sophisticated territory in the public and academic realms.

There's a lot to be said about the poor state of American public discourse. It's true, for instance, that the discourse about abortion often involves interlocutors talking past each other—with one side focusing on the well-being of women, and the other focusing on the well-being of fetuses presumed to be persons. Is this really, as Sandel suggests, the result of liberalism? It seems to me that the quality of this debate is really defined by a willingness of people to have more complex, nuanced, and essentially philosophical discussions in public forums where the philosophical sophistication of readers and writers is lacking. Are we really supposed to believe that the quality of such debates is less a function of sophistication than of people's willingness to talk about moral and religious ideals, and more generally, their identity? In fact their lack of sophistication is today typically premised on their willingness to hawk some conception of identity.

## Part V: The Poverty of Anti-Liberal Identity

The central argument in *Liberalism and the Limits of Justice* is incoherent. It erects an absurd straw man—the unencumbered self—and then berates it with *ad hominems*. I mean this seriously: the notion that justifications of political principles could work for or against one's identity (*Part III*), or that one's identity could work for or against one's political justifications (*Part IV*), is just to take the *ad hominem* fallacy and make a general principle of it.

But I think we can assume that this focus on identity is one of the reasons the book is so prized by the anti-liberal segment of the American left wing. It conforms to the current academic dogma—now also very common in American public discourse—that questions of identity trump liberal notions of equality, justice, and fairness. It constitutes a regression to the sort of tribalism for which justice and liberal institutions are meant to serve as a remedy. In fact, it's not just liberalism and deontology that provide no alibi to the hate for disfavored groups, disguised as compassion for the marginalized; it's any ethical theory—and any anti-authoritarian political stance—whatsoever. The warm-and-fuzzy concept of community is meant to put a happy face on all of this.

It is the individual, not community, that is the foundation for ethics. It is individuals, not communities, that can have thoughts and feelings, and consequently individuals that can be the objects of empathy. It is individuals that can be wronged, and individuals that—when you prick them—will bleed. It is individuals that deserve our dignity and respect, and individuals for which these ethical imperatives ought never to be compromised for the sake of loyalty to some community. Even if you believe that there is such a thing as a *community-Geist*, I hope you do not think that the community itself is a subjectivity. However much you wish to talk about "intersubjectivity," there is a stark and undeniable dividing line between my subjectivity and yours: You cannot feel my feelings or have my thoughts, and it is a rather unempathetic notion to believe that empathy can fully cross this boundary between us. "Individual" and "individuality" are not the bad words many humanities academics think they are, and there are versions of these concepts that have nothing to do with turning us into generic units fit for capitalist consumption. In fact, if we wish to avoid the generic, we cannot stop at community-based identity: Concreteness requires individuality.

Sandel seems to believe he is rescuing some richer version of the self than can be had by individuals liberally conceived. But his conception of identity—as primarily a matter of one's group identifications—is entirely generic, impoverished, and dehumanizing. To see why, consider the way in which Sandel's extension of virtue ethics—from human nature to community-based identity—can be deepened. Being courageous may be the virtue of human beings; and being a Muslim the virtue of someone formed by a certain community. But there are also goods, ends, and virtues based on formative influences—social and psychological— specific to individuals.

It might be the virtue of John, for instance, to be a doctor. Which is to say, John has the kind of character for which the profession of being a doctor would be suitable, and it would contribute profoundly to his well-being. But even this extension remains at the level of the generic: John's character, after all, is ultimately *sui generis*. In the same way that no one on Earth shares his genetic makeup, no one on Earth shares his unique pattern of influences and their consequences for who-John-is. Consequently, John's virtue is, ultimately, a specific pattern of living, being, thinking, and feeling: a specific path through life. Courage is certainly a virtue for John, and so might be being a Muslim or being a doctor. But his ultimate virtue is that of being-John, and actualizing potentialities that are more particular than these categories. You cannot do justice to John—to his unique character—by listing his group affiliations, or even by giving a list of generic character traits. To do justice to an actual, individual human character, you must be a good novelist, not a good taxonomist of political species. When novelists bring characters to life, they do so by making them more than stereotypes, more than generic examples of some group or trait. To do justice to identity, we need the individual in its full, glorious particularity. A good novelistic regime, like a good liberal regime, honors the individuality of its citizens, rather than obliterating them in the name of the plot-driven collective.

This means that culture is by itself a very poor way to understand identity. Whether I am stingy or generous is far more consequential than whether I am French or American, and whether I am Wes Alwan or Jacques Cousteau is far more consequential still. The least important thing about the formative experiences that forge my character—even if they are the most obvious—are the cultural garb they wear. What makes me different from you is a long succession of events in our personal biographies, beginning with genetic inheritance and intrauterine environment and extending to a series of stimuli directed at us both from within and without. Our characters have been forged by a succession of experiences of hunger and anger, love and lust, and the mechanisms we must use to cope with these experiences (these mechanisms can be divided into general categories of "defense," but there is an infinitely various symbolism to their manifestations). Especially important, psychically, is the behavior of early caretakers. Whether a person is neglected in French or English is not really the point, even if the effects of neglect on character manifest themselves differently according to certain cultural tropes. The essence of the situation is still neglect and characterological consequences, however signified. The same goes especially for the unique intersection of traits that is character in its full particularity.

The sketch of virtue I'm offering here is psychoanalytic and roughly Nietzschean. Here, for example is Nietzsche on the matter:

> The popular medical formulation of morality that goes back to Ariston of Chios, "virtue is the health of the soul," would have to be changed to become useful, at least to read: "Your virtue is the health of your soul." For there is no health as such, and all attempts to define a thing that way have been wretched failures. Even the determination of what is healthy for your body depends on your goal, your horizon, your energies, your impulses, your errors, and above all on the ideals and phantasms of your soul. (p. 120)

I say "roughly Nietzschean," because I don't think the more generic Stoic (which is to say neo-Aristotelian) account of virtue ("virtue is the health of the soul") is actually inconsistent with Nietzsche's more particular account ("your virtue is the health of your soul"). My account is also psychoanalytic, in that therapeutic effect of psychoanalysis is partly a function of identifying an idiosyncratic set of meanings specific to the individual: It involves becoming aware of one's own individual psychical culture, and through this culture one's own particular ends, and one's own particular version of health. Psychoanalysis might help you find out how to be generous, or that you ought to become a doctor. It might help you conquer neurosis or, with a great deal of work, a personality disorder (which is to say a disorder of character). But more importantly, it can help provide a more explicit interpretative frame for everything you do in the world. It might, for example, provide a new way of relating to a specific person, a set of behaviors that belong not to the generic category of "generosity," but are more finely tuned to that relationship (think of being able to sing a song rather than merely tapping along). Similarly, it might provide new ways of thinking and feeling and doing—in relation to particular aspects of the world—that defy generic categorizations in that they actualize not human nature, or community-defined ends, but ends entirely unique to a given character. If this seems too vague, consider what it means to be an artist or maker of things: ultimately, one is not merely "a writer" or "a painter," but whatever particularity it is that is manifested in the particular thing written or the particular thing painted.

And if you wish to make one term of the individual-community dyad the bad guy, why not pick community? What of the dark side of communities? What of the way in which they help us avoid knowledge of ourselves, or even enforce such self-alienation? Don't they accomplish this precisely by encouraging us to think of ourselves generically, and by encouraging us to conform not to our own ends, but to those of the group, however unsuited the ends of the group may be to our well-being? How many people's lives have been ruined by trying to fulfill the demands of the community over and against their own ends? What of the way in which communities are a source of stifling misery for those who don't fit in? And what of the way in which in-group identification encourages out-group demonization?

Consider, for example, the way in which the purveyors of identity politics—on the American political right and left—today talk about human beings. The thoughts and behaviors of others are never their own, but always represent their ethnicity, religion, or some other group affiliation (as if such groups were actually entirely uniform in their thinking and behavior). According to this logic, terrorism reflects poorly on Muslims, crime rates reflect poorly on African-Americans, and the suffering of every marginalized group reflects poorly on white people. Such politics conceive of people never as individuals, but as representatives of their groups, seen in the worst or best possible light, and collectively guilty or laudable for the behavior of any individual in that group. However much you dress these views up as a concern for "justice"—social or otherwise—they are a denial, both in their demonizing and idealizing modes, of humanity. This denial reflects an authoritarian frame of mind, the function of which is to control goodness by stamping out individuality, which is invariably too flawed for this ideal. It requires controlling others' thoughts, ensuring uniformity of communal ends, and ultimately stamping out individuality for the sake of the greater good. The point of liberal and psychoanalytic individuality, on the other hand, is not that we be denuded of all communal attachment, but that whatever our attachments, our fundamental dignity as human beings can never be held hostage to them.

Consider, in this light, Sandel's highly distorted reading of Kant, which makes individual dignity and ethical behavior seem entirely at odds with altruism and real human relationships. He restates Kant's moral maxim, that we ought never to use others merely as a means to our ends, as the maxim that we must not use others as a means to our ends, ever. Kant carefully worded this maxim to include "merely" with good reason. He knows very well that human beings use each other very frequently as a means to their ends. In having sex with someone, or even in having a conversation, we treat another person as a means to our pleasure. The point is that we also ought to respect their integrity as human beings by not, for example, forcing them to have sex with us. Sandel's misquoting of Kant neatly attempts to make the transcendental and empirical subjects inconsistent in just the way required for Sandel's argument to work. If human beings can't use each other for pleasure, then they can't ever have the kinds of social relations that embodied persons actually have.

Now take Sandel's notion that the Kantian conception of freedom involves our freely—and hence arbitrarily—choosing our ends, which for him is a way of illustrating the impoverishment of the unencumbered self. This absurd reading of Kant implies that we get to choose our moral precepts, for example, whether murder is wrong. But for Kant, it is not even the case that most of our choices are free. In limited cases where we can avoid heteronomy—functioning merely via our desires and impulses—we can make free choices. I might choose to refrain from murdering the person toward whom I have urgently vengeful impulses. And the general maxim—that murder is wrong—follows from the nature of the will. Over this I have no control. Consequently, there is a direct parallel to the way in which the ends of the thickly constituted empirical self are a function of identity. It is the nature of the will that defines these ends, not our arbitrary desires, as Sandel claims. Kant would agree with Sandel that most ends are not a matter of free will at all, but flow from the empirical self and its identity. A person's Catholicism is the product of a large number of formative influences, not of arbitrary willing. The same goes for liking football. But the same does not go, on the Kantian view, for a moment in which I reason my way away from a moral violation that I very much want to commit.

Finally, consider here the parallel between Sandel's treatment of Kant and the dehumanizing implications of community-based identity. Sandel's account shows no specific familiarity with Kant's actual work—with the individuality of the text—but instead treats him vaguely as the representative of certain general themes and vague associations, represented tendentiously in the worst possible light. Today this cynical approach to texts is not uncommon in humanities academia: Texts are to be read as the manifestations of certain cultural trends, or the biographies of their authors, not to be read as the highly specific and often well-motivated products of actual individuals with particular thoughts and feelings. And I do not mean literally read, but rather "read" via the game of interpretative telephone that is academic secondary literature: that's how your "merelys" drop out. There is no individual subjectivity behind the text: just the text as de-subjectified cultural product, subjugated by the authority of the social. That is why texts today are "interrogated" rather than heard: you do not listen to their testimony, but rather make them confess their crimes. This confession is necessarily in light of their lack of obvious conformity—in the case of texts that are truly great—to a certain set of simplistic political pieties that it is absolutely forbidden to question.

So here's a new political thesis: it's not shears chosen blindly that produce blind sheep, but rather intellectual shears applied carelessly in the service of the political dogma around identity. In this case, the sheep need no shepherd other than their community of fellow herd animals, whose ends—both intellectual and political—they dare not abandon, since that would mean leaving aside the comforting conformism of a thickly constituted (which is to say thick-headed, self-obscuring) way of life.

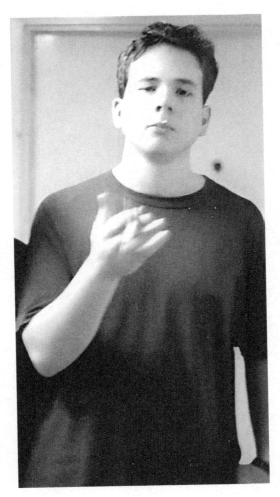

*1992, St. John's College, Annapolis, Maryland*

What are the appropriate limits of government power?

## READINGS

Nozick, Robert, *Anarchy, State, and Utopia,* Basic Books, 1974.

# Episode 104

*September 28, 2014*

*Genevieve Arnold*

## Stephen Metcalf on Nozick

*What moral limits should we put on government power? Nozick thinks that the only legitimate functions of government are protection and enforcement of contracts. Contra Rawls, Nozick's "entitlement" version of justice doesn't look at income inequality or any other pattern of holdings, but only at whether holdings were legitimately obtained.*

*- Mark*

# 104 - Metcalf on Nozick

**So, you guys love Nozick's writing style, huh?**

### Seth

It doesn't have the virtues of a good analytic writer. There are a number of meandering passages, and he has a tendency to use long, extended clauses, instead of just breaking things apart and making it more clear.

### Wes

His argument against utilitarianism, which you would think would be really his focus, amounts to some strange thought experiments. And he doesn't give you a full-fledged argument, just these little chapters. Overall, it's a very intricately argued, dry, analytic text. And that's what makes it difficult.

The only way I can get through these sorts of readings is to, as I read, summarize, responding to what he's saying. Otherwise, it's hard to maintain focus.

**At least he's someone you can take seriously.**

### Wes

Nozick says he didn't start out being a libertarian. He convinced himself by writing this book. I don't know how seriously we take *that.*

### Dylan

Once you insist on founding all human interactions by the actions of individuals, it's not so hard to see that you end up a libertarian. Basically, you discount the function of the social, and discount the function of the political. The fact that we're social beings is a kind of secondary byproduct, it's not something fundamental to our existence.

## Maybe we should let our guest opine?

**Stephen Metcalf**

I have recently been rereading Locke, and I see, in a new way, what Nozick was trying to do. He's making a *natural-rights* argument, but he's modifying Locke in two radical ways. The first is that he's trying to make an *invisible-hand* explanation for the advent of even a primitive state. So there's never a contractual moment (which is very big in Locke, Hobbes, and others, the moment where everyone "joins hands" and agrees to exit the state of nature). This is clearly the influence of the Austrian economists on his thinking, that even the contractual moment for the founding of something like a minimum state is totally unnecessary. Something more organic and spontaneous can happen.

## Which doesn't sound much like Locke

**Stephen**

To me, this shows the influence of Hayek and the Austrians coming into his thinking. Unlike Locke, who says that we exhibit reason in our ability to have these relatively spontaneous, very commercial and self-interested cooperative interactions. Much of what Nozick is doing rests on this Kantian halo of inviolability that he places around individuals.

It seems to me that's rhetorically persuasive. I feel Nozick had some deeply instinctive and sincere beliefs that human beings, at the end of the day, are ends and not means.

**Mark**

Maybe that's a good place to start, at the inviolability of rights of the individual. Whereas you might think that society has the right to—for instance—tax you to help somebody who's in great need, he thinks, *No, that would violate your rights.*

That's something fundamental. Even if it would only be a minor inconvenience to you, that's not the point. You can't look at the level of inconvenience versus the level of benefit. Society, without being unjust, can't do something like forcibly take your money for redistribution in this way. Taxation amounts to forced labor, which is a matter of using somebody's body against their will, which is a matter of your ownership of your own body.

### Seth

He ties this back to the Kantian notion of treating people as not simply a means, but also as an end, the *categorical imperative*. You can think of it as a constraint, a boundary as opposed to a positive action. Individuals are "ends" as well as "means," they have a right to self-determination. This is that whole conversation about *You have a right to treat your body like property. So you can dispose of it as you will.* And the point of that "side-constraint" means that nobody can take any action with respect to you that would infringe upon your right to self-determination. So the side-constraint is a boundary on what other people may do with respect to your Kantian individuality, which is to say, your right to self-determination.

It does not say, however, that anybody has any positive responsibilities or obligations towards you. In other words, I have no obligation to do anything that encourages your flourishing, or encourages you to actually exercise that self-determination.

### Mark

You might still have positive obligations toward people as individuals, but the state does not, because of its monopoly on force.

### Seth

I think he's saying that even individuals don't have positive obligations. The categorical imperative does not indicate that you have any positive obligations towards other individuals, simply that you have negative obligations not to infringe upon their self-determination.

### Wes

There are intuitions we can all accept about rights, that no one should have the right to kill me without reason. And that's one sense of the viability of my integrity. But with property, it becomes much more complicated. And it's not clear that Kant would think in that same sort of libertarian way that Nozick is thinking. That kind of entitlement theory doesn't flow from a Kantian conception of rights. He wants to relate the two, but it's not clear that one comes out of the other.

**Mark**

I think you need that intuitive chain that I laid out. If you believe that the Kantian thing means "people shouldn't be using you," what does that specifically mean?

## And why would we want a state at all?

**Dylan**

It does seem worth saying, "Well, you know, if you're going to say that the state is, in general, bad, why have a state at all?" The minimal state is okay, but the minimal state is the only justifiable state.

**Mark**

That's the "night-watchman state." It only can do protection.

## It sounds like he thinks it's immoral to help people in need

**Mark**

It's not that it's immoral to help them, you're free to give some of your money to this person, you're free to start an organization that solicits people for money to give to the poor, you could gift everything you have to the poor, you could gamble it away, you can do anything you want with your property. It's just the government can't tell you.

There's a distinction there between the morality of an action and what society can do. The government having a monopoly on force is very restricted.

## But you don't have a moral obligation to help at an individual level?

## Seth

No, because if you did, that leads to the state being immoral. He's trying to make the argument that it isn't.

## Mark

I could see a view that *Yeah, as individuals, we have a lot of responsibilities toward each other, "Honor your father and mother, blah, blah, blah."* But yet, it's not the government's business to make you honor your father and mother, or to honor your father and mother for you, or to be involved in that at all.

That, I think, would be a much more common libertarian position among people today. Does that mean Nozick is a lot crazier than real libertarians?

## Seth

In order to make his argument work, he has to commit himself to some impoverished notions about what human beings are and how they interact. And then he's just essentially projecting that onto theoretical apparatus that he's using.

> The clients of the protective agency, then, must compensate the independents for the disadvantages imposed upon them by being prohibited self-help enforcement of their own rights against the agency's clients. (110)

## Stephen

Effectively, it's a voucher-restitution system, where you quantify a disadvantage for being an independent forced to negotiate by someone who is part of the Protective Association.

## Wes

If you start out with the ultra-minimalist state, where only some people are paying for the service of being protected, this dominant protective agency cannot allow "independents," that is, people who aren't going to pay in.

When they protect their own clients, they're going to have to use force against independents who happen to be violating the rights of their clients. The question is how you screw with the lives of the independents without that being a violation of their rights. And the only way is to force them into the whole system, which is to say, you compensate them by providing them with protection services as well.

So yes, we're going to prevent you from murdering one of our clients. But we're also going to prevent someone else from murdering you. That's your compensation. But we're going to charge you the amount that you would have spent protecting yourself. So the price of guns, and the labor of sitting up at night in a paranoid sweat about who's coming to get you. So that's how you suck everyone into the dominant agency, and then charge them by taxing them.

### Mark

He, throughout this whole book, sees himself not as a far-right figure, but as a centrist, right between the anarchists on one side, the anarcho-capitalists and the state-ists on the other side.

## What about his entitlement theory?

### Seth

The entitlement theory basically says there are three ways that people can get things:

1. Acquisition, which is the simplistic model of there's something laying on the ground, and you pick up this driftwood, and you whittle it into a ship and stick it in a bottle, and then you own that ship in a bottle

2. You can then trade or sell that to somebody else, which is called transfer.

3. And the third way is rectification which is where you receive something as redress for something that was taken from you or stolen from you, based on the ultra minimal state.

Anything that you get via one of these means you are entitled to, and he thinks that this is a better way of thinking about ownership in the state model that he has, versus the distributive model, which is the Rawlsian position.

## What's this whole "micro" and "macro" thing he talks about, and how does that relate?

### Mark

So "micro" situations, means actual, concrete, real situations. You look at how your principles apply to that, and you apply the entitlement theory. And if you find that the transaction was "just" in one of those three ways that Seth mentioned, then the holdings that come out of that are "just." The famous example is this "Wilt Chamberlain" one, which I wanted to invite Stephen to give for us.

### Stephen

Nozick is trying to draw a distinction between what he calls "patterned" and "unpatterned" distributions. Patterned principles of distribution are inherently violations of liberty, of Kantian inviolability, because it's an end state to which individuals must sacrifice some of their liberty, or right to self-determination. Whereas an unpatterned one, by implication, is organic and spontaneous and doesn't require this abrogation of liberty.

The example that he gives is a thought experiment. Imagine a supremely talented basketball player named "Wilt Chamberlain." You can go watch a game that Wilt is playing and there's a tip jar. It's not even that you're paying a set fee in order to go see the game. You can put 25 cents in the jar, because that goes directly to Wilt Chamberlain, who's the principal reason you're going to watch the basketball game, and everyone puts 25 cents in. And if a million people go and see Wilt over the course of the year, Wilt takes home $250,000.

And this happens to be more in this thought experiment than any other person in this invented society. A patterned distributionist would say Wilt ought to be taxed to a certain degree, this is grossly disproportionate to what other people in the society have. Furthermore, maybe we can put to public use what we consider to be the excess monies that Wilt has.

So Nozick says "On what basis are you saying that?" Everyone puts the money completely voluntarily into the tip jar. No one of those contributions is unjust, so in the aggregate, they don't become unjust. Therefore, when Wilt has an enormous sum of money relative to his fellow citizens, since you cannot point to an unjust step along the way to that distribution, there's no basis to call it a "mal-distribution" and tax it.

And this links up to the other parts of Nozick theory by which taxing Wilt is roughly akin to coercing him to labor without remuneration.

### Wes

He says we would basically have to continually interfere in people's lives to enforce these distributions, and forbid capitalist acts between consenting adults. So he gives a pretty dark depiction of what's necessary if we're going to enforce a patterned conception of justice.

### Stephen

What I find amazing about this is that welfare states, all over the world, have responded to what they take to be the fundamental conditions of modernity by taxing their citizens in a way that does not overly enforce patterned life outcomes, including in the United States, which did it from roughly the 1930s until roughly the early 80s. It's an empirical question: *Did they ever forbid capitalist acts between consenting adults?* They were forbidden behind the Iron Curtain, but were they forbidden in Norway? Were they forbidden in Denmark, in France, in England?

I don't understand why libertarian arguments immediately go to an extremist case where it's a Road to Serfdom, or the specter of the gulag. These are the kinds of speeches that Reagan gave during his wilderness years, where it was always "darkness at noon." But if you looked around the United States, it was a radically free and open society in the 1950s and 1960s, even though your highest marginal tax rate was often north of 70%, and at one point was as high as 90%.

It's interesting to think about what had happened historically in the 1970s, that by the mid-70s, people were very open to an argument that had been a fringe argument before. This was a hugely bestselling book. And it won the National Book Award. It was legitimating arguments that had been seen as beyond the pale. This is one of these moments where you wonder, *What is it attaching to, in the imagination of many, many readers, that they thought that*

*that was a plausible thing for a reputable philosopher to say?*

### Wes

The idea that it's some "extreme of forbidding" doesn't seem accurate. These capitalist acts are having widespread effects on society. It's not as if they're happening in a vacuum, and it's not as if each transaction is as free as he makes it out to be. People, for instance, are acting out of need and desperation. So none of the sort of the entitlement principles and the way they're purely presented is an accurate description of the way things happen in the society.

### Stephen Metcalf

One should ask oneself why the emphasis in the book is on the coercive powers only of government. Do we think someone has an enlarged moral imagination if they can only see taxation for redistributive purposes as coercive, and they completely tune out how concentrations of private wealth can be coercive, that gross maldistribution of wealth that leaves some people without any meaningful economic power can end up being coercive? That the relationship between concentrated private wealth and state power means that you get the weak clients of the state economically disenfranchised, and the strong clients of the state get essentially what amounts to corporate socialism? All of these things impinge upon the moral imagination, if you open your eyes and see what happens in the real world. Why is this one form of coercion such a huge preoccupation? Look, it may have been in 1975, that the American welfare state was a propulsive Leviathan in need of a taming or shrinking or whatever. But this is an absolutist argument in the direction of doing away with the welfare state completely.

### Dylan

This preoccupation with constraint would point to a peculiar understanding of freedom for Nozick. I'm at a loss to how he's positively understanding freedom. It seems a naive understanding, a very simplistic freedom that's individual based.

### Stephen

The truth is, every human being is a bundle of complex inheritances, some of which are liberating, and some of which are profoundly inhibiting, and very many of which have absolutely nothing to do with their volition or their interaction with either themselves, their freedom, or their environment.

The Wilt Chamberlain example is fine if you live in such a hermetically sealed universe. But at some point, you have to break the seal on thought experiments and test them against one's own experience. And that's where this theory fails.

We all know there's a publicly educated child in the world somewhere who has been liberated into their own capacities for self-making and enlightenment in a way that they wouldn't have been if someone hadn't been taxed on their behalf.

### Dylan

Since the advent of public education in the US, the argument for using public money to do it was to create citizens that are able to run the country. So it would seem to be in the best interest of the government itself to have citizens that could do that.

### Wes

And again, I think you can use the same argument that he uses to get from the ultra-minimal to the minimal state to justify taxation for purposes other than protection. So if you start out and you say, *Well, look, I have the right to protect myself, and I have the right to hire someone to protect me, and we have these agencies, but the only way those agencies are going to work is if they interfere with others, and then they have to compensate them by protecting them, but then they also have to tax them,* you get this argument for taxation.

I think you can give a very similar argument for something like roads. The people have the right to get together and pay into a system where someone builds infrastructure that they can all enjoy. But in the same way that you're screwed if you end up in a society where there's a dominant protective agency, you're screwed if you end up in a society where there's dominant road agencies, and you're forced to buy into them. But you can make a Nozickian argument that you're forced, but that's okay, because it's the only way that other people can exercise their right to cooperate on infrastructure, because you're not going to be able to walk out of your house and not use roads, and all the other public sorts of things that people make use of.

### Dylan

The question is *Why is the line that Nozick draws physical harm? That's the only one we'll agree to? How is that line different than any number of other lines?*

### Mark

I think he gets this from Murray Rothbard. What I understand of Rothbard is that we all understand the government exerting physical force and having a physical monopoly, but anything that's beyond physical force becomes a slippery slope.

Even the company that owns the only water in town, and so you're gonna die of thirst unless you pay for it. And maybe you don't have any money and you can't pay for it. Well, you're just shit out of luck.

In contrast to somebody like Hayek, who would say, "Okay, that is actually a form of coercion," Rothbard wants to say, "No, it's only physical coercion. Because once you open the door, you have a moral obligation to help and then you open the door to somebody who has the moral permissibility to violate your rights by taking stuff and redistributing to others." And so everything just goes to hell out the window.

*Stephen Metcalf is a critic, essayist, podcaster, and screenwriter. His essays and columns have appeared in* The New York Times, New York Magazine, Slate, The Guardian, The Atlantic, *and* The New Yorker. *He is co-creator and host of the* Slate Culture Gabfest, *named one of the fifty best podcasts by* Time Magazine *and* The Guardian. *He is writing a book about the 1980s for Henry Holt, and a screenplay, an adaptation of the non-fiction book* Final Cut *by Steven Bach, for Amazon Studios. He has taught at Yale, University of Pennsylvania, and NYU. Metcalf was a visiting faculty member at Bennington for Fall 2018.* (Bennington College Website)

*Is science sufficient to give us a satisfying worldview?*

READINGS

Jaspers, Karl, "On My Philosophy", *Existentialism: From Dostoevsky to Sartre,* edited by Walter Kaufmann, New American Library, 1989.

# Episode 109

*December 29, 2014*

*Sterling Bartlett*

## Paul Provenza on Karl Jaspers

*O*n Karl Jaspers' "On My Philosophy" (1941), featuring comedian/ actor/director/author Paul Provenza. What's the relationship between science and philosophy? What about religion? Jaspers thinks that science gives you facts, but for an overarching world-view, you need philosophy. Living such a worldview requires "Existenz," or a leap towards transcendence, which is of course religion's stock-in-trade, though Jaspers is not a fan of dogmatism.

*- Mark*

# 109 - Provenza on Jaspers

**Paul Provenza**

This is Paul Provenza, not really sure about existing in Los Angeles.

### So who is Karl Jaspers?

**Mark**

This is a less familiar name to a lot of people than Sartre, or Heidegger, or these folks, but this guy was an older contemporary of Heidegger's. He and Heidegger met at Husserl's 61st birthday party. They found that they were kindred spirits, and they had a correspondence, from then all the way to the 60s, on-and-off, despite a violent disagreement over the whole Nazi thing, where Heidegger got to keep his job, and Jaspers, who had a Jewish wife, did not. And then, after all that blew over, Jaspers wrote a letter to say maybe Heidegger shouldn't be allowed to teach, but yet he still respected the guy. So they still continue to correspond and eventually warmed up by the 1960s.

**Paul**

Why let a little thing like Nazism get in the way of our friendship?

**Mark**

Apparently Heidegger did at least say he was ashamed at one point.

**Paul**

Yes. But apparently he said that to a mentor of his in a private conversation. And then the mentor went and brought that to the appropriate academic figures, and they went "Okay, are you like, Fifth Level Nazi? You're not?"

**Mark**

I think that mentor might have been Jaspers.

## Aren't you guys forgetting something?

**Dylan**

We should introduce Paul.

**Mark**

Come on. People know who Paul is.

**Paul**

You and I have the same crowd.

**Mark**

People who watched *VH1* in the 80s.

**Paul**

By the way, existence is determined by how much material is on the internet. If you existed before the internet, you didn't exist at all.

**Mark**

Well then, I'm glad that I got to see a number of episodes of your fairly recent show, *The Green Room,* on *YouTube.* For free.

**Paul**

Yeah... that's illegal.

**Seth**

*I* watched them legitimately, on *Showtime.*

**Paul**

A man who understands morals.

**Mark**

If you are not familiar with late 80s stand-up, then you might know Paul from the *Aristocrats* film.

## So, Paul what did you think of the book?

**Paul**

It was interesting, because going down the "Jaspers rabbit hole" raised a lot of questions. And I'm more confused about Jaspers after reading him. So I'm interested in talking about this... and finding out just how stupid I am.

**Mark**

A reason we don't limit ourselves to professional philosophers (or obsessed amateurs like ourselves) as guests is because we want this to be a reality check. It can't just be a community talking to itself, in some ridiculously insular way.

**Paul**

Isn't that the problem with philosophy in general? It's a snake eating its own tail. I actually started out at University of Pennsylvania as a philosophy major. And I left after two years, because it just wasn't funny enough.

**Mark**

You weren't reading the right philosophers!

**Paul**

I found it ideologically masturbatory. That's one of the problems I had with Jaspers. He uses words like "transcendence." There's so many different interpretations of what the word "transcendence" means! It's hard enough just to figure out what his definition of it is. And then when everybody else chimes in around it, it becomes more and more confusing. It seems to be obfuscating more than anything else.

**Seth**

I'm glad you brought that up, because I had a similar experience reading just this little snippet. A lot of people get exasperated by the fact that Jaspers doesn't define his terms, on purpose.

**Paul**

I'm so glad it's not just me. I would have stayed in philosophy if everybody got up and said, "You know what, I don't know what the hell's going on either." That would have been great.

**Mark**

You can describe the experience of transcendence, and the process of philosophy by which you leverage this, in interesting ways. But ultimately he thinks the doctrines that come out of philosophy are nothing that someone who didn't go through the process of figuring it out with you is going to be able to understand.

**Paul**

Zen koans make more sense to me.

### Where does science come into this?

**Mark**

If we're doing science, we're investigating particular things.

**Paul**

It's the general theory as opposed to the specific theory, right?

**Mark**

Science has the push toward more-and-more general. But it never gets, according to Jaspers, all the way to an actual worldview. Not even the scientific worldview itself, of "I will only believe things that I have good rational justification for." All the things of which a Dawkins would say *These are the guiding force of my life*—they are not themselves proved by scientific experiments.

In some way you learn about them through doing science, you learn about that attitude.

**Paul**

They accumulate to what ultimately one would hope is a worldview. But we're at a place in time, and technology, and scientific advancement, where we can seriously and concretely talk about things like parallel universes.

And those things are not abstractions, in the same way, that discussions of them are in philosophy. We've taken all the baby steps along the way to understand the concept in terms of the physical world, and the math of it all. I mean, "We have cell phones, they work, we know that," we're at that place.

So that gap seems to be shrinking, in terms of our understanding of vaguer, less concrete, less definitive aspects of science. Theoretical physics right now may as well be magic.

**Mark**

Dylan is the actual physicist....

**Dylan**

Have you seen the way physics gets made? The thing about science is that it accretes. It builds on itself. And there's always this kind of tie-back to stuff we can agree about. Every time a scientist says "I have a new theory," any scientist worth their salt will say, "Okay, let's agree about what we're going to measure, what we're going to be looking at together." If you get a different answer from me, for anything, then the way we sort it out is we go make a measurement of that thing, and that will tell us which one of us is right.

In that way, it ends up being a single worldview. There may be parts of it that don't relate to one another, you might not be able to calculate everything that goes on in a cell from first principles, or from particle physics, but the conceit of science is that you ought to be able to do that, in principle. It doesn't make sense that there are different sorts of entities and science going on at different scales.

**Wes**

Cosmology can get pretty speculative. And I don't think the many-worlds theory or theory of multiple universes is widely accepted. Some physicists think it's not a consequence of the mathematics.

**Paul**

But these kinds of ideas are no longer abstract in terms of our being able to understand them. You see where I'm going with that?

**Dylan**

You mean I can make a mathematical argument that would tie back to what I was imagining about parallel universes. It's not just a fanciful imagination or mythological story.

**Wes**

But they're entirely different concepts. The use of multiple universes in philosophy is a tool of modal logic. In physics, it's about possibilities.

**Paul**

That's what I mean. The world of science crossed over into so many of the abstract ideas about reality and consciousness that are the realm of philosophy. Now, even as part of the popular vernacular, we understand them in a different way. A lot of what has gone on in philosophy almost seems quaint.

**Wes**

I would argue that the "many worlds" hypothesis, which again, many physicists don't think highly of, is a more speculative and imprecise use of the concept of a "world" or "universe" than its use in modal logic. Just because it's more abstract with logic doesn't mean it's less precise, or ultimately, even less practical.

Remember, this development of logic also led to the technology of the computer. There's lots of fanciful sounding stuff that goes on in philosophy, that's a result of the fanciful kinds of stuff that goes on in higher mathematics. But some of these things have applications.

**Seth, can you save us from getting lost in the multiverse?**

**Seth**

Which is usually my job on the podcast.

**Right.**

**Seth**

What Jaspers is trying to say is *It doesn't really matter how much it expands, the total collection of scientific knowledge does not itself give a picture of our experience in the world, in its totality.* We can add up all the science together, and it's not going to tell us what it's like to be a human being, or to be this individual.

The other part is that scientific knowledge is historical. We do not need to reinterpret a scientific fact or a theorem in the light of every generation. Our experience in the world does not color how we see the constant flow of scientific theorems. Whereas the history of philosophy, and also things like art and poetry, are also always self-referencing and self-analyzing its own history in light of its current present.

### Paul

Isn't it also cultural? You can separate science from culture to a certain degree, but I don't believe you can separate philosophy from culture.

### Mark

He tells his "origin story" as a philosopher. He didn't become a philosopher until he was, like, 40 years old. He trained first as a lawyer, and then he switched to medicine, and psychiatry.

### Paul

That's fascinating, because of that "relationship is reality" stuff. He was so focused on delusions, and our perspectives on delusions, and separating our judgments about delusions, and all that sort of stuff, which I thought was really interesting.

### Mark

He was very conscious, as a psychiatrist, of the metaphors that they use in grounding their science. He says first, before psychoanalysis came along, it was talking about the brain. And clearly, at this point in the 1920s, or whatever, they weren't talking about neurons in the brain in any precise way. It's not even that much different than 100 years or so before when they're talking about the humors.

### Wes

Freud himself started out as a neurologist.

### Mark

Right. It's graduating then to psychoanalysis, which is non-verifiable. It's often used as an example of a scientific approach that is not scientific in a fundamental way—you can't test the basic assumptions.

Dylan was talking about how, before we engage in scientific work, we agree on this bunch of fundamentals, and then that gives us a shared grounding to investigate something specific. Jaspers thinks that makes all science hypothetical in a certain way. If you agree with this shared paradigm, then you can accept this alleged fact that we're putting forward. He thought, in observing his fellow scientists, that they did not put enough work into questioning these fundamental assumptions.

It's fine as long as you're aware of the chain by which you're supporting your current theory. He thought that it was much too common (and maybe scientists are less guilty of this now) for folks to elaborate some practical useful theory, and then take from that "Now we've discovered the nature of man." To give these sort of overweening statements that amount to a half-assed philosophy, done with no knowledge of actual philosophy.

This is what he's objecting to. He thinks science sets the standard for rigor, so he absolutely thinks that philosophers who ignore science are just fucking idiots. If you embrace irrationality or something like this, then you're just confused, you don't know what you're talking about. But at the same time, if a scientist goes beyond their scope, and puts forth philosophical statements, something is going wrong. Ultimately, most of the things we would talk about as philosophical generalizations, whether they're made by scientists or philosophers, are the wrong way of doing philosophy.

His point in philosophy is that you get to this personal existential statement of "This is my relationship to the world." And that is not characterized by a set of generalizations about the nature of man in the world." As soon as you take a dogma like that, and teach it to somebody else, there's something that's not true philosophy, according to him.

### Seth

He's not just complaining about philosophers. He's complaining about doctors, psychiatrists, scientists. He felt that, methodologically, all of these different disciplines were lacking. He talks about dream analysis, where he says we shouldn't be focusing on the content, but we should be looking at how the belief is held.

### Dylan

In section three of the essay, he says that philosophical thought is practical activity. He formulates his philosophies in terms of questions. In this section, he talks about Kant's "four questions" or "five questions," and then says, now for modernity, we have four different questions. The first question is the most important one, "What is science?" He goes on to talk about it along the lines of what you said, Mark.

> Neither skeptically to surrender everything, nor to seize something dogmatically as a conclusion in advance, but rather to retain the attitude of the researcher, accepting knowledge only on the way, with its reasons, and relative to its viewpoints and methods, turned out to be far from easy. This attitude of mind is attainable only with an ever-active intellectual conscience. (171)

So the activity of doing science is an attitude of mind. It's not theories themselves, it's a way of doing things. And to him, that's the same attitude you have in philosophy. It's a disposition of mind. It's not the particular theories. It's not the particular writers. It's a way of doing things.

### Seth

Because it's not knowledge. Philosophical knowledge isn't knowledge in the same way that scientific knowledge is. You wouldn't need to reinterpret it every generation, and each individual wouldn't have to do it for themselves if it was somehow something that could be grasped. It's a quintessential human activity. That's what philosophy is for him.

### Mark

Another quote here:

> ...scientific knowledge is always particularized, that it does not embrace the totality of Being but only a specific subject, that it affords no aim to life, has no answer to the essential problems that move man, that it cannot even furnish a compelling insight into its own importance and significance. (171)

In other words, in just investigating facts, where do values come from? You don't get values from science, you come with values already built in and you use them while you're doing science.

**Paul**

When it became clear that every atom in your body, my body, and everything around us comes from the same place, and goes back to the Big Bang, how does that not create a worldview? How is that separate from a worldview? How can you say We're stardust, we're all stardust and be inured to what that means?

**Dylan**

Darwin's evolution had a tremendous effect. People who objected to it saw it as directly attacking not just their Christian values...

**Paul**

...but an entire worldview, an entire belief system.

**Wes**

Arguably, though, that's a mistake. It doesn't actually have any implications for values. The advent of theory of evolution, or the idea that the earth is no longer at the center of the universe, those sorts of things may have affected values, and might have depressed people, or had any other effects you might imagine. But that doesn't mean that they actually have any demonstrative implications for values. I can't derive anything from the fact of evolution about what I morally ought to do.

**Paul**

If we find our common ancestor, our genome zero, we're all African over time, does that not affect us culturally, in terms of our values?

**Wes**

There's a difference between logical implication and causality. That the Earth is not the center of the universe might make us feel insignificant. But it doesn't actually demonstrate that. Nothing actually follows from that fact.

**Paul**

If we can scientifically arrive at, say, the classifications of race and all of those sorts of distinctions between people, and if we ultimately find out that no, in fact, *We are all related, we all come from the same ancestors,* how can that not change our values in terms of the way we exist in the world with others?

### Wes

You would need other values at work. You need a sort of moral or evaluative or normative premise at work in the first place to make that connection. You can't just pull values wholecloth out of facts.

When we work with science, we have to work with concepts that are established in non-scientific ways. The concept of happiness can be more or less sophisticated. And if I go out and test it, I might have some simplistic idea that happiness is just people experiencing pleasure. Or I might have a more sophisticated version of happiness, one that comes from Buddhism or Aristotelianism. And the science I do in testing those ideas is predicated on a lot of conceptual work that comes first.

Jaspers would say that there are genuine areas of philosophical concern where science cannot answer those questions. Only philosophy can answer those questions. And those areas have to do with thinking about myself as a human being. And the reason is because consciousness and subjectivity are cordoned off. They are not themselves empirical objects for scientific study. We have to get at them from the inside.

### Paul

When he talks about religion, is he talking about religion? Or is he talking about this sort of Zen kind of spirituality?

### Mark

I was hoping we would shift the discussion there. I'm in sympathy with a lot of what new Atheism is arguing, because if the alternative to believing in science is believing in religious superstition, then Come on! That we should even have to come forward and say "No, no, we should pay attention to science and reason" is ridiculous.

But certainly everybody who's religious is not just a superstitious nut job. There are plenty of really smart religious people. Kierkegaard, in particular, was a guy that Jaspers ran into and said, *Wow, this guy, I don't ultimately buy any of his Christianity, but he was such a crazily impressive, smart human being. And these things that I'm reading in him are motivating to me.* In fact, he sketches a lot of very tight parallels with things that Nietzsche had to say, a guy who believed exactly the opposite, who was very anti-religious.

Jaspers thought that, ultimately, the content of their religious belief is of no consequence. The thing that he was interested in is their existential attitude, how they did philosophy on the margins, the fact that they were thinkers outside their times.

### Seth

He, at one point says, I'm talking about "real truth" versus the "merely correct." This goes back to this idea that knowledge of facts or knowledge of things, which is the way he's characterized the body of scientific knowledge, is not going to get you to morality, ethics, right action, happiness, fulfillment—all the things that are really interesting about what it is to exist in this world.

*Paul Provenza is an American television presenter, actor, radio panelist, stand-up comedian, filmmaker, and skeptic based in Los Angeles. He has appeared on several podcasts and in recent years has interviewed other stand-up comedians. In 2005 he became a director, in 2010 an author and in 2011 he started producing for comedy festivals and television.* (Wikipedia)

*Editor's Note: I wasn't able to clear a picture of Paul in time, so instead please enjoy this one of a handsome young devil named "Mark"—probably around the age when he was watching Paul on VH1.*

*What connects these thinkers?*

## READINGS

Gleick, James, *Chaos: Making a New Science*, Cardinal, 1991.

Jaspers, Karl, "On My Philosophy", *Existentialism: From Dostoevsky to Sartre*, edited by Walter Kaufmann, New American Library, 1989.

Huxley, Aldous, *The Perennial Philosophy*, Harper Perennial Modern Classics, 2009.

Brentano, Franz, "The Four Phases of Philosophy and Its Current State" in Balazs M. Mezei, and Barry Smith, *The Four Phases of Philosophy*, Rodopi, 1998.

# The Cycle of Philosophers

*2024 (based on material from 1999)*

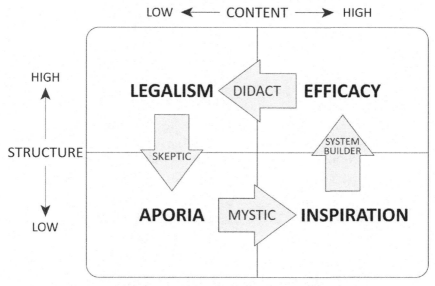

*Cycle of Philosophers* ©2024 Sunami

## Christopher Sunami

*I* *had long been fascinated by the archetypal triad of Ancient Greek philosophy: Socrates, Plato, and Aristotle. They were all so different, and arguably in opposition to each other's aims, yet their close association could hardly be coincidental. Armed with my new model, I was able to see that the three of them formed a logical progression.*

*Years later, I discovered this same "cycle of philosophers" had been proposed, a century earlier, by a German philosopher named Franz Brentano—universality at work! Our two theories were much the same... except for one crucial detail.*

*- Kitoba*

# The Cycle of Philosophers

> Since the basic questions of philosophy grow, as practical
> activity, from life, their form is at any given moment in
> keeping with the historical situation; but this situation
> is part of the continuity of tradition. The questions put
> earlier in history are still ours; in part identical with
> present ones, word for word, after thousands of years...
> so that we make them our own only by translation.
> (Jaspers, 166)

"On My Philosophy" (the Karl Jaspers essay discussed in the preceding podcast) is concerned, among other things, with a comparison-and-contrast between science and philosophy. As Jaspers notes, where science is a roughly linear historical progression (as Dylan Casey says, it "accretes"), philosophy is cyclical, and returns again-and-again to the same questions and concepts. This is often seen as a deficiency in philosophy, perhaps even as a demonstration that progress in philosophy is impossible. More severely, there have been thinkers who have accused philosophy of being a mere epiphenomenon of science, or even of being worthless nonsense (or at best, Humean entertainment).

Nature, however, is full of generative cycles, and we don't accuse the Earth of making self-indulgent gyrations just because she progresses through the same four seasons year after wearying year. So too, the fact that philosophers return repeatedly to the same well is no certification that they are failing to make progress. Like the Biblical householder, they are able to bring out of their storehouse things both "old and new" (*Matthew 13*). And one of the things philosophy characteristically brings out of its storehouse is brand new sciences, from Physics in antiquity, to

Formal Logic, in the recent past.

Given, however, that philosophy does not progress in a linear fashion, how then does it progress productively? As the late nineteenth-century German philosopher Franz Brentano discovered, it passes repeatedly through four identifiably distinct phases, schematized by Mezei and Smith as follows:

> 1. The first phase is that of rapid progress. Its characteristics are the expression of a purely theoretical interest... on the one hand, and the application of scientific method (openness to the richness of empirical cases) on the other.
>
> 2. The second phase is that of practical interest: there prevails, in the philosophical investigation of nature not the search for truth, but rather the motives of "relevance," social benefit and the motives of "applied philosophy."
>
> 3. The third phase arises as a reaction to the phase of prevailing practicality. It is the phase of scepticism...
>
> 4. The fourth phase, that of mysticism, arises in turn as a reaction to scepticism. Its main characteristic is the invention of new methods, the discovery of special "powers" in man through which radically new types of knowledge are deemed to become somehow accessible. (Mezei and Smith, 10-11)

Brentano and I agree that the first phase is the most scientific, and therefore the most historical. Philosophers of this type, which I call SYSTEM-BUILDING, such as Aristotle, Newton or Russell, are inventors of new sciences. Their work is full of vitality, and is compelling and accessible to the contemporary audience. Yet, as their work recedes into the past, it becomes a historical curiosity in a way that is not true of all philosophy. It is well-suited to a certain time and place, indeed it has a transformative impact on that time and that place, but it is vulnerable to obsolescence due to existential drift.

We also largely agree on the second phase, which I call DIDACTIC. Philosophers of this type, from Confucius, Moses and Hammurabi to

Peter Singer, and modern self-help gurus, are primarily interested in the problems of the ordinary world, and while they may have an interest in larger principles, they express this interest solely in the form of precepts and guidelines for practical behaviors. Because their guidelines can be followed by rote, without any greater understanding, these types of philosophies can be hugely influential, and reach a mass audience beyond that of dedicated philosophers. But as the world changes, these philosophies are unable to change with them, and become not only obsolete, but increasingly inaccessible.

Where Brentano and I diverge is with regards to the third phase, which we both call SKEPTICAL. Brentano sees it as purely destructive, a cynical abandonment of the true mission of philosophy, and an embrace of nihilism. But while I think Brentano's negative view is apt in the case of a destructive, Humean skepticism, I see the productive skepticism of a Socrates, Sextus Empiricus, Zhaungzi or Descartes in a more positive light. Such skepticism serves a housekeeping role in the progression of philosophy. As didactic and system-building philosophies age, and go obsolete, productive skepticism clears them from the mental landscape, breaking down entrenched dogmas, and freeing people's minds. In this way, skepticism is the most evergreen of all philosophical modes—the provocations of Socrates are as fresh today as when they first enraged the good citizens of Athens.

That brings us to the final phase of the cycle, the MYSTICAL, where Brentano and I diverge most sharply. Brentano describes this phase (which is the target of Humean skepticism) as a point of maximal decline:

> With pathologically intensified enthusiasm people start once more to construct philosophical dogmas. In addition to the natural means employed in the first phase, however, they now invent entirely unnatural means of gaining knowledge on the basis of "principles" lacking in all insight... so that very soon people suppose themselves to be in possession of the most exalted truths that are beyond all human powers. The period of decline thereby reaches its extreme point. (Brentano, 86-87)

For Brentano, this fourth phase is worthless. In dismissing it this way, however, he creates for himself two significant and insoluble problems. First, he cannot explain what makes philosophy of unique value outside the realm of science, given that he views the most science-like phase of philosophy to be the most valuable, and everything else as a decline. Second, he cannot explain how the cycle returns to a state of renewal and revival following such decline.

Both problems can be solved when we find the value in mysticism, rather than dismissing it as worthless. Many of the greatest philosophers in history—Plato, Lao Tzu, the Buddha—were mystics. It is true that mysticism is a relatively inaccessible phase of philosophy, esoteric in a way that can seem needlessly alienating, and obscure in a way that invites dismissal, if not mockery. But if we see mysticism as the well to which philosophy keeps returning, we can understand that the flowering and rebirth of the vital philosophy of the first phase is made possible only by the return to the Source represented by the last phase.

Jaspers alludes to this in his essay:

> Philosophizing, as it occurs in each historical age, involves the penetration, without limit, into the unity of the revelation of Being... Though too immense to be envisaged as a pattern, it encompasses us nevertheless as a world... The immensity of the Whole and the evocative tones of its unity are indispensable for achieving universal philosophic communication as well as for realizing the truth of each individual's concrete understanding. (Jaspers, 162)

Or, as Aldous Huxley describes it in the introduction to his tribute to the great mystical traditions of the world, *The Perennial Philosophy*:

> ...the metaphysic that recognizes a divine Reality substantial to the world of things and lives and minds; the psychology that finds in the soul something similar to, or even identical with divine Reality; the ethic that places man's final end in the knowledge of the immanent and transcendent Ground of all being...is immemorial and universal (Huxley, *vii*).

*What's the relationship between sexism and racism?*

READINGS

hooks, bell, *ain't i a woman: black women and feminism, 2nd Edition,* Routledge, 2014.

hooks, bell, *black looks: race and representation, 2nd Edition,* Routledge, 2014.

Ortega y Gasset, José, *The Dehumanization of Art and Other Essays on Art, Culture and Literature,* Princeton Classics, 2019.

# EPISODE 139

*April 24, 2016*

*Chris Warr*

## MYISHA CHERRY *ON* bell hooks

*b*ell hooks (aka Gloria Watkins) describes black women as having been excluded both from mainstream historical feminism (which was led by White women who didn't want to alienate Southern whites) and Black civil-rights struggles (which were permeated with patriarchy). This removal of them from narratives of liberation puts them in a challenging position when it comes to achieving self-actualization and social justice. black looks is one of many books in which hooks engages in the cultural critique that she thinks is part of the solution: Marginalized groups need to reclaim the narrative about themselves so that they aren't cast as "Other" in their own minds. These limiting images need to be replaced in people's psyches by a story rooted in the historical struggle for liberation.

*- Mark*

# 139 - Cherry on hooks

**Mark**

Welcome our guest, Myisha Cherry, whom folks might have heard on her podcast. Tell us about that.

**Myisha Cherry**

*The UnMute Podcast.* It's a podcast that seeks to bring philosophy out of the academy, and to talk about issues that affect the real world.

Currently, I am a PhD student in the Philosophy Department at the University of Illinois in Chicago. Prior to coming to the University of Illinois, I was an adjunct in the New York City area, teaching philosophy. Before doing that, I was working in the nonprofit sector. I've always been passionate for disenfranchised communities, "the marginalized and the oppressed." As I transitioned from the nonprofit world to academia, it wasn't to turn my back on those particular communities, but to still work with them in a very different way.

As much as I am into academia, and philosophical research, I'm also interested in public philosophy. I've been writing for *The Huffington Post* for the last five years or so. I've also done a lot of op-ed pieces for *salon.com* and the *LA Times*, and written a few pieces for public philosophy books in social and political philosophy.

The focus of the podcast is to talk about those kinds of socio-political issues. We have a podcast coming out soon on pornography. We've talked about slurs, we've talked about propaganda, we've talked about ignorance. I interview a particular philosopher, and we talk about one particular topic throughout the podcast. It's been a great companion piece in classrooms.

## What's bell hooks' project in these books?

**Mark**

*ain't i a woman* is, for the most part, a historical overview. There's something about 19th-century Black female political awareness that she thinks is more radical than today's—within feminism or among Black women generally. She wrote this as an undergraduate, apparently. She was 19.

The reason why she wrote this is because she's a voracious reader, and was looking in the library, like *Where are books about the experiences of Black women?* and wasn't finding them. Her significant other at the time said, *Well, why don't you just write one?*

There are five chapters, and each one goes through a different aspect or historical point. Chapters *One* and *Two* are on sexism, and the Black female slave experience, and the continued devaluation of Black womanhood.

The official reading here was chapters *Three* through *Five*.

**Chapter Three**: "The imperialism of patriarchy." This is mostly about how sexist those great civil-rights folks were. Yes, they were fighting against racial oppression. But when you hear Richard Wright talking about "the Negro," it means *Black men*.

**Chapter Four:** The same thing, these people that are revered as the old-time feminists—not Sojourner Truth, obviously, but Susan B. Anthony, and folks like that—were either racist themselves, or made political compromises because they wanted to gain the support of White women in the South, so they ignored the experience and plight of Black women.

**Chapter Five, "Black women and feminism":** The most overtly political. *Hey, Black women, raise your political consciousness, get involved in this. You may have distanced yourself from the whole movement in the past, because they were so racist, but this is our call to action.*

**Seth**

You're making it sound like she was making an attack on these people. There's a broader theme. She's trying to make the point that Black women's experience during slavery, and then post-slavery, was completely overlooked. There's an assumption that feminists were fighting for the rights for all women, and they weren't. And people who are working towards emancipation are not necessarily considering Black women's experience. She's saying they're victims of both sexism and racism. And each one of those worked against the other. If they stood up to fight against sexism, they were told *Now you need to focus on racism.* And if you start to fight against racism, it erased the whole notion that they were being oppressed as women. So it's a broader theme. She uses as an example that the suffragettes were all White women, and that Black women were not included in those caucuses, and were not welcomed.

### Mark

Why should we be aware of this history? Why is she presenting it like this? It's part of this raising of historical consciousness: *How are our minds still messed up from this?*

This is where that second work that we read, *black looks: race and representation* comes in, written two decades later. And she gives us a little more of her program of media critique. It's about the stories we tell ourselves. To have an identity is to be able to tell a story about yourself, and your background, and your group identifications.

And as long as those are infected with White supremacy, patriarchy...

### Dylan

...and capitalism. That's the triplet.

### Mark

Yes, even right now, people fighting for women's liberation are, she thinks, fighting for *We want to have the good capitalist jobs, like the men do.* And that that's not going to be the route to self-actualization. And since Black women are being pelted on all sides by these historical injustices, they are in a position where they're already having to critique the whole culture. In doing so, why not reject the capitalist imperialism as well?

**Dylan**

One of the things that's clearly in there is the psychology of how oppressive cultural institutions affect the way the individuals who are oppressed see themselves, and try to actualize themselves. She spends a lot of time in *ain't i a woman* talking about mistaken ways of actualizing oneself, that amount to assuming the role of an oppressor.

**Mark**

Adopting their whole framework. *I don't reject the framework. I just reject my position in the framework.*

**Dylan**

The example that stood out was her discussion about the relationships between Black women and White women during slavery times. The White women were oppressed in this patriarchy. But they didn't identify themselves as women in solidarity with Black women, but became oppressors. There's a psychology going on there about escaping from domination. And the way to do that is *not* to become part of that.

**Mark**

She really keys in on Martin Luther King's view of love as the solution. So it's self-actualization, and openness, and trying to get into a place where you can have real dialog with each other. She's very positive. She's critical, but in a way that is a part of love. People say she hates Spike Lee. *No, it's only because he's worth critiquing. Because he has so many good qualities about his movies, it's worth talking about the way that he portrays women.*

**Myisha**

As I was reading *black looks*, she doesn't give a prescription on how to self-actualize. But she asked those who have self-actualized to produce narratives, so people can have an account of how they did that for themselves. One of the things that I enjoy about reading bell hooks is that she writes from a first-person perspective. What she's telling us about her experiences lays out for us how she self-actualized, perhaps how we can.

I think of her mentioning Angela Davis' autobiography.

And begging for a feminist like June Jordan to also write these autobiographies, to allow black women in particular—and other people as well—to see *What does their self-actualizing entail? And what does it look like?*

### Dylan

That's her call to action at the end of the "revolutionary black woman" essay in *black looks*: "Write some books!"

### Seth

She also says it should be backed by theory, as well as revolutionary practice. She says she always has been a Marxist. If your goal is to self-actualize outside of the framework, then you need to somehow overcome or get rid of the framework, which requires revolutionary action, which requires organization.

She frames the whole historical narrative of *ain't i a woman* about reactions to the capitalist—but really more colonialist—framework that was brought over and institutionalized. During slavery, there's obvious terrorism and oppression; following slavery, there's psychological terror, there's the desire to conform. So she's framing everybody in terms of them wanting to play roles that they think they're supposed to assume. That causes this very conflicted consciousness and self-image.

That book ends with *We've never told these stories, we've never considered this perspective. And we don't really have a theoretical framework for even acknowledging black women as subjects.*

*black looks* doesn't sound like she has a prescription. I don't think there *is* a prescription like *Go do this, and you will become a self-actualized person.* Rather, there needs to be a movement of expression which will find its way, as people push against the boundaries, but also simultaneously organize and collect in a way that's productive.

**Myisha, what does bell hooks mean to you? Had you read much of her work before this episode?**

### Myisha

I think every black woman has read bell hooks, but that's going to be a generalization. At different points of my life, I read different kinds of books by bell hooks. When trying to reimagine myself as an instructor in the classroom, I read her series of pedagogical books. And then I was doing some research on masculinity, and her book on black masculinity is just brilliant. I'm also interested in political anger, and she has a book on rage. And so, at different points of my life, as a Black woman, I tend to "hook."

### Dylan

I had never read her before, and found it super-interesting. First of all, she's a really good writer. Just from that perspective, it was interesting to read. And then in *ain't i a woman*, it's clear that she has read all kinds of books that were deep in the library, but not in *every* library, and looked, in particular, for personal, individual accounts. So it's a kind of history, a kind of genealogy, and also a kind of reporting, in the future, of the past. I found it engrossing to have someone distill these first-person accounts, along with the analysis that went along with them to bring it together. It made me want to read more of her books.

### Myisha

She mentioned, in her critique of White feminism, about upper middle-class women only wanting to theorize about and present their experiences. In the feminist canon, you do have lots of work by White women. What the Black feminist today is trying to recover is that White feminists were not the first feminists. And they were not the only feminists in the 19th and 20th century.

I'm still trying to catch up, because I wasn't taught this in high school, or in undergrad. And so I feel, as I read bell hooks, and a lot of contemporary feminists, that I'm also digging deep in the archives. It's unfortunate that we have to dig. But I'm glad she's bringing it to the forefront.

## Is bell hooks a philosopher?

### Mark

She doesn't call herself a philosopher. She's a professor of English, and she's in women's studies departments. I don't know if she has an essay on this, but I think she would find the whole *Is it philosophy?* question part of the problem.

### Seth

*ain't i a woman* reads a lot like an undergrad version of Foucault—I wish I wrote that well, when I was 19. She's telling a story about a hidden and forgotten narrative. And one of the things that she does really well in that essay is point out how language is used to reinforce ideology and the dominant paradigm without being obvious about it.

It's a brilliant job of saying, *Here you see how they use the word "man," or they use the word "woman," but what they really mean is "White women," "Black men,"* that sort of thing. You read the quotes, she makes that point, you go back and reread the quote, and you're like *Oh, my God, yeah.*

In the later essays, 20 years later, it's clear she's been in a critical-theory department. She uses the term "deconstruction." There's an evolution there.

### Mark

Different books are aimed at different audiences. But certainly both the books that we read are supposed to be accessible as widely as possible. She would never want to say that this can only be read by somebody with the appropriate graduate degree. It's supposed to be consciousness-raising for regular people.

### Dylan

Myisha, have you taught bell hooks classes, or used her in any classes that you've put together?

### Myisha

Now that I think about it, I've never used hooks before. That's pretty selfish of me—I feel bad!

### Dylan

But it sounds like you've used her thinking about the role of teaching.

### Myisha

I've benefited from her work.

## How did you decide to read these books?

**Mark**

I feel this is a great way into a discourse that's very common now—but not as well-done—in popular culture. I think about religion. You could read the core religious texts, and those will make sense. And you'll say, *Okay, I get where you're coming from.* But then you'll hear regular people talking about them, and it'll sound like absolute garbage. But when you go back to see what they're bastardizing, then *Oh, okay, I see where that's coming from.*

So, in particular, the focus of *black looks* is about media portrayal. And this is one of the things that often causes a lot of eye-rolling, but *black looks* made the whole thing make sense to me. If a lot of the persistent historical issues are the stories we tell about ourselves, then our aesthetics may be a symptom of this. And maybe the main way of addressing it is to have more control over images, to be able to have more control over the way different groups are depicted in the media. Every time that there's something that's a stereotype, or whatever, it's not just a matter of *Oh, this quirky character in this sitcom!* It's another reinforcement of the imperialist patriarchy, whether it was made by White people, or by self-loathing Black people that have internalized this.

**Myisha**

I believe that representation matters. And people who believe that it doesn't, either they're just blind, or they have been privileged by seeing images that represent them until it's just a norm.

Prior to our conversation I was listening to a geek podcast. There's a movie coming out based on a Japanese anime character, and a mainstream White actress is going to play the role. And the whole question of the podcast segment was "Is this 'whitewashing' the movie? And is anything problematic with that?"

One person said, "Yes."

The other person says, "Well, this is going to sell movies, right?"

And we've seen that with several roles. The movie with Nina Simone being played by a Black actress, but a Black actress who doesn't look like Nina Simone. People are up in arms about that, because—particularly with Nina Simone—representation mattered to her. Just Black and *gritty*.

We've seen studies of young Black kids that have a negative perspective about other Black kids, such as the "Doll project." You've got to ask yourself, "Why do they feel like that? Why do they think that Black doll is ugly?" Because they've seen the media portray that *Black people are ugly, bad people, are thieves, are violent*. This kind of self-hatred has all come through representation. So representation does indeed matter.

Even today, it's still an issue. I don't know how many of you have heard of "colorism." bell hooks talks about the situation when she goes to another island, and her friend's daughter basically hates her skin and wants to become lighter. In other parts of the world, people do believe that lighter skin is best. People are even bleaching their Black skin to become lighter. And this all has to do with the images, and this myth that whiteness is beautiful, and whiteness is the best thing that one ought to be. And so why not try to be like that?

### Dylan

At the end of the introduction of *black looks*, she says many audiences in the United States resist the idea that images have ideological content. It makes me think of Socrates in the *Republic*, saying *We ought to regulate what the poets say, because it's bad for people to be taught the wrong things, because it corrupts their souls.*

And there's something in common with that idea that what the media says matters. When you're a student, you resist this idea that there should be any kind of censorship. But there's other ways, without talking about censorship. Just the effect of the way we speak—and of media, and images, and poetry—on how we think of ourselves, and the way in which that's used as a purposeful force. When you're steeped in it, it has an effect on you.

### Mark

I guess the source of resistance with all of this is that people don't like to consider themselves as being manipulated and subjected to things. If you ask explicitly the question of anybody that's reasonable "Do you think whiteness is more beautiful than blackness? Or is better morally?" "No, no, no!" In the 21st century, if you're educated at all, you're not going to say that. And this is why people say, "Oh, racism doesn't exist anymore."

Certain advances have been made. Women got the right to vote, and now women are in positions of power. Minorities are in positions of power. Every time there's advances, there's a number of voices to say "The goal has been achieved." And people like bell hooks want us to engage in consciousness-raising, to realize that *No, no, the problem is still deeper than that, that you are more messed up than you realize, whatever you may logically assent to. Whatever your position is, no matter how liberal you may think you are, even if you are yourself a civil-rights leader, there might be still something that is not properly decolonized.*

### Myisha

Ideology is "a hell of a drug." Believing it gives you some sense of comfort, but in other ways, it's a danger to your own self-actualization. And the question is, what do we do with it? I think that's the ethical question, what do we do? Do we resist it, to decolonize our own thinking? Or do we continue to allow it to have its way? I think that's a challenge for us.

### Mark

The way that bell hooks puts it, most people think that racism is a matter of race hatred, and they think, *I don't have any explicit race hatred, so that's fine.* Or, if you are a Black person, *No, of course I don't have any hatred toward Black people. So what's the problem? Get off my back.* No, because still there's a colonialist mindset here.

### Myisha

Getting decolonized has several parts to it. One way is exposing the truth of the narrative. For example, in our textbooks, we learned that the Europeans came over and had a wonderful feast with the Native Americans and everything was peachy. And the decolonizing process exposes the truth of that encounter. It exposes the messiness of imperialism, the messiness of sexism and racism.

In other ways, decolonizing is trying to do surgery on ourselves. You think about when an imperialist comes over, or a colonizer comes over, to colonize a particular land. They give the natives a different kind of education, a different way of living and being that takes away their true identity. And so when the colonizer leaves, you still have the problem of that mindset and that education. How do you set yourself free? How do you become yourself again? How do you begin to think like yourself again, without thinking with the lens of whiteness?

### Mark

She talks about it as part of sexism. There's no historical event by which men colonized women, but the dominant narrative was constructed by men with their own opportunistic self-interest in mind. No matter how well-intentioned, you end up lionizing your own group. So decolonizing would be removing the effects of that.

### Dylan

But the decolonization would not be just going backwards, because you couldn't get rid of the effects of the colonization. It's a different kind of freeing that has to go through a colonized thinking. Decolonizing isn't removing that, it's getting beyond it, so that the effects of colonization aren't guiding your soul anymore. And it would be true for both the oppressed and the oppressor as well.

She talks about that some in the book. It does seem a little bit weird to talk about how bad the oppressor feels, you know, and *Gosh, they have some work to do to free themselves.*

### Myisha

She does say that being an oppressor is being a victim.

### Seth

She talks about people that recognize that everybody is victimized by the structure, and then use that as a strategy to say, *Hey, do you realize even though as a White male, you benefit from everything that's happening, and you have no incentive to alter the power structure, you're actually being harmed by this?* She says that that's a terrible tendency. That's not what she wants to do. And that's not what she thinks is effective.

### Mark

As a tactical matter, you shouldn't be doing that because that's not the right reason to change. She says that already groups that have power will deflect attention from the real problem by saying *We have problems too.*

She talks about this at length. White women in the women's movement would compare their situation to Black men—an implicit reference that leaves Black women not identified at all, invisible.

> Many unlearning racism workshops focus on helping white individuals to see that they too are wounded by racism and as a consequence have something to gain from participating in anti-racist struggle. While in some ways true, a construction of political solidarity that is rooted in a narrative of shared victimization not only acts to recenter whites, it risks obscuring the particular ways racist domination impacts on the lives of marginalized groups. Implicit in the assumption that even those who are privileged *via* racist hierarchy suffer is the notion that it is only when those in power get in touch with how they too are victimized will they rebel against structures of domination. The truth is that many folks benefit greatly from dominating others and are not suffering a wound that is in any way similar to the condition of the exploited and oppressed. (*black looks* 13)

Let me add to that the quote by Ortega y Gasset:

> A strange thing indeed, the existence in man of this mental activity which substitutes one thing for another— from an urge not so much to get at the first as to get rid of the second. The metaphor disposes of an object by having it masquerade as something else. Such a procedure would make no sense if we did not discern beneath it an instinctive avoidance of certain realities. (Ortega y Gasset 33)

**Mark**

So you might think that you're highlighting the struggle of women by saying they're treated like Black people were treated, but no, what that really does is just make you forget about how horribly Black women—Black people—were treated.

**Myisha**

Outside of the comparison context, she says this:

> Unfortunately, our over-emphasis on the male as oppressor often obscures the fact that men are victimized. To be an oppressor is dehumanizing and anti human in nature, as it is to be a victim. Patriarchy forces fathers to act as monsters, encourages husbands and lovers to be racist in disguise. It teaches our blood brothers to feel ashamed that they care for us and denies all men the emotional life that would act as a humanizing, self affirming force in their lives. (*ain't i a woman*, 114)

This is outside the comparison context. *Let us not forget that the oppressor and oppressing us is also a victim, because in doing that he or she dehumanizes their own selves.* It's a separate point.

**Seth**

That's totally valid. It's consistent with the idea that the system itself victimizes everybody, but, like it says in *Animal Farm*, "All animals are equal, but some are more equal than others." People are victimized in different ways. And there are people that benefit from the structure. Everybody's victimized, but some people benefit.

It's a theoretical move to say, *Hey, everybody's a victim.* But in practice, we have to acknowledge the fact that some people stand to gain, and they have no incentive to overthrow the system that benefits them. If you piece all of her points together, her thesis is that decolonization may take place at an individual level first, in terms of awareness, *I'm not a racist, but I benefit from the colonial capitalist racist structure that exists.* But to be fully decolonized, the system itself is going to have to be overthrown.

I can't imagine her even suggesting you could be fully decolonized and self-actualized and still function within the system. This ties back to our previous discussions around the culture industry. If you're outside the system, you have to get appropriated inside the system. There's very few narratives of people who successfully resist the system and end up living happily ever after. And that's because ideology expresses itself through those forms of culture.

Decolonization requires a revolutionary action that overthrows colonial capitalism.

### Dylan

It certainly requires outward action in your community, specifically, political action. Activism, for her, is not a duty, *You should go out and do this because it will help people.* It's part of decolonizing oneself. It's not for your community, it may be partly for that, but it's also part of decolonizing yourself.

### Seth

She's saying you can't self-emancipate. It's not a religious or an intellectual exercise. In one of the essays, she mentions this need to create narratives, so that Black women can see stories about a variety of different Black female experiences, so that they can begin to have role models, and have examples and opportunities. We need this narrative structure. Decolonization is not strictly a theoretical act that takes place in the individual, it's a social act, because you have to see that played out in other people's lives, and then you emulate it, and then you share that with others. It's a process that involves other people.

### Mark

No matter how enlightened and free you think you are, unless you connect your struggle to a historical tradition of liberation, then you're missing something.

But one of the points of "Essay Three" in *black looks* is black female subjectivity. What does that mean? If you are colonized, and you're in a minority group, then you see yourself as "the Other." It's some weird form of psychological dissociation. The perspective that you're trying to come from—that has invaded your mind—is not something that actually lines up with your own interests.

### Would you be willing to explain intersectionality?

### Myisha

It's the intersection of multiple identities affecting the way in which we're treated. I can be a Black man and experience a kind of oppression. But I can be a Black woman and experience a different kind of oppression. It's because the identities of my womaness and my African-Americaness have intersected.

This was one of the criticisms of the White feminist movement, that not all women are the same. As Black women, we're saying, *Yeah, we experience the same "as women," but our experience as women takes on a different feature than your experience as women.* It's not necessarily worse than yours, but it's the kind of oppression that can occur when one's identities intersect.

What bell hooks is trying to get us to see that there's a difference. First of all, stop excluding Black women from getting liberation, but also take into consideration that they experience a different kind of oppression than we imagine.

As I was reading the essays, I couldn't help but think about "Black Lives Matter." Although it was started by two Black, lesbian women, the narrative of police brutality against Blacks was constructed around this narrative that "Blacks" really meant "Black boys" and "Black men." Women were being excluded from the conversation. It wasn't until Sandra Bland that the hashtag *#sayHerName* brought these Black women into the conversation. And that's an ongoing effort.

Patriarchy is also a hell of a drug. There's so much work to do to decolonize.

*Myisha Cherry is Associate Professor of Philosophy at the University of California, Riverside. She is also the Director of the Emotion and Society Lab. Her research is primarily concerned with the role of emotions and attitudes in public life. Cherry's books include* The Case for Rage: Why Anger is Essential to Anti-racist Struggle *(Oxford University Press),* UnMuted: Conversations on Prejudice, Oppression, and Social Justice *(Oxford University Press) and, co-edited with Owen Flanagan,* The Moral Psychology of Anger *(Rowman & Littlefield). Her latest book is* Failures of Forgiveness *(Princeton University). Her forthcoming book,* How to Love *is currently under contract at Riverhead Books (US) and Basic Books (UK). Her work on emotions and race has appeared in* The Atlantic, Boston Review, Los Angeles Times, Salon, Huffington Post, WomanKind, *and* New Philosopher Magazine. *Cherry is also the host of the* UnMute Podcast, *where she interviews philosophers about the social and political issues of our day.*

*To what extent are we obligated to give to the poor?*

## Readings

MacIntyre, Alasdair, *After Virtue: A Study in Moral Theory*, University of Notre Dame Press, 1981.

Singer, Peter, *Famine, Affluence, and Morality*, Oxford University Press, 2015.

Singer, Peter, *The Life You Can Save: How to Do Your Part to End World Poverty*, Random House, 2009.

# EPISODE 150

*September 13, 2016*

*Chris Warr*

## PETER SINGER *ON* POVERTY

*O*ur focus is the newly reissued/repackaged 1971 essay "Famine, Affluence, and Morality," which argues that just as we would regard it as unethical to fail to save a drowning child because you don't want to ruin your expensive shoes, so it's unethical to let someone die of preventable illness or hunger when an expensive-shoe-level donation would save that life. The new publication includes supplementary essays, and Peter has spent much of the rest of his career elaborating and arguing for and preaching about the practical upshot of this essay, which is that our priorities in this consumerist society are very out of whack: We don't give nearly enough to charitable causes, and we don't judge our charitable giving by the standard of helping the most people in the most substantial ways.

*- Mark*

# 150 - Singer on Poverty

**Peter Singer**

I think we should just start with a brief summary of the core of the argument in this famous famine article, and then we could go from there:

At one level, my argument is about an analogy, the story that I tell of the child drowning in the pond. To put that story very briefly, you're walking across the park, there's a shallow ornamental pond in the park. You know it's shallow, because you've seen kids splashing around it in the summer. But it's not summer. Now, you don't expect to see anybody in the pond. But, to your surprise, there is something or someone splashing in the pond. And when you look more closely, it's a very small child. Although the pond is shallow, this child is not going to be able to stand—seems likely to be drowning. You look around and say, "Who's looking out for this child? Where are the parents? Where's the babysitter?" But there's nobody there. You don't know why, but you can't see anybody looking after this child at all.

Your next thought is "I better jump into the pond and save the child." But then you have this much less noble thought that if you do that, you're going to ruin your fancy clothes, your nice expensive shoes that you put on this morning. And you say "Do I really have to do that? After all, this child is not my responsibility. I've never seen this child before. And nobody asked me to look after the child. Why can I just forget about the child and go on my way without having to replace my expensive clothes, and be late for my appointment?"

Now, at that point, I want the reader to ask themselves, *Would it be wrong if you did that? Would it be wrong if you did walk past, leaving the child to drown?* When I put that to audiences, pretty much unanimously—sometimes there's one or two dissenters in an audience of hundreds—they say *Yes, that would be wrong. That would be very seriously wrong if you were to do that.*

**Mark**

Right.

**Peter**

So then I say, "Well, are we so much better than the person who walks past the child?" Because we know that there are children dying from preventable poverty-related causes elsewhere in the world. We know that they're dying from lack of nutritious food, or poor sanitation, or malaria, or measles. All things that we know how to prevent, and that if we put more resources towards it, we would be able to prevent a lot of these deaths, if not all of them.

And if we're enjoying our comfortable life, spending money on nice clothes that we don't really need, or vacations, or whatever else it might be, then are we really so different from the person who walks past the pond? Does it make a difference that these children are so far away that we can't see them, that we don't know what they look like? Why should those things matter morally?

In the article, I consider reasons why people might think it matters morally that you're close to the child, that you can see the child. But I argue that none of those things really hold up in terms of a justification for non-action, in the case of giving to organizations that would help the children in developing countries. So I think the only solution to that is actually to change the way we live, to start giving significantly to help save lives of strangers, where we know that we can save those lives at relatively modest cost to ourselves.

**Mark**

We've got big moral issues that jump out right away:

1. The difference between duty and charity, between the morally required and the merely morally virtuous. Of course, it would be good to give to charity. But past a certain point, we're not morally required, according to conventional wisdom. You are challenging that.

2. The intuition of "impartialism." You're known as a utilitarian. But you argue that utilitarianism is the least complicated form of *impartialism*. Impartialism is shared by Rawls, by Kant, it's the principle that my interests don't matter any more than anybody else's, everybody's interests are equal. Therefore, from a moral point of view—from God's point of view, from the point of view of the universe—if you are going to act morally, you can't favor your own interests over someone else's. Looking objectively at the value of a human life versus your shoes, or the $200 in your pocket, or whatever, then you're going to have to choose the human life. Given the state of the world, with so many lives that are savable with a minimum financial outlay, then we should not just do the equivalent of jumping into the pond once, and saving a child, but as many times as we can do so—without significantly morally harming ourselves or our families by running out of funds.

### Peter

Right. Where do you draw the line, when have you done enough? When can you stop? That's one of the really difficult issues that's raised in the article, and that I've continued to grapple with, perhaps not in a fully satisfactory way, over the years and in various works.

### Mark

Is that something people jump on a *reductio ad absurdum* against the argument? That it can't possibly work? Because thinking about the good life, and whatever it would be, would mean attention to things besides helping the very worst-off? It's like you're doing triage in an emergency room, and completely burning yourself out. Even worrying about *What is the good life?* seems trivialized by the amount of starving.

### Wes

The pond example is meant to make the costs as low as possible, and the certainty about future consequences as great as possible. But what if my life were to be simply a series of drowning kids in ponds? What if that were to occupy every minute of my day for the rest of my life, to the detriment of any other projects I had, any other things I thought would make me happy? In that limiting case, I think many people would reject the idea that they are obligated to give up their lives in that way. And to do that instead of, for example, studying philosophy. I think many people's intuitions would likewise be that we're not obligated to kill ourselves if that means saving one person, or even many people.

Peter, your intuitions may differ on that, but I don't think it's as uncontroversial and intuitive as the pond example. There really is a hidden cost in saving someone in a pond. Every act of altruism is a demand on my time and attention. It's a little piece of my life. And where I draw the line on what I get out of my life—and what other people get—is a very difficult question.

If asked about a particular instance of what I'm willing to sacrifice, it's clear. But if you started at the other end, and asked me if I was willing to sacrifice an entire lifetime of experiences, I would reject that. Then the question is, where, between those two extremes, does the line lie?

### Peter

That's a discussion that we have to have. If the article prompts people to think about where we draw the line, then it's already achieved part of its purpose, because initially, people don't really think about that at all. They don't see themselves as having an obligation to save even one life of a distant stranger. So, somewhere between "one" and "every possible life that you can save for the rest of your life" is already starting to make progress.

If you look at the responses to the article, various books and articles that have been written on this theme, many of them say *This is how far I should go*. Garrett Cullity—his book talks about the things that are central to my life, the most important projects he thinks you're justified in not sacrificing. But, for most of us, there would be a large area that, on his view, we still ought to be doing.

So it's interesting to look at those attempts to draw the line. And there are various other ways of framing the issue too. This sort of thing has led Alastair Norcross to abandon the idea of *Morality is just black and white. So either you're doing what's right, or you're doing what's wrong, and it's one or the other.* He suggests a scalar form of consequentialism, where it's shades of gray all the way along. And so we should just look at where we are in terms of this continuum, between doing the best thing we could do and the worst thing we could do. And what we should be trying to do is to aim to be closer to that best end of the continuum, rather than seeing it in terms of This is what I have an obligation to do, and the rest of it is optional.

### Wes

This seems a backtrack to the idea that there's what we're obligated to do, and then there's the ideal virtuous thing that we might want to do.

### Peter

There's just degrees of rightness, if you like, all the way along. That's one way. Another way is the distinction between what we're obligated to do, and what we ought to praise or blame people for doing. That's a distinction that was made by Henry Sidgwick in *The Methods of Ethics*, because (for utilitarians) blaming and praising somebody is itself an act. And you have to think about the consequences of that act.

Let's say that you're the kind of person who says, "Okay, I'm going to spend eight hours a day saving lives. And I've got to sleep eight hours. The other eight hours, I'm not going to save lives, I'm going to educate myself in philosophy, or go surfing or whatever it might be."

Am I going to blame you for that? Well, not really, because most people don't even spend five minutes a day saving lives. And here you are spending eight hours a day saving lives. It wouldn't make sense for me to blame you. That would just discourage other people from even getting started and going in your direction. Rather, I should praise you for doing so much more than most people do. And try to encourage other people to do more as well.

### Mark

This was a distinction you made at the end of *The Life You Can Save*. Strictly speaking, you should be doing as much as you can, without giving up something that's morally significant. However, that's going to be different than the rule that we're going to suggest be imposed. You'd have to take into account not just what is morally correct, but what will work. You have to take into account people's psychology, their human nature. What is going to be too much of a requirement, that people are going to just be discouraged and say "The hell with the whole thing?"

### Peter

It is about the standards that you want to set. The standards are very low in our society in terms of what you ought to be doing to help people in vastly greater need. What we want to try to do is to raise those standards. How are we going to do that best?

You're fortunate enough to live in an affluent society, but in a world in which there are a billion people who are in extreme poverty, and few of those affluent people are helping them. You could try to raise the standard by saying, look, it would be relatively easy for us to do a little bit more. So you set some low standard, asking if everybody gave 10%, or even 5% of their income, we could together eliminate global poverty. You might set that up as a realistic standard. And maybe in that way, you'll end up doing more good than if you said "Unless you give most of your income, or most of your time, to saving lives, then you're just not an ethical person at all."

### Wes

It seems from your original article that you had a pretty firm line, and a demanding criterion, for what we're obligated to do. Is that less clear to you now? Because, to take one of the examples in your *New York Times* articles, it sounded like spending $200 on a TV, if that could save a life, is equivalent to killing someone. At the very least, we're obligated to choose the life over the TV.

And if we moved into other domains, like spending an afternoon with the kids, when I could have just gotten another job to make money to save more lives, the line is less clear. So is that an open question for you, where that line lies? What we're obligated to do versus what is just virtuous, but non obligatory? It's unclear to me where you stand.

### Peter

At the moment, my view would be that there is a proper sense of the term in which you could say "We're doing wrong" if we are spending money on things that don't save lives, that are just sort of conveniences or luxuries for ourselves. But I have to acknowledge that, by that standard, I'm doing what's wrong, because I'm certainly spending money on things that are not necessities.

That leads me to say *How do I think about the fact that, by my own standards, I'm not doing what's right?* I do think about it, to some extent, in the terms that I mentioned before. I know I'm doing a lot more than most people in this society. So I don't feel too bad about that.

Do I say to myself, *Well, that's a kind of an excuse. I know I should be doing more?* How much time do I spend feeling guilty, because I'm not doing everything I should be doing? And how much time do I feel comfortable saying, *See, I'm doing so much more than most people, in this society in which I'm living?* That's not a very stable position.

But I wouldn't say that I have a stable position. I'm generally aiming to do more. I'm increasing the amount that I'm giving progressively. 40 years ago, I started off giving 10%. Now I'm giving maybe 35% to 40% of what I earn, because I'm more comfortably off than I was 40 years ago. So that's a lot easier to do.

### Wes

On the other hand, what if I were to say, *Well, I'm killing a certain number of people a year, but everyone else is killing a lot more people than me. Therefore, I don't feel too bad about that?* The point of that example is to reemphasize what someone might think of as an obligation, which would be hard-and-fast: *Thou shalt not kill.* There is no spectrum there. There is no scalar approach. If I've killed anyone, that's wrong. And that's something I have to take very seriously. I don't get off the hook by saying other people have killed more than me.

## Let's muddy the waters.

### Mark

To bring in the other thing that Peter is famous for, I agree with some of Peter's argument, at least with regards to animals like pigs and cows, that approach dog-like levels of emotionality, and ability to suffer. I mostly don't eat those, but it's such a widespread practice, and my not doing so in a particular circumstance, or even with my whole life, is not going to make that much difference. So it has the feeling, like you're talking about, where I'm "murdering less" than most people. I don't feel so bad that I'll try to eat less chicken, or whatever.

### Wes

If lessening is relevant, then it can't be a matter of obligation. It has to be a matter of virtue or imperfect duty, in Kantian terms.

### Peter

Yes. But that's not the way that I think about morality, I do think that we face choices. And there are circumstances in which you may be doing things that are wrong, but by doing less, that makes an important difference.

In terms of what you have to be praised or blamed for, what are the differences between letting people die through my inaction, and actually going and killing people? There was a difference in the motivation. My motivation for letting people die is that I want to have this vacation. In a different world that would not be a bad motivation at all, it just happens to be bad because of the way the world is set up, and the number of people in need. Going to one of these developing countries, and killing a lot of people, is a very different motivation. We can feel that would be terribly wrong, because of what it would say about the kind of person that I am. You can't really imagine a world in which that kind of motivation could be acceptable in the way that having the motivation to enjoy your vacation would be acceptable, if only the world had a better distribution of wealth.

### Mark

In the TV show *Dexter,* you had somebody that the only way they can feel good is to kill someone. How can this be channeled to do good? *I'll kill only killers, and somehow bring a greater amount of overall happiness by removing these people.*

### Peter

In a case where, for some reason, there is a compulsion to kill that you cannot escape, then it seems to me clearly better to do what you were suggesting, to kill only people who, if you don't kill them, will go on and kill others. Even though this is still wrong, it's definitely better to redirect this activity, which you cannot just entirely avoid, in order to do less harm than you would be otherwise.

### Mark

I like the role that guilt seems to play, or not play, in your books. On the one hand, presenting this thought experiment to people, and saying, *Why don't you just stop right now and pay the $200 before you even go to the next page?* That sounds like it's all based on guilt.

But the utilitarian take would be *Guilt is only valuable insofar as that actually motivates one to do something more.* Even if you do enjoy some conveniences, enjoy some luxuries, and not all of those can be justified. Even if you are doing the wrong thing, by your own standards, if more guilt is not going to help you do more of the right thing, don't feel guilty.

### Peter

That's an accurate account of the way I think about guilt. I think for some people, it's a useful motivator. But where it's not a useful motivator, then it's purely negative.

### Mark

I found the extreme demands of your ethic comforting. I have a lot of sympathy for Alasdair MacIntyre's update of Aristotle, where he gave me this clean view of morality where it's not gray. *They're actually conflicting duties. And if we're choosing to fulfill one thing, we're neglecting something else.* One could be discouraged by that. One could say *We're always doing wrong, so there's no point in even thinking morally.* But the existential challenge is to think about which of these duties wins in a particular circumstance. The duty you talk about between caring for your family, being a good husband, being a good father, versus the duty of charity, of caring about the whole world of suffering people? These are things that maybe just cannot be reconciled.

**Peter**

I think it's true that they can't be. And the question then is, so what does ethics have to say about that? Some people, like MacIntyre, might just say *Well, there's these conflicting duties. And there's always this moral dilemma. It's an insoluble moral dilemma.* So you can't, even in principle, say what would be the right thing to do. Even if you had complete knowledge of all the morally relevant facts.

I'm not happy with that outcome. I don't know whether I can justify it. But I want more ability to reason your way through to what is the right answer, even if, in practice, we're not going to be able to know what it is. Even if we're not going to know the facts. I want an overarching normative theory that would say *If you knew all the facts, then you could put it into this normative theory, and it would tell you what is the right thing to choose.*

*Alana Holmberg*

*P*eter Singer is known as the "world's most influential living philosopher" for his work on the ethics of our treatment of animals, his emphasis on effective altruism and his controversial critique of the sanctity of life in bioethics. Winner of the 2021 Berggruen Prize for Philosophy and Culture. Author of Animal Liberation, *author or contributor to 50 other books, and founder of The Life You Can Save foundation. Ira W. DeCamp Professor of Bioethics in the University Center for Human Values at Princeton University.*

*What can the perspective of ancient China add to our understanding of ethics?*

READINGS

Confucius, *The Analects,* translated by D. C. Lau, Penguin Classics, 1998.

De Tocqueville, Alexis, *Democracy in America,* translated by Henry Reeve, Albert A. Knopf, 1945.

# EPISODE 159

*February 5, 2017*

*Chris Warr*

## TZUCHIEN THO on CONFUCIUS 孔子

*H*ow should we act? What's the relation between ethics and politics? Can a bunch of aphorisms written in the distant past for an unapologetically hierarchical culture emphasizing traditional rituals actually give us relevant, welcome advice on these matters? Are we even in a position to determine the meaning of these sayings?

*Mark, Seth, and Wes are joined by Tzuchien Tho, who studies Leibniz but grew up in a household where Confucian texts were revered, to do the best we can to figure out Confucius's fundamental ethical concepts, make notions like "ritual propriety" and "filial piety" relevant, and learn what to do with all our wisdom in a corrupt political climate.*

*- Mark*

# 159 - Tho on Confucius

**Mark**

Thank you, Tzuchien, for joining us. Tell us a little about who you are, and your background. I know you're not a Confucius (孔子) scholar, but someone that grew up reading this text.

**Tzuchien**

I'm from many places. I'm ethnically Chinese, but my father is Chinese diaspora from Malaysia, and my mom is Han Chinese-ish from Taiwan. So I grew up within this kind of context. I don't have to say how deeply influential Confucianism is to so-called "Chinese culture." And my father put a huge emphasis on knowledge of the classical texts. So we spent a lot of time memorizing and studying Confucian texts, not just this one.

**Mark**

Did you read *The Book of Songs*, the one Confucius tells us to read?

**Tzuchien**

We don't really have the one that he had. But we have a version of it compiled later. So, I have some knowledge of that. We studied a lot. When other kids participated in sports, we spent Saturday studying Chinese classics.

**Mark**

We are not knowledgeable enough to know how geeky that actually was for your culture.

**Tzuchien**

It was standard for my father's generation. I was born in 1980. In my generation, it's like, *Wow, your dad makes you do that!* Other adults, they'll sort of pat you on the head and say how knowledgeable you are. It's a cute thing as well, for him to be able to parade his kids who know Confucius, and can quote you the answer.

My father is extremely conservative. He has all these ideas about how you are supposed to raise your children. So that was my past, and then I ended up studying philosophy at University, and encountering these texts, again, as an adult, and interacting with them in a totally different way.

**Mark**

You teach Hume, right?

**Tzuchien**

I'm a Leibniz scholar. In general, I'm an early modern scholar. So I do Galileo, Descartes, Spinoza and Leibniz. I'm generally interested in philosophy of science, philosophy of mathematics. That's what I wrote my PhD on.

I was always told to study Chinese philosophy, because I was Chinese. And I could read the text. I had some marginal interest in it, but *You're Chinese, thus you should do Chinese philosophy* was the thing I really wanted to get away from.

**Seth**

The piece I didn't understand is the notion of him training people for government, but not being in government himself. He seemed to be resentful, and I couldn't quite get the context for that.

**Tzuchien**

That's one of the key conundrums surrounding Confucianism as a tradition. One of the main tropes in Chinese history, and Chinese intellectual tradition, is this figure of somebody full of moral insights, and wanting to serve some lord, or some sort of state, for the greater good. And then entering into government service and finding politics too corrupt, the power struggles too aggressive, and becoming a hermit. And then just complaining.

Within the same period as Confucius, you have Qu Yuan (屈原),

who was famously one of these scholars, who wanted to serve the government but was pushed out by the corrupt officials in a power struggle. He becomes a hermit, writes a bunch of texts complaining about his lot in life, and then kills himself. And the villagers who sympathize with him went and tried to dig his body out of the lake. And that's where you get this tradition of the Dragon Boat Festival, because these villagers went in with their boats.

So you have all these traditions based around this figure of the maligned scholar, who would have otherwise brought about the greater good. It's definitely a theme.

## Can we talk about what *ren* (仁) means?

### Mark

That's translated here as authoritative conduct.

### Wes

I think there's someone who translated it "co-humanity," which I like. Does that get at the essence of it?

### Tzuchien

With a lot of ancient texts, we only know the meaning of the words through the way it's used in those texts. The Greek *oikonomos* and the contemporary "economy" are the same word, but they have different meanings because of the way in which they're used in the text. So there isn't a way to say what *ren* is—if that makes sense to you?

### Mark

He was innovating about it. So it almost doesn't matter that much.

### Tzuchien

If you look it up in a proper Chinese dictionary, it's your "humanness," your "virtue." But it isn't exactly "virtue" in the Greek sense. It's associated with love, as well as love for those who surround you. All of those things.

**Wes**

When I see that association with love and benevolence and humanity, I wonder if "authoritative conduct" is the right translation. Or if it's the translators trying to be too clever.

**Tzuchien**

It's also that Confucianism gets reinvented several times, and *ren* means something slightly different. It has something of this sort of "primary comportment." First you have *ren*, and then you learn *li* (禮). So you have a basic orientation towards the good, towards virtue or love. And then you learn the proper way in which to employ them. But ren is a kind of pre-political, pre-ethical orientation towards goodness. It's very comportmental. It isn't something that conforms to a set of rules, but a kind of behavioral thing.

**Wes**

I was reminded of Levinas, and this idea of a fundamental moment of facing others, and ethics growing out of that. When we talk about *li* ("ritual propriety"), you might see it as this dead thing transmitted through tradition. At a certain point, no one even knows why they do it anymore. It's just the rules. It's an interesting notion that to say, well, actually, there's *ren* which is the source of that.

## Isn't Confucius just a lot of strange little rules?

**Mark**

It's very rare for us when we're doing ethics to actually talk about ethics, as opposed to meta-ethics: "Why would there be ethical obligations in the first place? What does that mean?"

What we get in this book, and what makes it hard for us, is

> The Master said, 'It is rare, indeed, for a man with cunning words and an ingratiating face to be benevolent.' (1.3)

Lots of individual little things like that. One of the chapters is just Here's how the exemplary person dresses, here's exactly how you bow entering the room. Some detailed, and for us, anachronistic, not particularly interesting stuff.

**Wes**

It's got a lot of straightforward, ethical pronouncements. You could look at this as "self-help," in some sense. There's not much ethical theory or meta-ethics here. That sort of thing that we have to infer from the sort of recommendations that the Master is making.

**Tzuchien**

Even somebody within the Confucian tradition, reading it 200 or 300 years afterwards, would have the same struggle, because the times were different. In a way, the Confucian tradition is constituted by generations upon generations of people having this exact problem.

**Seth**

I want to say something about this notion of propriety. There's an uncharitable way to look at it, as ritual. And to think of it in terms of being a straitjacket. You have to stand here, and bow at this particular distance from your quote "betters." But I thought of it in the same way as how Burke thought of tradition, as the stabilizing force. It's the thing against which we react, but you react against it with respect.

I can imagine that the rituals need to evolve, or that a part of the ritual propriety is the ability for certain actors inside of that system to establish new rituals or change rituals.

**Tzuchien**

Confucius saw his age as a decadent one. So the question is "How do we return to a time when people had more tendencies towards embracing good things, rather than bad things?" He singled out the decay of ritual as one of the symptoms of his age. The fact that it is so prominent in the text is due to his view of his own time, and the attempt to try to restore virtue in his society.

*Is ritual an organic extension of virtue, which can be cultivated through reading* The Odes, *and things that you can learn? Or is there some other thing? Does there need to be a righteous ruler? Are there political conditions for the reestablishment of morality within the land?*

All this harks back to some earlier time, when people knew

instinctively how to act, versus now, when all of these morals have become decadent. Whereas the people in the past would see it as natural to mourn, for three years, the death of a parent, now we have to explicitly underline mourn for three years.

### Seth

The part that I'm seeing flexibility is where he says *When the Dao prevails, the authoritative person does X, when the Dao does not prevail, the authoritative person does Y.* It's okay to speak your mind openly when the Dao prevails, because the righteous rulers will understand that you're gently instructing them in good behavior. That indicates a nuance, and a recognition of the relationship with the other, but also the context of what's happening socially and politically.

### Tzuchien

Think of there being something more primordial in terms of human behavior associated with *ren*, and then *li* as being something that coordinates human society in an ethical life. And then there's *fa* (法), which is "law," which is prohibitive. *Don't do this, don't do that.* And so you have three levels of social coordination. One that is a little bit more "organic," as part of your behavior. Then, at the second level, establish rules, like the rites. Then, the stronger intervention of the state that says, *You have to pay this many taxes, and you have to not do this, and not that.* So, three different levels.

Plato's *Republic* is also trying to deal with some of these questions. If you think of yourself as living in a time where everyone is unethical, how do you create the conditions where you can move towards a city of virtue? *What kind of resources do you have? Do you begin with the individuals? Do you begin with the state?* You can see him as embracing the rites as one of the places that mediates human behavior.

### Mark

He's writing, as you said, in a time where he thinks that he's being a light of virtue in a sea of non-virtue, that he has to look back to the ancients for models.

But were there points where they felt like *Now we have the unified*

*Chinese Empire, with the Emperor with the mandate of heaven? Now we actually are in a state where the ruler is governing successfully according to Confucian norms, with the ministers in place that can advise him, and cover all the different things? And for the most part, the state is ordered?* Did they actually feel like they succeeded at some point? Or was it always *No, we still have to look back to the ancients. We're always falling short?*

### Tzuchien

The period right after Confucius, the "Warring States" period, ended in a very bloody way. And the establishment of the First Emperor, Qin Shi Huang (秦始皇), didn't solve the political problems of China. This is the same emperor who burned all the Confucian classics, and politically persecuted anyone who would quote from *The Songs* and such.

So the way in which people use philosophy after that point, there's always a strong dimension of propaganda. And even today's government in China uses Confucius and Mencius as propaganda, to justify what they're doing.

### Mark

Nazis ruin Nietzsche for a lot of people. But can modern propagandists ruin Confucius for you?

### Tzuchien

Maybe. I think of it in a tarnished way. Me, personally, I mean. This goes all the way down to funding—which professors get hired, which scholarly projects are funded by the government. They want to promote a kind of Neo-Confucianism, as the counterpart of so-called Socialism with Chinese Characteristics.

The big counterpoint to Confucianism is Daoism. They were emerging literally at the same time. There were dynasties that embraced Daoism, for a lot of different reasons. So there's always a back-and-forth. But one of the key aspects is that an intelligentsia, whose goal is to participate in government, was established right after this period.

And these guys took on the model, like I said, of complaining. There's a lot of complaining in the *Analects*. The history of Chinese intellectualism is complaining about the government.

Was there ever a time where they thought *We're pretty close to reestablishing the classical dynasty*? I don't think there was ever any agreement to that. When emperors themselves, and the ministers say *Oh, now we have restored, finally, the virtuous society,* it was always propagandists.

### Wes

When you guys were talking about earlier about ritual, I thought about a very famous quote from De Tocqueville:

> Men living in democratic ages do not readily comprehend the utility of forms: they feel an instinctive contempt for them... Forms excite their contempt and often their hatred; as they commonly aspire to none but easy and present gratifications, they rush onwards to the object of their desires, and the slightest delay exasperates them. This same temper, carried with them into political life, renders them hostile to forms, which perpetually retard or arrest them in some of their projects. (De Tocqueville, V2.B4.7, p. 325-326)

He's talking about everything from manners to other sorts of kinds of social rituals. Things which don't rise to the level of moral commandments, *Thou shall not,* but play a very important role in the cohesion of the social fabric. Ultimately, De Tocqueville thought they were as important as institutions to sustaining democracy, even though the democratic attitude tends to undo them.

So what is the function of ritual propriety? In the same way that De Tocqueville talks about forms, maybe it stands between us and simply acting on our individual desires.

> Of the things brought about by the rites, harmony is the most valuable. Of the ways of the Former Kings, this is the most beautiful, and is followed alike in matters great and small, yet this will not always work: to aim always at harmony without regulating it by the rites simply because one knows only about harmony will not, in fact, work. (Confucius, 1:12)

## Wes

When we talk about maintaining harmony, we're also talking about hierarchy. We're talking about the things that lead to sort of filial virtues, filial piety. That's also something that's related to standing between us and our own individual desires.

For Burke, as Seth mentioned, this idea of hierarchy was also very important. He thought the fabric couldn't be the fabric, unless those relations were there.

## Seth

There's definitely a notion that the general populace needs to be guided and ruled. And he makes the claim in several places that that's better done through the moral character of the rulers than through laws. That's part of the harmony you just described. The hierarchical harmony is that not everybody can be an exemplary person and exert that moral force. So part of the hierarchy is to make sure that the persons who are responsible for governing and ruling do exert that force, because they are the ones that bring everybody else along in that path.

## Mark

If the rulers have this virtue, then it will flow out.

> Guide them by edicts, keep them in line with punishments, and the common people will stay out of trouble but will have no sense of shame. Guide them by virtue, keep them in line with the rites, and they will, besides having a sense of shame, reform themselves. (2:3)

## Tzuchien

One of the rival schools at the time was the "legalist" school, which became the ruling ideology of the Qin Emperor. *Make laws clear, make punishments clear, and make rewards clear.* If you have a society completely governed by clear laws, prohibitions and rewards, everyone will be organized. It's kind of a Hobbesean hierarchy, where everyone's place in society is neatly cut out by laws.

They were the main rival school against the Confucian school, so later disciples might have put that in there to make Confucius say something explicitly against the legalist. And point out the blind spot of legalism, which is that beyond laws, you need to have some kind of innate affective dimension to morality, which is shame. Or, what we would call an authoritative behavior, *ren*, which is, in a way, the opposite of shame. There needs to be something organic, arising out of feelings and comportment, that is more than just laws from the top down.

> Chi K'ang Tzu asked Confucius about government, saying, "What would you think if, in order to move closer to those who possess the Way, I were to kill those who do not follow the Way?"

> Confucius answered, "In administering your government, what need is there for you to kill? Just desire the good yourself and the common people will be good. The virtue of the gentleman is like wind; the virtue of the small man is like grass. Let the wind blow over the grass and it is sure to bend." (12:19)

## Tzuchien

If you are an exemplary person, people naturally gravitate towards you, and your speech will naturally be accepted by others. The proper ruler doesn't have to do anything. They simply sit there on the throne oriented towards the North Pole. That's exemplary, the person for whom virtue is effortless, so that they don't have to do anything specifically. They don't have to say, "Here's the five-step plan to virtue," they simply just do it effortlessly.

> The rule of virtue can be compared to the Pole Star, which commands the homage of the multitude of stars without leaving its place. (2:1)

*Tzuchien Tho is a philosopher and historian of mathematics and physics. He continues to work on the core issues of mathematical ontology, and the impact of modern mathematics on contemporary philosophy. He currently teaches at the University of Bristol.*

*Previously, he has been affiliated with the Jan van Eyck Academie in Maastricht (NL), the École Normale Supérieure in Paris (Rue D'Ulm), the Max Planck Institute for the History of Science (Berlin), Berlin-Brandenburg Academy of Sciences, the Institute for Research in the Humanities (University of Bucharest) and the University of Milan.*

*He is currently working on a research project on causality in 18th century physics, focusing on the development of analytical mechanics. He is also currently working on issues related to Badiou's mathematical ontology, the philosophy of algebra, Leibniz' reception in the 20th century, and the critique of contextualism as historical methodology.*

*Pittsburgh, September 2015*

*How can we better understand the dynamic of race in America?*

## READINGS

Baldwin, James, *The Fire Next Time,* Vintage International, 1962.

Baldwin, James, *Notes of a Native Son,* Beacon Press, 2012.

Baldwin James, "The Dick Cavett Show," June 13, 1968, *I Am Not Your Negro*, distributed by Magnolia Pictures, 2016.

Coates, Ta-Nehisi, *Between the World and Me,* One World, 2015.

# EPISODE 162

*March 21, 2017*

Chris Warr

## LAWRENCE WARE ON JAMES BALDWIN

*B*aldwin is a go-to figure at this point in discussions of race; his essays, stories, and speeches provide a key touchstone in discussing how racism has warped our culture. So, how do we translate his testimony into philosophical theory? The full foursome are rejoined by Lawrence Ware to shed new light on Baldwin's middle way between MLK's love and Malcolm X's rage and his critique of the American dream. How do you oppose the inhumanity of others without demonizing them, and thereby becoming inhuman yourself?

*- Mark*

# 162 - Ware on Baldwin

**Lawrence Ware**

This is Lawrence Ware, still fighting the power in Oklahoma City.

**Mark**

This was gonna be just a little appendix to the previous episode. But as we started reading Baldwin, we felt we needed to do a full-on episode of him.

**Dylan**

He's freaking awesome.

**Mark**

He's known as much as an essayist, perhaps more so, than as a fiction writer.

**Lawrence**

Incredible writer, legitimately one of the best writers I've ever read.

**Mark**

The line between his essays and his fiction is not that wide. It might be about characters who are not him. But still there's things about fleeing America to live in Paris, because American racism is so bad, and then having to go back to America and what that's like, and situations like the father in *Notes of a Native Son*, that kind of damaged authority figure.

**Wes**

The overall theme is that White people have to face reality, that racial progress is not simply a matter of elevating the standards-of-living of Black people. It's a matter of White people actually coming to terms with the mythology of White supremacy, and the sense of superiority to Black people that is soul-killing for everyone, and disastrous for the nation.

### Dylan

The scourge of racism and White supremacy is a corruption of the soul of Americans.

### Lawrence

The relationship with America that many Black Americans have is a relationship that many White Americans don't understand, nor do they understand the history. Baldwin does a good job of giving a voice to that difficult relationship that Black folks have with America, how we have this kind of uncomfortable relationship with the notion of patriotism, or an uncomfortable relationship with the history of race in this country, and what that means for us.

### Mark

This ignorance he's trying to get us to get over is not necessarily some subconscious "You may think you're not a racist, but actually, if you look deep, you'll see that you, in fact, really are racist." It's not so much of that, because he's reacting to people who were completely racist. He's reacting to cops stepping on his neck when he was a 12 year old.

### Wes

He does talk about well-meaning Whites as well.

### Mark

He did break with the White liberals. The thing he's trying to get them to recognize is more than an external situation. You might insist "We should just ignore race. And we should just pay attention to people's individual characteristics." But that is ignoring the external historical situation, and the testimony of Black people.

There's a scene in the documentary: He's just gotten done talking, and this older, White philosophy guy is like, *I don't understand why you keep bringing race into it. We all have our individual problems. Everybody has it hard. And everybody has their own unique challenges.* His response was:

> I left this country for one reason only, one reason...I
> ended up on the streets of Paris with $40 in my pocket
> on theory that nothing worse could happen to me there
> than what had already happened to me here.... Once you
> turn your back on this society, you may die. You may die.
> And it's very hard to sit at a typewriter and concentrate
> on that if you're afraid of the world around you. The
> years I lived in Paris did one thing for me, they released
> me from that particular social terror which was not the
> paranoia of my own mind, but a real social danger visible
> in the face of every cop, every boss, everybody... I don't
> know what most white people in this country feel, but I
> can only conclude what they feel from the state of their
> institutions... You want me to make an act of faith risking
> myself, my wife, my woman, my sister, my children, on
> some idealism which you assure me exists in America—
> which I have never seen.

To ignore that testimony is wrong. Part of looking into yourself is recognizing how the historical situation has shaped you and your attitudes. But a prime portion of this ignorance is actually recognizing historical facts, and the facts of other people's experiences, and the external situation. Not just navel-gazing.

### Wes

I don't think it's just ignoring historical context. On one theory, what needs to happen is that we get rid of certain inequalities, and we make sure injustice doesn't occur. If we can say there's no discrimination, and that things aren't unfair, then that's enough.

But Baldwin is arguing this isn't just about that sort of externality. White people have to change the way they look at themselves. And in some way, so do Black people. This is about the importance of altering the way you look at the world, as essential to racial justice. It's not just about economic equality, or ensuring that people aren't discriminated against in jobs. He talks a lot about the horrible acts of humiliation that went on, the way police treated him, for instance, and just all the other horrible, horrible stuff.

But even apart from all that nastiness, and the most obvious stuff, the argument is there's something inherently structurally oppressive in the situation. If White people, even at some unconscious level, think of their history in this whitewashed way, if they think of themselves as pure, and if they have this sort of demonized "Other," the Black person, as the counterpoint to that, the background against which they can feel superior, even at some very unconscious level, then something is still wrong.

As with White privilege, a lot of this has to do with how African-Americans are perceived, and how they perceive themselves, and how White people perceive African-Americans in themselves.

### Mark

The first part of the book *The Fire Next Time* is actually two essays. One is called "My Dungeon Shook: Letter to my Nephew on the One Hundredth Anniversary of the Emancipation." That's pretty direct, in terms of talking to this young person, this 13-year-old, about how the world is hard and has hardened the guy's father, Baldwin's brother. I've got a quote here:

> There is no reason for you to try to become like white people and there's no basis whatsoever for their impertinent assumption that they must accept you. The really terrible thing, old buddy, is that you must accept them... and accept them with love. For these innocent people have no other hope. They are, in effect, still trapped in history, which they do not understand; and until they understand it, they cannot be released from it. They have had to believe for many years, and for innumerable reasons, that black men are inferior to white men. Many of them, indeed, know better, but, as you will discover, people find it very difficult to act on what they know... In this case, the danger, in the minds of most white Americans, is the loss of identity... Any upheaval in the universe is terrifying because it so profoundly attacks one's sense of one's own reality. Well, the black man has functioned in the white man's world as a fixed

star, as an immovable pillar: and as he moves out of his place, Heaven and Earth are shaken to their foundations. (*Fire*, 8-9)

### Lawrence

There is a truth here that, although he's writing 50 years ago, still resonates with me deeply. Because while, yes, there are a number of individuals who are relatively enlightened, there is still what Fanon calls the "Fact of Blackness." And the "Fact of Blackness" clouds the way White people see Black bodies, and interact with Black bodies.

He's expressing something that has always been said to me. It's kind of a precursor to what will be called "respectability politics," the fact that you can bang your head up against this wall if you want to, or you can find a way to circumnavigate it, and live within the fact of your Blackness, and the fact of how they're going to see you.

That's something I've always been taught. I've gotten away from it now, because I've come into my own. But as a very young child, this is a reality that you've got to learn to circumnavigate: *They're going to see you as a threat. They're going to see you as someone who is unintelligent, someone who is inarticulate, someone who has limited possibilities.* You've got to find a way to circumnavigate that.

The many speeches that I heard as a young Black boy came to mind—from my mother, from my grandmother—telling me how to survive in this world. What he's saying is very similar to what Ta-Nehisi Coates writes, in *Between the World and Me*, just *This is the reality that you have to deal with.* Not many other people will have that speech given to them. But being a Black boy, it's a fact of life.

### Wes

The quotation spoke to the way in which African-Americans are a fixed star for the White person. It's about their inability to see reality, because facing that reality in themselves is a loss of identity. But the essay starts out about how terrible his own father's life was. And there's a quote here: "...he really believed what white people said about him" (*Fire*, 4). He talks about how you can be destroyed by that.

So it's a dialectic between Black self-understanding and White understanding, reminiscent of Hegel's master-slave dialectic, where the self-perceived supremacy of one party is as self-degrading as when the other party looks at themselves through those degrading eyes.

## Dylan

He explicitly draws out that parallel with his father. The fact that he believed what White people thought about him as a Black man was, in some decisive way, the source of his pain and his many failures. And White people have the same kind of parallel problem of believing what is said about them, and it has a corrosive effect on them, to corrupt their souls. Think about the way bullies are corrupted by the way they understand themselves.

## Wes

There's a really good quotation on this in the next essay, "Down at the Cross," the sense in which it's corrupting to the White soul. He's talking about the way in which Black people could sometimes achieve freedom, and something close to love within the oppressive limits that had been set for them. And then he talks about the freedom, for instance, in jazz.

> To be sensual, I think, is to respect and rejoice in the force of life, of life itself, and to be present in all that one does... Something very sinister happens to the people of a country when they begin to distrust their own reactions as deeply as they do here, and become as joyless as they have become. (*Fire*, 43)

## Wes

He begins talking about how White people are terrified of sensuality, terrified of that part of themselves. And the way in which they project those sorts of fears onto African Americans. This is one of the ways in which he thinks that souls become corrupted.

## Seth

I feel Baldwin is trying to say that the particular experience of people of African descent, brought to the United States against their will, is an inalienable, incontrovertible fact of the American experience. It's not a category of *Other-and-self* where you're trying to take this frame and apply it to your own experience. He's saying *My experience as a Black man in the United States at this period of time is not only irreducible, or inexplicable, but also an inescapable fact of the American experience.* When you say *I just didn't think that way about Black people, because I didn't have any in my sphere of influence or my sphere of experience,* it's missing the point.

### To what extent is this all about economics?

**Dylan**

The threads of the economic argument, at least in what we read, seemed to fall more in the category of rampant and perpetual kinds of social humiliations: Going to go get a mortgage, and being denied that because you were Black, as a way of keeping the social order in place. It was an explicit humiliation of the Black patron who was trying to get a loan.

Baldwin gives the example of going to a restaurant somewhere. He and his buddy had just wandered in, and nobody's serving them. Eventually, somebody clues them in, *We don't serve Negroes here.* It's a perpetual social humiliation. He had several different stories that just articulate the kind of rage you feel when you are humiliated in that way, or just simply ignored, where your teeth are gnashing, and you want to scream and lash out. You're angry at the situation, you're angry at the particular people who are embodying that situation.

**Wes**

There's a good passage where he's talking about growing up, and his friends becoming adolescents, taking to drinking and cursing and fighting.

> ...lost, and unable to say what it was that oppressed them, except that they knew it was "the man"—the white man. And there seemed to be no way whatever to remove this cloud that stood between them and the sun, between them and love and life and power, between them and whatever it was that they wanted. One did not have to be very bright to realize how little one could do to change one's

situation; one did not have to be abnormally sensitive to be worn down to a cutting edge by the incessant and gratuitous humiliation and danger... (*Fire*, 19)

I think The Fire Next Time is almost entirely about the effects of humiliation on the souls of the people at the receiving end of it and the people who were doing it.

### Mark

My point is, to the extent that he's giving a specific psychological account of the way things were happening to him and his peers, and the way people were treating them, and humiliation all day long, then that's about that specific time period.

### Wes

I don't agree.

### Lawrence

I don't either. I had an uncle who was a Vietnam vet. He was your standard Black-male conspiracy theorist, the guy who would always talk about *The Man*. He didn't play pool, because he thought that pool was a game that was rigged to teach Black people to be subjugated—the table was green and represented the earth, and the goal was to take the white ball and knock all the other colors off the table. And how would you win the game? When the white ball hit the black ball off the green table: *White dominance.*

He was that kind of dude. And I thought he was crazy my entire life. Until I realized that he had been reared in a Southern culture, where he was constantly told "you are less than." One of the things that he saw was his father (my grandfather) who went and fought in World War II. When he comes back home, he can't buy a home, not in certain areas, because of redlining. You have this man who's gone to war, fought for the country, got shot, got a Purple Heart, came back, and is still a second-class citizen. That breeds suspicion, it breeds animosity with the country, with White people.

He's talking about a very specific time period. But, to be honest, I cannot think of a time period, even in my life, where I was not, on some level, aware of the humiliation. Just being pulled over at random times, being treated like I'm not supposed to be in philosophy as a Black man, being treated like I'm not supposed to be at a predominately White campus as a Black man. No one spits in my face. No one calls me *the N word* to my face (although I *have* been called *the N word* not long ago). But that humiliation is still there. It's just the ways in which those things are communicated that have changed.

I still see the same things that my grandfather dealt with and my uncle dealt with. They're still communicated to me. Even as a Black man teaching at a university, living in a suburban neighborhood, driving an Ultima, it's still there. It still colors the way that I see the world. Even in a suburban environment, my sons are going to have to deal with being Black men in this world.

### Let's have another quote:

> The glorification of one race and the consequent debasement of another—or others—always has been, and always will be a recipe for murder. There is no way around this. If one is permitted to treat any group of people with special disfavor because of their race or the color of their skin, there is no limit to what one will force them to endure, and, since the entire race has been mysteriously indicted, no reason not to attempt to destroy it, root and branch. This is precisely what the Nazis attempted... Whoever debases others is debasing himself. That is not a mystical statement, but a most realistic one, which is proved by the eyes of any Alabama sheriff... (*Fire*, 83)

**Wes**

It's very Platonic, that principle in the *Republic*: To do injustice to others is worse than being the victim of injustice, it's more soul-deforming.

**Lawrence**

That, to me, is the moral force of Baldwin. It's very similar to King. Even as he's been very clear in telling the truth to power in a very prophetic way, he's also very intentional about saying *We must respect the humanity of everyone. We cannot allow ourselves to have hate and to harbor hate, and allow that to be the driving force behind what we do. Even if we were to get into a position of power, we cannot treat them the way that they have treated us.* And that still resonates with me even now.

### Mark

We value you, Lawrence, and not merely as a representative. I'm sure we'll have another topic—that's not race related!—that will come back to you.

### Seth

He'll be too big and famous.

### Lawrence

Whatever guys, but just for the record, I am not your Negro philosopher!

## Anything else for the record?

### Dylan

Go read his essays. Go read all of his novels. I feel like I've missed out. I'd never read James Baldwin before. And I was so impressed, his writing was absolutely fantastic.

### Wes

He's both an artist and a thinker. It's one of these rare things you see in a Nietzsche, or a Shakespeare. There's the elements of being a great artist, and a storyteller and a novelist, the ability to pull out these details, and make you feel things, and do all of that stuff. But it's also a really structured thesis. It's remarkable how virtuoso this is, when you're looking at the fact that he's methodically building and arguing for a certain thesis. It's easy to get sucked into making a very dry, boring, academic argument out of that sort of thing. So, to be able to sustain that on the one hand, and to talk about personal experience on the other, and weave them together in this intricate way is a rare kind of talent.

**Lawrence**

What frustrates me is so many people viewed Baldwin as not really doing anything worth wrestling with. He wasn't taught very much.

I would put him beside many great American philosophical thinkers. What he's doing is not as rigorous as some of their things. But his ability to tell a story while wrestling with weighty ideas is unparalleled. I teach him in philosophy courses—I hope that others will do so as well.

*Lawrence Ware is Associate Director of the Oklahoma State University Africana Studies Program and Teaching Assistant Professor and Diversity Coordinator in the Department of Philosophy. He is a contributing writer to* Slate Magazine, *the* New York Times *and* The Root. *He has been a commentator on race and politics for* MSNBC, NPR, *and* CNN.

*Lawrence has taught and lectured across the country on issues ranging from race to economic policy.*

*What is involved in fully recognizing the existence of other minds?*

## READINGS

Fonagy, Peter and Mary Target, "Attachment and reflective function: their role in self-organization," *Development and Psychopathology*, February 1997.

Schore , Allan N., "Attachment and the regulation of the right brain," *Attachment & Human Development*, Vol. 2, No. 1, April 2000.

Schore , Allan N., "Right-Brain Affect Regulation: An essential mechanism of development, trauma, dissociation, and psychotherapy," *The Healing Power of Emotion: Affective Neuroscience, Development & Clinical Practice* edited by D. Fosha, D. J. Siegel, & M. F. Solomon, W. W. Norton & Company, 2009.

# Episode 172

*October 26, 2017*

*Genevieve Arnold*

## Dr. Drew on Peter Fonagy

*"Theory of Mind"* is not what philosophers talk about when dealing with the philosophy of mind, but a term in psychology referring to how we impute intentions, desires, and goals to other people. Fonagy uses the term *"reflective function"* to describe our ability to *"read people's minds,"* in the sense that we can predict others' behavior based on our ability to think of them as having minds. Much of the story here is developmental, like learning language. Reflective function is a built-in human ability, with a number of predetermined steps in its development, but individuals can vary in how it develops, and certainly things can go wrong for various reasons.

*- Mark*

# 172 - Dr. Drew on Fonagy

**Mark**

We are pleased to be joined by a radio legend, Dr. Drew Pinsky

**Dr. Drew**

This is Drew Pinsky being thrown into PEL. If I were thrown into the Pacific Ocean, I'd be less anxious than I am today. Because I'm a huge fan.

## What's the topic today?

**Mark**

Theory of mind, which sounds like a philosophy topic, but is really a psychology topic: How do infants get the idea that other people have intentions and goals? So it's kind of related to the Cartesian topic of *Can we doubt that other people exist?*

**Wes**

Being able to understand that other people have intentions, and are aware that we know that they know, is critical to self-awareness, to thinking of myself as a self, or developing self-consciousness. And that turns out to be dependent on early interactions between an infant and a caregiver.

**Dr. Drew**

It does come close to the things that several philosophers were messing with. And, much to my surprise, the one that came closest, at least as you guys were reading it, was Hegel, in the sense that the *Other* was the critical ontological ingredient to prevent the tautology of "I am." To that end, I want to be careful to define our terms. As I listened to you guys, there's a lot of talk about "consciousness" and "self-consciousness," but no definition of "self." And there's the "I" and the "me" and the "I am" and the "person of the ego," and "the mind." Each of these things, in my opinion, is different. I want us to be really careful about defining those things. I think it'll help us to find the ontological landscape, in addition to the psychological landscape.

## Uh oh...

**Mark**

A lot of people approach philosophy and say "To start off, you have to give definitions of all the terms you're going to use." It's true, we need to be clear about how we're using the term, with respect to a particular author. But that's as far as we can generally go as a preliminary matter: "How does this author define the *I* versus the *Me*?" Because figuring out a generally applicable definition for those things, *that's the whole task of philosophy.* You can't just do that right off the bat.

**Dr. Drew**

Let me fall on my sword. It's my confusion I'm addressing, because I come with these preconceived ideas about what these terms mean. And then I'm trying to figure out what this or that philosopher is saying, and it gets confusing,

**Dylan**

When we come up to these definitions, the best we can do is articulate what we mean, or what we think that this philosopher means, or what this paper is saying about this particular idea. We might not come to any conclusion, ultimately about the bigger part of it, but we'll at least be able to follow the conversation.

**Mark**

Let me read something from near the beginning of the paper. He actually does start by trying to define terms.

> Psychological interest in the self is usually traced to
> James' distinction of two aspects of the self, the "I" (self

as subject) and the "Me" (self as object). The I is the active agent responsible for constructing the self-concept of Me. To paraphrase in the terms of current cognitive neuroscience, the Me is the mental representation, while the I embodies the mental processes or functions which underpin representations of the self. (Fonagy 679)

**Wes**

This is very similar to the distinction we saw in Sartre.

**Mark**

The difference being that Sartre is unapologetically being phenomenological. That's his whole method. He's describing experience. He's saying there's this idea of my character over time, *Who am I really?* But there's also the "I" that unifies experience in the first place, that makes this perception, or that perception, and is the doing. So Sartre's whole puzzle is Is that "I"—which Kant called the "transcendental ego"—a real thing?

Whereas *this* jumps immediately to it's "the active agent responsible for constructing the self-concept of Me." In other words, it gives a causal account. So it's not talking phenomenologically.

Is there a separate part that is the thinker of the thoughts? And then there's the character that is built up over time and referred to as "Me," and that other people point out as "Me" because they can't see the "I"? They can't see the magic thing behind my eyes.

I think it's a real question: Can you take that directly to a causal mechanistic distinction between the two types of things and say, "There's certain brain processes that cause thoughts. And then there's a different representation that is built up in the brain in some different way that's the Me"?

**Wes**

The *I* as a set of functions, including the function of being conscious, is, by itself, something bare and undifferentiated. It doesn't say anything about me, in particular, Wes. Then there's personal *Me*. And then there's the representation of that personal *Me* to myself. If we think of the *I* as subject, we're thinking of something more abstract, more general, we're thinking about something like the Lockean consciousness that's unified through time. And then, once we drill down into actual self-consciousness, representations of myself, personal qualities, we're at the level of *Me*.

### Dylan

But isn't there an aspect where the *Me* then reflects on the *I* as well?

### Wes

*Me* is a representation. Fonagy talks about "working models"— we have a bunch of self-representations. And we don't always have them in mind. They can be unconscious, or tacit, yet they will shape the way I look at the world, and then, in turn, shape the way I look at myself.

### Dylan

I take the distinction here, between *I* and *Me,* as "the subject" and "the object." And what's nice about this reflective function is it's allowing us a way to talk about the back-and-forth between those things.

### Mark

But does the *Me* actually do anything? I'm not sure I like what Wes was just saying about how the *Me* affects how we see things. It seems like the *I* is supposedly the thing that's doing the seeing.

### Dylan

There's a way in which the subjects become objects themselves, and the objects become subjects. I know that's too abstract. But I think that's the kind of problem that the language of reflective function is trying to get around. We have to get over that strict *subject-object* distinction.

### Dr. Drew

Is it worth talking about subjectivity and consciousness at this point?

### Mark

The thing that people are worried about when they say "How could minds emerge out of matter?" is *How could there be this fundamental experience that we have?*—the thing that Descartes was pointing to, that all of the subsequent phenomenologists were pointing to, consciousness in that sense.

### Dr. Drew

Let me show all my cards. I believe consciousness and self both emerge in an intersubjective context. That's why I'm so fascinated by this material. I don't believe there is a *self* without an *Other*. I don't believe consciousness, in the sense that it's commonly understood, particularly self-consciousness, can emerge without the *Other*. When you read the Fonagy article, that's part of what he's talking about. And the biology of how we communicate non-verbally, and how that has a deep impact on our theory of minds.

### Wes

If we're talking about the emergence of self-consciousness, and the ability—this reflective function—to attribute consciousness to others, that has to emerge out of something non-mentalistic, and pre-symbolic. It's a difficult subject, because we have to start with something that doesn't rise to that level. One of the interesting things Fonagy does when he's talking about the acquisition of reflective function is talk about the ability to look at other people's behaviors in terms of teleology. It's pretty symbolic. It's not mentalistic.

For instance, if you show a child the age of six months an animation, in which they're doing people-like things, if it does something irrational, the child of six months will be surprised. Even though they're not able to represent all this stuff linguistically, there's still some sense in which they are already attuned to a theory of mind at the teleological level. They already understand that other people have goals and intentions, and so on. Reflective function comes about, basically, when they have a teleology about the *Other*. Reflective function comes about when they understand that other people's intentions involve seeing their intentions. And that ultimately will give them a vocabulary for talking about their own emotions, their own intentions. It brings the teleological to the level of mentalization.

## Dr. Drew

I'll go back to the paper. He says the principle of rational action—he calls it "the teleological stance"—is applied by infants to humans and nonhumans alike. This language of teleology confused me a little bit, because I thought it was explicitly goal-oriented. But it really amounts to having a kind of predictive model. And in this case, before it becomes mental expectations regarding the activities of other minds, it's just expectations for how something will happen.

## Wes

It's expectations specifically involving a reference to goals or intentions. It's not just an expectation, like *If I hit the billiard ball in a certain way, it's going to do X.*

## Mark

*If I touch the hot thing, then it will burn me.*

## Dylan

The example given in the paper that Wes articulated was you have some animated objects, and they're moving in a certain way. And there'll be cases where their behavior makes sense. And there'll be cases where that behavior is surprising. And the interpretation of it being surprising is that it's not behaving according to the teleological model that the infant has.

## Wes

According to an implied goal in the scene for those blobs.

## Dylan

Whatever is going on, if you want to call it a model, if you want to call it an intuition, or whatever it is, all of that is going on inside them such that it comports with their expectation, or it surprises them. The force of those experiments is that they have that expectation. And then the next step is that those kinds of expectations, those kinds of modelmaking, that kind of construction of behaviors, extends to other rational entities, not just animated objects, or objects that are moving around in the world.

And it's actually very similar to the expectations of causality of the sort that you just mentioned, of hitting a ball or getting your hand burned, or any of these other things, that it's an expectation of a certain result, that's based upon some implicit understanding of causality.

### Wes

The difference is if we had a scene in which the movement of the billiard ball violated our expectation, it would violate it with respect to our past experience, that has given us a model of how things should bounce off each other. It's sort of an intuitive sense of the physics of it.

But in the teleological case, the regularities at stake are not just these physical laws, they have to involve rules about how goal-oriented beings will behave. So that's the teleological part of it.

### Mark

Adults curse at the computer, "The computer is stymieing me." We tend to apply these teleological things to inanimate objects. But would we want to describe our perception of that ball, or the thing on the screen, as teleological?

### Dr. Drew

We, at the very least, make narrative. And that narrative has a teleological quality to it. Children who have an expectation based on how humans behave, if it's disappointed, or it's altered in some surprising way, they react to it long before they should understand. The research shows there's something hardwired that gives us a teleological stance.

## Let's talk about the 4 kinds of attachment and what that theory is based on...

### Dr. Drew

This is all based on observations, not just of infants, but adults. We carry these attachment styles into our adulthood, and then of course, into our parenting style as well. One of the goals of treatment is to try to develop a secure attachment. So that model of security then gets reflected back into the interpersonal context, and that person's life, whether it's in their romantic relationships, their friend relationships, or their parenting relationships.

> There is general agreement that, as the self exists only in the context of the other, the development of the self is tantamount to the aggregations of experience of self in relationships. (Fonagy, 684)

Those experiences of self can be parsed into four broad categories of relating. One of the ways they examine this is by looking at the "still face" paradigm, where the mom just sits there with a blank face, and looks at the child, and they see how the child responds to that.

It's so stressful to a child just to have a face go flaccid, that they become acutely distressed within minutes. That's how much interaction goes back-and-forth with the child even pre-verbally, in face-to-face interaction.

### Dylan

Emphasizing how much of who we are depends upon the *Other,* that from infants all the way up to adults, we get our understanding of ourselves by seeing it reflected in other people. We don't just do it by ourselves.

### Dr. Drew

And there's templates that are left behind. People think about this as "procedural memory."

> Given these features [of attachment]... the schematic representations postulated by attachment and object relation theorists are most usefully construed as procedural memories" (Fonagy, 685).

In other words, not explicit memories, but just experiential templates that we automatically engage with.

### Mark

It seems surprising, given a lay understanding of attachment, that this would be so different than attachment to my security blanket.

### Dr. Drew

There are paradigms of attachment, and they're healthy and

unhealthy attachments, and the unhealthy ones fall into specific categories, like "avoidant" or "disorganized." Disorganized, unfortunately, is one of the more common things that we see today. Where the attachment is disorganized, the self is disorganized. The love and attachment is to an object, which is also the source of distress and disorganization.

The four types are "secure", "preoccupied", "dismissive", and "fearful-avoidant." Those are the four common ways in which these things are categorized. If you want to think of it practically: *A child is stressed, and then mom comes back and tries to reregulate with the child, and the child diverts its head 90 degrees and becomes flat with its aspect, and doesn't engage*—That's an attachment. That's evidence of an attachment style.

### Mark

Reading this made me feel better about my over-attentive parenting when my kids were small. You get the feeling, the moment when you're around a little baby, that as long as they're awake I should be there, making faces, paying attention to them, really locking eyes, and not necessarily jumping to their every whim, but attending to them.

After some time of that, I shifted more to the camp of "No, throughout history, parents have not been that spastically attentive to their kids. And they did just fine." Reading this, my initial instinct seems justified.

### Dr. Drew

Yes, we don't do enough of it. And so the child is abandoned, and abandoned is actually considered the most significant trauma you can possibly perpetrate. Because they are left with no access to all of these mechanisms we're talking about.

Now, I disagree with that, I think that you can be active in your abuse, and that ends up being more shattering. But we have a lot of trouble with kids not being adequately attuned during the early development, when they really need lots of this.

### Mark

I just want to tell all the new parents listening *If you do feel like you're burned out and you just need to let the kid cry and go watch TV... you are a bad parent.*

**Dr. Drew**

No!

A lot of the really good parenting is about repair—leaving and coming back. How you repair the departures or the ruptures is where a lot of the important stuff goes on, as it turns out.

## Can you become conscious of the procedural aspects of your own psychology?

**Dr. Drew**

To an extent you can. There's aspects you are not aware of, that you're not seeing, that another person can reflect back to you. And we think of it almost as the other person "metabolizing" it and then handing it to you. You can then go *Hmm, I didn't see that. That's a blind spot. I guess you're right. I* do *do that.* Wes, have you ever had that on the couch?

**Wes**

Yeah. The way it happens is through emotional communication, where it's not that your therapist "tells" you that there's something that you do, but it's revealed to you in the relationship.

**Dr. Drew**

When you're the patient, it's mysterious, because it seems to come out of nowhere. When you're the doctor, I find it more explicit, in the sense that I will have thoughts, feelings, hear music, smell things, that are "not mine"—it's something that I'm creating with the patient. And at the right moment, I'll go, "I'm having an experience, what of this has meaning to you?" They will just walk right into it, even though it's some disavowed part of them that they didn't ever express. They will just matter-of-factly walk with you into the shared space of that experience.

**Wes**

It's sort of a parallel process to what goes on with mothering, this development of reflective function. Language can be helpful, but only insofar as it's doing something emotionally. And the problem is not being able to represent your own feelings to yourself, not knowing what you're feeling. And because of that, not having the tools to regulate it.

### Dylan

It's not just that the mother is reflecting their anxiety directly to them—it's reflecting their anxiety, but also with this coping mechanism to get them out of it. It not being merely verbal makes a big difference in my own experience with my own kids, especially when they're hardly talking, and can't articulate in words what they're doing. It's often just the faces, or the physical proximity, and touching of them, where you're providing them a safe, context-holding environment. Literally holding or emotionally holding.

### Which is great, but can we get more philosophical?

### Dr. Drew

I was curious about how you guys would interpret the ontology of all this, how it reflects on the phenomenological continental heritage.

### Mark

You brought up Sartre, his issue with freedom. You'd have to say that all this kind of programming is part of our "facticity." Psychologically, we've got all these patterns, and things that we're unaware of, that are pushing us this way or that. But, nonetheless, you could still, from an ethical point of view, have absolute freedom to choose whatever you want.

It could be really difficult. I can't just choose to be not addicted to cocaine, but you could choose to point yourself in that direction and try. Even if you're chained up, you still have freedom of choice.

### Dr. Drew

That's interesting, because it drives back towards the Stoics a little bit. I think of Epictetus when you say that.

### Mark

My rant is that's "pretty weak tea." If you really have a lot of hard psychological problems, then simply wheeling yourself in the right direction? The freedom is thin.

Existentially, we often talk about the isolation. Wow, we're all fundamentally different from each other, our minds can never connect. Even sex, even in that physical relationship, you're relating your own sensations into an image you have of them. We're all fundamentally isolated in this way.

That seems to have an emotional connotation and not merely an ontological connotation. Why you'd say that is because you actually do feel I am so bleak, and I must sit at the café and smoke my cigarettes, and we're all isolated. If it was purely an abstraction, then existentialism wouldn't have caught on as a thing.

But, reading all this stuff about attachment, it does seem like *No, actually, if you feel that isolated, there's something wrong with you. You didn't have the correct attachment, when you were a kid, and that's what's going on right now.* And maybe some therapy can address that, even if not completely undo it.

### Dr. Drew

I have my own interpretation of the "brain in the vat" paradigm, which is not so much about the brain-in-the-vat, but about the process of signing up to become the brain-in-the-vat.

There's one thing about the phenomena that can't be escaped. You are experiencing the perfect life, you think you are in the world, you think you are with all your loved ones. But the raw fact is that you would not exist to others. And that fact is so powerful to human beings.

I go out there and ask people this question all the time, particularly drug addicts, and 90% of people would not sign up to be the brain-in-the-vat. Because it's so powerfully important to us to exist to others. We have to exist to others to make meaning of life.

*David Drew Pinsky, commonly known as "Dr. Drew," is an American media personality, internist, and addiction-medicine specialist best known for the nationally syndicated radio talk show* Loveline, *and the* VH1 *show* Celebrity Rehab with Dr. Drew. *Pinsky currently hosts several podcasts, including* Ask Dr. Drew (Wikipedia).

*How much can people be blamed for their actions when the whole system they're a part of is corrupt?*

## READINGS

Arendt, Hannah, *Eichmann in Jerusalem: A Report on the Banality of Evil*, Penguin Classics, 1977.

# EPISODE 181

*December 31, 2017*

*Shane Wood*

## HANNAH ARENDT

*Are we still morally culpable if our entire society is corrupt? Arendt definitely thinks so, but has a number of criticisms of the handling of the 1961 trial of Nazi war criminal Adolf Eichmann. Israel used the spectacle to remind people of the horrors of the Holocaust, but missed the opportunity to explore what would make a rather ordinary man a party to such heinous acts. They were committed to the view that he was a monster, when the reality, says Arendt, is more frightening. He was really more of a clown: a status-obsessed, cliche-spouting, self-pitying bureaucrat who, far from having no moral compass, was extremely dedicated to obeying a warped version of the* Categorical Imperative: *"Act in such a way that the Führer, if he knew your action, would approve it."*

*- Mark*

# 181 - Arendt

**Mark**

So why did we read this?

**Wes**

What prompted it was an article in *The New York Times* about a neo-Nazi as an ordinary guy. You know, *Going with him on a trip to the grocery store, and documenting his family life,* and things like that. It produced a lot of outrage, along lines of normalizing being a Nazi, and humanizing Nazis, and how there's something wrong with that.

I noticed people were preemptively arguing against the whole "banality of evil" angle. It's as if the author of the article had said *Look, I'm just illustrating the dangers of this sort of thing. It's actually your next-door neighbor, and no matter how normal and how nice they might seem, they might have these sorts of opinions.* And I saw comments to the effect that *Yes, we all know about the banality of evil. And we don't need to be reminded of that.* So I wanted to get into the details of whether our popular conception of that is a misunderstanding.

**Mark**

Seth, you said you'd read this a couple times before.

**Seth**

I read it, of my own volition, when I was still in college, and then I read it again, when I was in graduate school, and then I read it once more, about a decade ago. Part of it was my own curiosity, being Jewish—part of my own intellectual engagement with "my tradition," or "my history." But the other part is, during the 1980s, when what constituted the classical canon came up, when Bloom wrote *The Closing of the American Mind*, this book was part of the conversation. It was part of the conversation because it was written by a woman, who was also a philosopher. It was controversial in its time, because thesis challenged our standard understanding of what constitutes normal.

As we saw from our previous Hannah Arendt readings, she's a tremendous writer, a sharp thinker and social critic. And so, I wanted to engage with the book for my own edification.

Also, in my circles, the title itself, *Eichmann in Jerusalem*, is a cultural touchstone. It's a meme in our culture, and I wanted to understand what that meant. I liked it as much this time as I have every other time I've read it.

### Mark

When this came out, it was very controversial, and condemned by some Jewish groups because it wasn't taking the Israeli line. It's a report on the trial of Eichmann that took place in Israel. He couldn't be found for Nuremberg, he was hiding out in Argentina. But when the State of Israel was firmly established, he was found in Argentina, and they kidnapped him and brought him to trial.

This is Arendt's commentary (originally written for *The New Yorker*, but then expanded) on how the trial went. But it doesn't go into detail. We don't hear the statements of a lot of the witnesses, or anything. And it's critical of Ben-Gurion, the Prime Minister of Israel at the time—his reasons for having the trial. She characterizes it as having aspects of a show trial. Not that it was a sham, or that the verdict was already determined beforehand. She was complimentary of the judges. But certainly, there were a lot of purposes ulterior to simply finding the guilt of this one person.

It was meant to present to the world that Israel can do this thing, has the jurisdiction, has the independence. *Finally, the Jews can have a nation to prosecute based on their interests.* And to remind young Jews, and everybody else, exactly how horrible the Holocaust was. It was pro-Zionist, that Jews need to be militant in resisting this kind of thing in the future.

So Arendt was critical. And some of what we read did, in fact, mischaracterize Iran's positions regarding aspects of Jewish resistance, or Jewish collaboration with the Nazis, etcetera. But despite that initial controversy, this book is revered as necessary. Understanding that somebody like Eichmann was not terribly uncommon, that he was not a sadist, out there making his own law, that he was just a cog in the machinery—that's a really necessary lesson: We need to make sure this kind of thing doesn't happen again.

### Seth

That's part of it. She wrestles with a couple of parallel themes. She's making the point that the purpose of a trial is to determine guilt or innocence. And Eichmann's guilt had been firmly established and documented, because this was 12 years after the war. So, she's making the point that the purpose of the trial was not to determine whether he was guilty or innocent. The purpose of the trial was to make a statement to the world.

Immediately after the war, when the Nuremberg Trials happened (and some follow-up trials of war criminals), they took place in the countries where those crimes occurred, and were adjudicated by the international tribunal of the victor nations. At the time, the Jews didn't have a state. So they weren't in a position to actually have a trial themselves, and mete out justice against any of the perpetrators of the crimes against them.

So she was claiming the purpose of this trial was not to determine Eichmann's guilt. The purpose of the trial was to show the world that Israel had the right and the ability as a state to have this kind of a legal proceeding to accomplish the same task that the Nuremberg trials and the other trials did.

That having been said, Eichmann was different than the people who were tried at Nuremberg. He was not a high party official, a general, a minister, or anything like that. The perception was that he was the mastermind behind the Final Solution. And what she does is point out that he was not the mastermind. He wasn't in a position to make those kinds of decisions.

The issue was that he just did what he was told, because he was trying to advance his career. And it was this sense in which he divorced his moral faculty, or his conscience, from what was actually occurring. *Individuals can do this,* but more importantly, *An entire civilization did this very thing.* He was indicative of the collapse of the entire moral order, first in Germany, and then the entirety of Eastern and Western Europe. The Eastern states, once they started collaborating with (and then ultimately were annexed by) Germany, more than enthusiastically participated in sending their Jews off to the gas chambers. And the Western countries that knew this was happening didn't take actions to stop it immediately.

So her question in this book is, how do we understand the complete collapse of 2000 years of development of culture and morality, as personified by this one person, and identify that the collapse itself is due to the fact that people refuse to think.

**Wes**

Specifically Eichmann, what she calls his inability to think from the standpoint of someone else.

### What about her thoughts on theatrics of the trial?

**Wes**

A show trial is contrary to procedural justice in the strict sense.

> Justice demands that the accused be prosecuted, defended and judged...On trial are his deeds, not the sufferings of the Jews, not the German people, or mankind, not even anti-Semitism and racism. (5)

The trial was built on what the Jews had suffered, not on what Eichmann had done, which in her mind is a deviation from the question of justice. If he suffers, he must suffer for what he has done, not for what he has caused others to suffer.

I want to emphasize that assumption of hers: *Justice doesn't exist to satisfy victims. Justice is there to meet the demands of society, which aren't necessarily the same as the demands of the victims.*

**Dylan**

To me, the brilliance of the book is as a report of things more-or-less directly related to Eichmann, and the circumstances of his guilt, and thinking about what kind of man he is, and how he came to be. There's a lot of facts in the book. It's all the more horrible because of all the facts. But it's not a giant's-eye view of big topics, like "How did the Germans do this?" To the extent it has psychology, it's *Eichmann's* psychology.

**Wes**

She does say that the trial is an opportunity to understand Eichmann, and his motivations, and the implications of those motivations. And by making it a show trial, and making him a monster, it passed up that opportunity.

She takes that opportunity in this book, and it's something that created a huge controversy and got her in a lot of trouble, people accusing her of normalizing the terrible and the atrocious.

**Dylan**

I didn't find myself feeling it was normalized. It was one of the most horrifying things I've ever read in my life.

**Wes**

It was very depressing.

**Mark**

There are large sections of it that are of historical interest, but are not chock-full of philosophy. As a philosopher, if you really wanted to get to the nub of this, it's just a couple of the chapters, just the beginning and the end. And a couple of chapters in the middle about the Final Solution itself, chapters *Six* through *Eight*.

*Chapter Eight* is called "Duties of a Law-Abiding Citizen." Eichmann even name-drops Kant, and the fact that he was consistently doing "his duty." He even is able to give to the judge some version of the *categorical imperative*. He was not undermining the society in which he was a part. He was not like a thief, where, if everybody stole, property wouldn't be possible. No, he was within his environment. He was doing his duty, the best that he could.

And, in fact, they point out that he was not just following orders, as claimed by a lot of the Nuremberg defendants. He even went against explicit orders, on the grounds of *What would the Führer actually want? What was his true duty?* He was super-zealous in going ahead with additional deportations, even though the trains were all broken down. This is the thing he was most directly responsible for, in terms of his own initiative. He wasn't just following orders, and wasn't claiming that.

### Wes

Regardless of Eichmann having been a cog in the machine, there's a point in 1944, when his boss Himmler is saying *Break off the sending of Jews to extermination camps, we've got to think about how we're going to negotiate with the Allies once they take over*. Because everyone had seen the writing on the wall. The way it's characterized in this chapter is not that Eichmann was going above-and-beyond what Hitler wanted. There wasn't a lot of paper trail, there wasn't a lot of evidence of Hitler explicitly putting it down as a law that *You shall deport Jews to the extermination camps*. But everyone knew what Hitler wanted, and they acted on that.

And even after everyone else had stopped acting on that, he continued to act on that principle. And that's the sense in which he thought of himself as a Kantian, following his duty, even after everyone else was thinking pragmatically about what was going to happen after the end of the war.

### Mark

We should clarify that the thing that he was involved with was transportation. He didn't run the camps himself. It wasn't just the fact that he couldn't be found that he wasn't tried at Nuremberg. He was not in the position where he was obviously directly responsible.

A lot of the argument was *You were in charge of transportation, you knew what would happen to these people if you successfully did your job and transported them.* So that's enough to make you responsible.

### Wes

There's a conflict between what he said before trial, that comment about hanging himself, and then his feeling at the end of the trial, which is it was an injustice. In the beginning, he had this braggadocio about "Repentance is for children." But then he writes this plea for clemency. I went online and read that, and it's the same sort of thing. *I didn't do these things. I wasn't responsible. I didn't pull any triggers.*

He was responsible for different things at different times during the war. In the beginning, it was so-called emigration. He facilitated emigration.

**Mark**

And worked with Zionists.

**Wes**

And went to visit Palestine, and learned a smattering of Hebrew, and thought of himself as a Zionist. All of this is part of his blindness. There are people who are fearful, and being persecuted, and that's why they're emigrating, in large part. Some of it is straightforward Zionism, or it's a mixture, but he thinks of himself as doing a good deed here.

Later on, it becomes forced deportation, and concentration of Jews, and ghettos, for the purpose of deporting them to other areas in the future. And then, explicitly in 1941, it becomes the *Final Solution,* where he knows he's deporting people to death camps. And he didn't deny that he knew what he was doing, when he put people on trains. Sending people to their deaths. So that's the sense in which he was implicated and involved.

In the beginning of the trial, his plea is "not guilty," in the sense of the indictment. And Arendt reflects about what that means. For his defense, lawyers make the argument that in a way, these are acts of state. They weren't illegal under Hitler's regime. And so, Eichmann can't be prosecuted for something that wasn't illegal.

Eichmann just aided and abetted murder, he wasn't the actual murderer. And that was a very important distinction to Eichmann. That was the thing that had him feeling this was all a great injustice. He never actually went up to someone and shot them, or pulled the lever to release the gas.

**Mark**

One of the things Arendt was criticized for was spreading the guilt around. She considers *Could he have made a defense that if he hadn't gone along with this, his life would have been in imminent danger?* and concludes that's not the case. It was just that success was defined in that structure as doing what Eichmann was trying to do.

### Dylan

This is one of the most interesting parts of her discussion, and his psychology. Within the Nazi regime, was it so brutal that anybody who deviated would be considered traitors, and strung up or killed? Were they pulling a trigger because they had a gun to their head? She makes the point that is simply not true. You could refuse to participate. You get a transfer. You say, *Well, I don't like this kind of work.*

There's this deeply horrifying aspect of it just being a corporation. And if you didn't like doing some of the work, if you didn't like working downstairs, you could just transfer somewhere else. In Eichmann's case, he had a sense, not just of duty, but of bureaucratic achievement. He wanted to excel, and get the accolades of excelling as a bureaucrat. That's why he didn't want to leave, he wanted to do a good job and get promoted and make a little bit more money, and was irritated about not getting promoted, and would essentially stand around the watercooler and talk to people about how he deserved to get another promotion.

### Wes

As Arendt mentions, there's no evidence that anyone was ever imprisoned or executed for saying, *I don't want to be part of an execution squad,* or *I don't want to be part of the bureaucratic mechanisms that are getting millions of people killed.* There's no evidence that anyone was ever punished. But Eichmann says it would be "unthinkable" to quit his job.

Arendt makes a lot of the fact Eichmann was this lower middle-class guy. He had been a traveling salesman, and he got that job because of the connections of Jewish members of his family. And even that wasn't going well. Being a Nazi allowed him to start over and start a successful career.

For him, pursuing that successful career was everything. And that motivation was exacerbated by class differences—the sense that in many ways, he was the social inferior of people around him. He wanted to live up to the prevailing values, and sense of what was respectable in that society.

Because of his situation, he was an extraordinary conformist. And if the whole project was to exterminate Jews, his conscience wasn't going to reject that, because his conscience was entirely tied up in approval from superiors, and respectability, and all that stuff.

His whole devotion to Hitler, by the way, was made worse by the fact that Hitler was also a bumpkin, essentially, who became powerful and Eichmann identified with that.

### Mark

The Lance Corporal who became the Führer.

### Wes

Exactly. So that class thing is interesting, especially in light of our episode on Orwell, where Orwell emphasizes the fact that totalitarianism is sort of the cancerous growth of this idea of status, and respectability. If you remember, he claims that the source of totalitarianism will be middle-class and upper middle-class bureaucrats, who are essentially meritocratic careerists. Totalitarianism is the final result of that hierarchy, the worst possible case of the growth of that hierarchy into something terrible.

### Dylan

Part of that horribleness is, even though Hitler is behind it, and in the case of Eichmann, his own sense of duty, it's also the case that this bureaucratic mechanism is a faceless state. In some sense, nobody's responsible, because there isn't anybody who is identified as running something. There is an aspect of it that there is a machine that's moving along and people are just making the machine run.

The Holocaust happened in a step-by-step manner. In particular, there's the Wannsee Conference, where you have this group of high-ranking National Socialists get together and work out the logistics of the Final Solution. *Who's going to make sure the trains run on time? Who's going to arrange for the soldiers to get fed?* Imagining that room, and that conversation—after which they have drinks—was the most horrifying part of the whole book for me.

### Seth

This idea that there's an agentless state, there's a lot to the mechanics of that. The first is that the Nazis invented a language for describing the Final Solution, which took the sting out of actual words like "gassing" or "killing." They had a whole nomenclature of the way they spoke about it, in very neutral terms.

The original characterization, way back, even before Hitler came to power, was the "Jewish question." Which already makes it ambiguous. There's a way that they spoke about it that took the sting out of the conscience, as they were working through the mechanics. And often Hitler's instructions were verbal. There's this complicated system where Hitler speaks, and then his agents and ministers actually enact legislation or rules. It all points back to Hitler, but with no written record of his accountability.

Arendt talks about an "idealist" as being somebody who's willing to sacrifice people for an idea. It's the way that she characterizes Eichmann.

### Wes

It's the way he thinks of the Jewish Zionists that he's dealing with. He thinks *Hey, these guys are idealists, just like me. They're prepared to sacrifice everything and everybody to this idea*l.

### Dylan

It's Eichmann who talks of himself as an "idealist." So Arendt puts the word in quotes.

### Seth

It's this idea that he has fidelity to—the idea of solving the Jewish question, because that's critical to the future of Europe and the Reich. Everything subordinates itself to the accomplishment of that particular task.

The question can be formulated as Arendt saying *You think of Hitler as being the one who could sacrifice others for an idea, but how is it that millions and millions of people were persuaded to that way of thinking?*

She says, in the book, everybody had their "good Jew." Everybody says, *Yeah, we have to solve the Jewish question. But my neighbor fought in World War I. He's one of the good ones, right?* And so part of the question is: How is that relationship, that actual concrete human relationship, outweighed by subordination to this abstract idea that permits you to just essentially wipe away your conscience?

### Wes

Abstraction is the key, the willingness to think in generalities. This idea of being able to think from the standpoint of someone else, by the exercise of imagination, which is not just to empathize with them, but really think about a given situation, instead of subsuming particulars under some universal category. That's what she accuses Eichmann of not being able to do. He has a defect in thinking from the standpoint of other people. And it's reflected in his language.

### Seth

Part of the question is, was there anybody who was external to Eichmann who said, *Oh, my God,* that challenged the conscience? Is there any societal, or super-ego, or parental, or some kind of external conscience that would hold him in check? The argument for the defense is there was no external conscience. There was nobody in society telling him that he was doing something wrong, so he couldn't judge that he was doing something wrong.

If you connect this back to the idea of *I and Thou,* or Levinas' "responsibility in the face of the other," the individual themselves carries with them the weight of conscience. Your interaction with another individual should be sufficient to generate a sense of responsibility, or external conscience. That's all that's required for you to recognize their humanity, or recognize their dignity.

The Jewish intellectual tradition is skeptical of the abstract. It's skeptical of generalization, precisely because it contains within it the seeds of totalitarianism and cruelty. This has been a thread that weaves through and informs my view of the world. It's why I'm less interested in ontology and metaphysics, and more interested in this kind of stuff.

### Wes

Cliches are a preeminent example of generalization, of the inability to think in concrete terms. What she calls "stock phrases," which defended Eichmann against reality, and the consciousness of his self-deception. A lot has to do with his view of the Jews as his "respectable enemies." They're on the same level as him and it's just *We were enemies, we respected each other, we went to battle, let's move on.*

He prided himself on his relationships with certain Jewish representatives, for instance, the guy he went to visit in the concentration camp, who tried to run and appealed to Eichmann for help.

And Eichmann went and said *What rotten luck!* And then he said, *It was a great inner joy to me that I can at least see the man with whom I had worked for so many long years, and that we could speak to each other.*

These are the sorts of stock phrases that Eichmann is prone to, including the story that he is this unfortunate guy, and that if he just unloads this tale of misfortune to his Israeli captors, they're going to sympathize with him. Arendt goes concretely into his way of thinking—this idea that he was pulling together with the Jews, that they were sort of his comrades, this inability to think of it from their perspective, this absurd way of understanding it.

### Mark

Hitler hardly ever attempted to justify things in ideological terms. And if he did, it was apparently quickly forgotten. What stuck in the minds of these men, who had become murderers, was simply the notion of being involved in something historic, grandiose, unique, a great task that occurs once in 2000 years, which must therefore be difficult to bear.

This is important because the murderers were not sadists or killers by nature. On the contrary, a systematic effort was made to weed out all those who derived physical pleasure from what they did. Hence, the problem was how to overcome not so much their conscience, but rather the animal pity by which all normal men are affected in the presence of physical suffering.

The trick used by Himmler, who was strongly afflicted with these instinctive reactions himself, was very simple, and probably very effective. It consisted in turning these instincts around, in directing them towards the self. So instead of saying *What horrible things I did to people*, the murderers would be able to say, *What horrible things I had to watch in the pursuance of my duties,* and *How heavily the test weighed upon my shoulders.*

### Wes

A good example of the failure of judgment here, and the way it can be deformed or impaired—this "reversal of pity."

### Dylan

It's not normalizing the activity of the killing, but acknowledging that it's not normal, but then appealing to a "supernormal" time. You're being asked to do something, and your inner instincts are that this is terrible, and this is wrong. The way you're going to get around it is *Hold on to your duty. Tough things have to be done in order to get to the other side.*

### Seth

This wasn't simply nationalism, in the sense of *Do this for Germany!* The Third Reich was to be the "Thousand Year Reich." It was a religious mission, almost. It's not as simple as appealing to a normal instinct, like fidelity to family or community. It wasn't even fidelity to Germany as a nation, it was fidelity to the fear. They're going to acknowledge that the act is morally bankrupt, or corrupt, or evil, or wrong, but claim that it needs to be done in the service of something else. And then you come up with a language and a process that systematizes the process. Execution of those actions allows you to divorce yourself from agency.

And so, when you think about each stage of that process: *How it would be possible to get there?* If you think of yourself as an individual: *How could I stand by or even participate in doing something that I know was wrong?* First, you'd have to have the conviction that doing it was for some kind of a greater good. It's not simply because Germany needs it to defend its borders, it's because you're doing something unprecedented, with massive historical ramifications. It can't be left to your direct agency, where you're constantly having to make judgments, and be faced with the reality of what you're doing. It has to be systematized in such a way that you can participate, and essentially, divorce yourself as an agent from the actual actions.

### Wes

It's not that Eichmann didn't have a conscience, it's that his conscience was the voice of society around him. One of the most potent factors in soothing his conscience was that he couldn't see anyone around him who was against the Final Solution. It wasn't just the Nazis, who thought this was normal. It was Germans in general. It was even the victims, whose lack of resistance made it seem normal.

By the way, she's not judging them for the lack of resistance. This is one of the things that got her in trouble. She doesn't think any group of people would have acted any differently, or could have, out of the circumstances. But she does take note of it.

**Mark**

Some Dutch Jews actually did kill some Nazis, and they were tortured, horribly, such that she says they would have envied the folks in Auschwitz.

**Dylan**

But she does have harsh words for the Jewish leadership in Germany.

**Wes**

Like Eichmann, they enjoyed their status and power, they enjoyed the fact that it put them in a leadership role.

### Did anyone put up a successful resistance?

**Wes**

Denmark is the famous example where they just said "No." Bulgaria is another standout example. Bulgarians totally resisted.

**Mark**

There's a lot of moving parts in making something like this happen. Unless there's cooperation from a lot of people, you do not get this kind of horror going on.

**Wes**

They didn't even suffer any reprisals for it. The Germans on the ground didn't have the heart to continue if there was any resistance. So when they met resistance in Bulgaria and Denmark, they just gave up.

**Seth**

This goes back to what I was saying about having to institute the system where you can divorce yourself from agency. Cooperation makes it possible, lack of friction in the process. It's about momentum. It's not that there were moral monsters, or there was mass hypnosis, or something like that. All this was made possible simply by the fact that people didn't say "No."

**Seth, you feel Arendt has a strong message for us?**

**Seth**

Any time something's unprecedented, you don't understand it, you don't know how to deal with it. So, genocide was unprecedented. There had been mass exterminations of ethnic groups previously. But it all took place within the borders of a sovereign state. What differentiated this was the attempt to wipe one individual group off the face of the earth, regardless of national borders...

**Wes**

...for no utilitarian purpose.

**Seth**

There's a temptation to say *Because it's unprecedented, because it's exceptional, there was something exceptional in the cause, and it can't happen again.* And she says *No, now it is precedented. We should not only worry, but we should expect the same thing to happen again. And so, we must understand how it was possible that this happened.* That narrative—where we have monsters, evil and unique circumstances that give birth to the situation—if we read exceptionalism into it, we will miss the opportunity to understand, and to be able to safeguard against the recurrence of this in the future.

*Live at Manhattan's Caveat, 10th Anniversary Show, April 6, 2019*

*What is it to live wisely?*

READINGS

Maitra, Keya, *The Philosophy of the Bhagavad-Gita*: A Contemporary Introduction, Bloomsbury Academic, 2018.

Vyasa, *The Song of God: Bhagavad-Gita*, translated by Swami Prabhavananda and Christopher Isherwood. Mentor, 1972.

# EPISODE 204

*October 18, 2018*

*Chris Warr*

# SHAAN AMIN *ON* THE BHAGAVAD-GITA भगवद्गीता

*On the classic Hindu text from possibly around the third century BCE, which is a part of the Indian Epic poem* Mahabharata, *attributed to Vyasa, though that probably wasn't a single person. The text is a conversation on the eve of battle between the archer-hero Arjuna and his charioteer, Krishna, who in the course of the text reveals himself to be the supreme God.*

*- Mark*

# 204 - Bhagavad-Gita

**Shaan Amin**

This is Shaan, ever-deluded.

**Mark**

Are you a one-named guest, like Cher?

**Shaan**

Shaan Amin.

**Mark**

Shaan Amin, what is your deal?

**Shaan**

I'm a graduate student studying political science. But I'm interested in the political outcomes associated with religious and ethnic identities in South Asia and Southeast Asia. I'm also a practicing Hindu from a Hindu family, and I grew up immersed in the *Bhagavad-Gita* (भगवद्गीता), the *Mahabharata* (महाभारतम्), which surrounds it, and various others—the mythos of Hinduism.

I emailed somewhat out of the blue, but I remember you saying in an earlier podcast that you were excited to sink your teeth into non-Western philosophical work.

**Mark**

Why don't you give us a little background, how this fits in with the other Hindu holy texts, why we picked this one in particular.

**Shaan Amin**

The *Gita* is situated in the broader text of the great epic, the *Mahabharata*. There's various datings, between 400 BCE and 550

CE. So we don't know. And there's a lot of uncertainty about it. It's not one of the foundational texts of Hinduism, interestingly enough. The foundational texts are the *Vedas* (वेदः), which are compiled around 1500 BCE, and then over the next couple of centuries, the *Upanishads* (उपनिषद्), which are getting more into philosophy, the metaphysical implications of the nature of God and the nature of the cosmos (whereas the *Vedas* were more ritualistic). And then the *Gita* comes along and synthesizes a lot of these early forms of the schools of Hindu philosophy.

### Mark

This is the most popular Hindu text now. But only as of the early 20th century. Famously, Gandhi referred to this a lot, as his favorite text, and the people that shot Gandhi used this text to defend their actions. So, like many religious texts, you can get a lot out of it.

### Wes

The frame for this is a situation in which Arjuna is hesitating to kill his enemies in war. And his charioteer turns out to be Krishna (God). Arjuna doesn't want to kill all of his kinsmen, all these people who are fathers, grandfathers, teachers, uncles, and so on. He gives a few reasons for that, the surrounding the killing of law, the corrupting of family and the mixing of caste, and things like that, and then Krishna says, *No, kill them.*

### Dylan

*Do it, because no one really dies.*

### Wes

And why you should do this ultimately has to do with the fact that to be "pious" (and that's my word, that's not a word that occurs here) is not to refrain from acting. It's to have a certain comportment towards one's actions. One that involves not being oriented towards the fruits of one's actions.

And there's a larger theme of not being attached in general to objects of the senses, potential objects of desire. The whole thing is framed around this argument that *Wisdom is not inaction, go ahead and be who you are, be that warrior, and kill all these guys.* That's the frame for this, which drew me in and was immediately fascinating.

### Shaan

To give context, the *Mahabharata* is a long story of this succession crisis in a kingdom, between one faction of five brothers, and their cousins, who are a faction of one-hundred brothers. The five brothers are the good guys. Arjuna is arguably their greatest warrior, he's the most charismatic hero—not the most virtuous one. Krishna is the ruler of a neighboring kingdom, who befriends these five princes while they're in exile, earlier in the epic. He becomes their negotiator in the weeks leading up to the war, trying to defuse the conflict—or so it seems. And when this doesn't happen, both of the sides come to him asking for his kingdom's aid.

He offers to one side his entire army, the other will just get him as a noncombatant. The good guys choose God as their charioteer, and the bad guys choose this insanely powerful army. This is why God is in a non-combatant role. It's not clear who knows that he is God-on-Earth in the *Gita*. As you saw, Arjuna is pretty freaking shocked when he sees who his buddy Krishna really is. So that might help understand the dynamic between these two people.

### Mark

Just one other thing about the framing device. This whole conversation is being relayed by another charioteer, Sanjaya to his master, the blind Kuru-King Dhritarashtra. Somebody on the bad side, basically. So this whole thing is being related secondhand.

### Shaan

There's this whole symbolic thing where Sanjaya is a servant endowed with divine vision. So he has no authority, and infinite sight, versus the blind king Dhritarashtra, who has great authority, and is literally blind. So there's this tension, which is a symbolic frame to ideas of enlightenment, and what it means to see.

### Dylan

It reminded me of lots of stuff that I've read out of the Western tradition. And I'm interested to find out how much of that is my Western-tinted glasses missing things. Its themes are resonant in lots of different kinds of philosophy regarding action-and-inaction, what one's duties are, what nature is—those metaphysical and epistemological questions.

There's a tension throughout, between the notion of action rightly understood as "unattached action," and complete detachment, which seem to be at odds with one another. Arjuna, at one point, asks *Which is better: Unattachment, or right action?* But it turns out that both will get you to Krishna.

And there's this role of devotion, and the notion of self. The focus one has on oneself and one's action seems to be one conduit towards getting out of the cycle of rebirth. That seems to be the big carrot—getting out of the cycle of rebirth and becoming one with the universe. That seems to be the one thing that's constant throughout, what the primary end of a person ought to be.

### Shaan

I've always struggled with the idea that an endless cycle of increasingly awesome lives of pleasure would leave me wanting to strive for non-existence. That level of hedonism would probably lead me to be hurled through ever-lower rebirths.

But that's something which I would love to talk about—if this actually seems like an effective carrot.

### Wes

The theory here is that desire, attachment, whatever one's pleasure is, ultimately leads to frustration and to anger. It leads to more pain than pleasure. Is that the premise that you want to see whether we ought to reject?

### Shaan

Different than some of the Buddhist texts, it seems a lot less pessimistic about the experience of earthly life. When they're talking about moving on, and recognizing that this is all illusionary, it doesn't seem to be explicitly motivated by suffering.

### Wes

In *Chapter Eight*, Krishna calls the world "a world of sorrow and pain," which, I think, is the only global characterization of the world as such. I was struck by that, and also by this long list of sort of causal relations: If you dwell on the objects of a sentence, there's a danger of becoming attached to them, which arouses desire, which arouses anger, and then confusion, problems with memory, it messes up your understanding, and then the result is ruin.

We do get this picture of a life of attachment being ruinous and causing a lot of suffering. That's the thing to be avoided. The word "freedom" comes up a lot. And it seems to be freedom from suffering, it seems to be equanimity.

### Shaan

One of the motivations is to motivate people to act rightly, and to act devoid of attachments to the fruits of actions. An interesting piece of context is that Arjuna, at the end of the epic, does not achieve what in Hinduism is called *moksha*, which is the equivalent concept to *nirvana*, oneness. He goes to heaven. But he doesn't make it to this oneness and reunion with God. He doesn't transcend. Moreover, at the end of the battle, there's this scene where Arjuna says—and it might be an example of satire—he doesn't remember the content of the *Gita*. He says, *Hey, Krishna, could you refresh me on what you said before the battle, because it seemed really important. And I remember really valuing it. But we've been in the middle of this really intense battle, and I just lost it.* Krishna is really annoyed. He recapitulates some of the ideas, but the prince doesn't reach that goal.

### Wes

I want to get back to your question of whether we buy into the premise. You were saying you might be tempted by hedonism? Is there enough here to draw us away from hedonism? Do we buy that we can't just pleasure our way through the world?

### Dylan

According to Krishna, it corrupts you. And so you end up being the lowest of the low. You fail, in the eyes of Krishna, in your devotion, and your right action, and so you end up getting punished in your sequences of rebirth, going into lower and lower forms of existence. It reminded me of the kind of argument you get in the *Republic* for why you should be dedicated to the Good and why the nature of the Just Man and the Just City is oriented towards the truth. It's better for your soul.

**Mark**

There's a lot of teleology built in here. Everybody has, due to their nature, certain duties. For the character in question, his caste was that of a warrior. What society expected of him corresponded with his internal nature, and his internal teleology. And everybody has something that they're supposed to do. And the ones on top are the Brahmins, the priests, who have more duties than anybody else. It's not that once you get to be the top of the heap, then your teleology is to bow before no one and serve only yourself.

**Dylan**

Right action is performing your duty. And performing your duty poorly is better than performing someone else's duty well. And *that* seems to be a straight-up political argument for keeping people in their places. At least, that's the way my liberal democratic soul reads it.

**Shaan**

In many ways, the *Gita* is a response to the challenge of Buddhism. Ambedkar, leader of the Dalit independence movement, urged the conversion of low-caste individuals to Buddhism, to escape the hierarchy of the caste system, and to move into the equality of the *sangha* (संघ) of the Buddhist community.

So this is a forceful argument for the legitimacy of this stringent system of inequality. People are designed to operate at certain levels, and in certain ways, and that is what they should do. That is a spot-on observation.

**Mark**

There's an interesting parallel between this and Marcus Aurelius. The things that Wes was quoting sound exactly out of the Stoic playbook: *Pleasure ultimately leads to pain, so to hell with it all, rise above your desires.* But, like with Stoicism, this is supposed to be a practical philosophy, whereas if you read the *Upanishads*, you might think that you should become a monk and retreat.

According to Marcus, you've got your duty, but you've also just got your nature as a human being, which, like a lot of teleological stories, mixes up the descriptive and the prescriptive. Even just taking care of your body requires that you do stuff. Your essence as a physical body means you're going to be constantly in motion. So you don't just act any old way. You've got a particular place in the social hierarchy, a particular situation regarding your family, your duties, that will direct what your proper action is.

I saw this as an attempt to compromise between past traditions. The whole distinction here between what you must do by your nature, and what you're just caused to do (because you are the kind of person you are) is mixed together here.

Aristotle mixes those things, too. But he's very specific and critical about it. This was more just stating doctrines.

### Wes

I think *Chapter Three* is illuminating here. It starts out with the idea that no one can exist without acting. And we are compelled to act by nature, more specifically, by these three strands, these gunas, which will turn out to be different qualities. The point isn't to refrain from action. Refraining from action could even leave you susceptible to becoming focused on passive sensory experience, which would be disastrous.

The other part is that worship requires action. Action is a form of worship. So it's essential to the right comportment of one's mind. It's not just that we're going to do it anyway. It's that we actually need it, as long as we're doing it as a form of worship, and without being oriented towards its fruits.

### Mark

It doesn't go on-and-on about your caste-specific duties. It is more *Whatever it is, you're going to do, you have to do it with the right attitude. You have to do it non-attached.* If you can do that, then you don't need to learn some super-advanced yogic technique. The yoga of everyday life, of walking around concentrating on whatever you're doing without attachment, or doing it as a sacrifice to God, it's enough.

### Shaan

There's something to the relationship between the yoga of devotion, the *bhakti* (भक्ति) yoga, and the yoga of action, the *karma*

(कर्म) yoga. Oftentimes, when I read them, the only real difference is just that: *Acting and renouncing the fruits of action*. It seems almost pragmatic:

> It is more arduous for those whose minds are set on the unmanifest; for the path to the unmanifest is hard to attain for embodied beings. But those who renounce all actions to me, regard me as their supreme goal, worship me by meditating on me with unwavering yoga (Maitra, 118)

That seems very much the same thing. You're still not attaching in any way to the actions of what you're doing. You just now have an entity that you can hand off these fruits to, so you don't have to psychically deal with them in any way, shape, or form.

### Wes

What's the difference here between devotion and worship? There are two different words in my translation. Which is better, loving you with devotion or loving the unmanifest?

### Mark

The unmanifest is a more philosophical, and hence esoteric, way of getting at God. Whereas love introduces the idea of a personal God. The metaphysics here is very much like we saw in Spinoza, where there's really just one substance. It has a mind-like aspect, and has a physical-like aspect.

It's not the same breakdown as in Descartes or Spinoza, because a lot of your character is actually part of the physical, it's part of "the changing," whereas the mind part has no change at all. So it is more like Plato's "World of the Forms" versus the phenomenal world, than Spinoza's *mind-versus-body*, where they both run in parallel.

It's not exactly the same as Spinoza, but it's similar. Spinoza was accused of being an atheist, but he denied it. It seemed to be optional, whether you identify a personal God, that you say "Hi" to, and you love. As long as you're acting with the right comportment, whether you personify God is up to the particular sect.

I'm seeing something similar here. If you're in the *Upanishads*, pre-Hindu tradition, then you acknowledge it all as One. But why would you "draw a smiley-face" on that One, and worship it in that way?

You described the old Vedas as like any ancient worship of God: We do the sacrifices, the gods are personal. In fact, there are a lot of them and there are stories about them, the normal kind of mythology stuff. In the *Upanishads*, we get a very intellectual *Yes, there's a Supreme God, but does it have a personality or not? Maybe not. I don't know enough about that.*

But here, we're trying to slam the two together. So we acknowledge what the *Upanishads* have concluded that, yes, all is One. So *You're God, and I'm God and everything is God,* but the emphasis is having God actually appear in the avatar of Krishna. Here, Vishnu appears as Krishna, and says *In fact, I subsume all the other gods, I have all the gods within me,* but he's still a personality, who shows back up on Earth. Whenever he is needed he is reborn. He has motivations.

So there's an account of how can He be eternal and unchanging, but yet also have this lower nature that is changing, that is born in various places, and driven seemingly by the gunas in the same way that we are. They're trying to have it all.

### Shaan

I also thought of Spinoza, his propositions about getting to the idea of the Earth: *This earth, can it be God, but also not be God? How absurd they are, to think that this corporate real substance is apart from the Divine.* So I think Spinoza would be sympathetic to the "having it all" sentiment. I like the *prakriti/purusha* dichotomy.

### Mark

Let's slow down and spell those two terms out.

### Shaan

The *prakriti* (प्रकृति) and the *purusha* (पुरुष) are a way of getting at the mind/body problem, but the *prakriti i*sn't just the body. It's also your intellect, your emotion, your energy, and a lot of other things that we would think to be the seat of the personality or the mind.

### Mark

Anything that changes.

**Shaan**

And the *purusha* is a fixed awareness or consciousness—the capacity to be a witness.

### Can you make that more concrete?

**Shaan**

Once I had a concussion, and the entire way I thought about things, the way I structured my sentences, the way I talked, significantly changed. That really made me think, *Oh, I'm sort of made out of meat and my brain is made out of meat.* And I thought that this is a really interesting way of getting at the idea that our intellect and emotion and energy and a lot of the things that we consider to be personality are intertwined.

But there's also room for something extra, something that's sitting outside of that—that might be motivating it.

*S̲haan Amin is a data scientist, investigative journalist, and essayist completing a doctoral program in political science at the University of Wisconsin-Madison. His work has been published in* The Atlantic, The Caravan, The New Republic, *and several small presses.*

## *Can Mind and Body be reconciled?*

### READINGS

Berkeley, George, *A Treatise Concerning the Principles of Human Knowledge & Three Dialogs between Hylas and Philonous*, Open Court Classics, 1962.

Bostrom, Nick. "Are You Living in a Computer Simulation?" *Philosophical Quarterly*, Vol. 53, No. 211, 2003.

Boswell, James, *Boswell's Life of Samuel Johnson*, edited by Anne and Irvin Ehrenpreis, Washington Square Press, 1965.

Descartes, René, *Meditations on First Philosophy*, translated by Donald A. Cress, Hackett Publishing Company, 1979.

Eagleman, David, *Incognito: The Secret Lives of the Brain*, Vintage Books, 2011.

Hamilton, Sue, *Indian Philosophy: A Very Short Introduction*, Oxford, 2001.

Keith, A Berriedale, *The Samkhya System*, Oxford, 1918.

# Conceptions of Consciousness

## *2024*

*Esther Derksen*

# Christopher Sunami

*Since both the preceeding and the subsequent podcast touch on the mind/body issue, I thought it would be worth mediating between them with a refresher on the history of this problem, and its centrality in modern Western philosophy, as well as some alternate—and potentially more productive!—ways of conceptualizing it.*

*- Kitoba*

# Conceptions of Consciousness

## Cartesian Dualism

The "mind/body" problem is arguably the most characteristic challenge of modern Western philosophy. Although its roots go back to the ancient Greeks, the form we know it in is most closely associated with French philosopher (and master-mathematician) René Descartes. In his seminal work, *The Meditations*, Descartes undertakes a mental journey to try to understand the world by first doubting everything he possibly can (with shades of Ibn Sina's "flying man" experiment). At the end of that journey, he has reached three significant conclusions.

1. Human beings, at their most fundamental, exist as beings that think, that are grounded in a non-physical reality of ideas and concepts.

2. The external physical world nevertheless does exist, largely as we perceive it (when guided by our rational judgment).

3. The mental and the physical are two wholly different things, neither of which reduces to the other.

Taken together, these ideas—that mind and body both exist, and are fundamentally different from each other—form a concept known as *Cartesian Dualism*. ("Dualism" expresses the idea that the universe, at its roots, is made of two fundamentally different substances. Other dualisms exist, including the moral dualism of Zoroastrianism, where the fundamental substances are *good* and *evil*, and the complementary dualism of Daoism, where the fundamental substances are *yin* and *yang*.) Even during Descartes' life, however, Cartesian Dualism came under attack for two major reasons:

1.  It fails to provide a good explanation of why and how the mind and body interact with each other.

2.  The incomplete reductionism of two fundamental substances (instead of one) feels arbitrary, and unsatisfying.

## Ideal Monism

*Monism* (meaning "one substance") appeals to the desire to find a single unified explanation for everything. For an *idealist* or "ideal monist," that fundamental substance is mind, intellect or soul. The concept traces back, in European philosophy, to Plato, who held that what is *real* in the world is ideas, concepts and ideals, because they are perfect and eternal, and that the physical world, with its constant changes, is nothing more than a malign illusion, "shadows on the wall." This viewpoint was repopularized in the English-speaking world by Bishop George Berkeley, who described the universe as existing within the Mind of God.

Idealism also suffers from two main deficits:

1.  It has no strong explanation for why the physical world would even seem to exist, other than the ineffable will of God.

2.  It seems critically out of touch with our everyday experience of the world—it forces us to imagine that the true nature of the world is very different from how it appears to us.

It was this second object that provided the vigor behind the famous "refutation" of Berkeley by his contemporary, Samuel Johnson.

> I never shall forget the alacrity with which Johnson answered, striking his foot with mighty force against a large stone, till he rebounded from it, "I refute it thus." (Boswell, 218)

Outside of a brief revival in the "spiritualist" movement of the nineteenth century, idealism has suffered a long slow decline in the Western world, perhaps because of its "unscientific" reputation. A notable exception is in the world of mathematics (many notable mathematicians believe that abstract concepts such as number have a deeper and more fundamental reality than do the physical phenomena of the world).

## Physical Monism

The counterpart of the decline of idealism has been the rise in another monism. "Physical monism" or *physicalism* is the concept that the world is fundamentally made up of one substance, and that substance is physical matter (including light and energy as other forms of matter). Closely allied with this is the concept of empiricism, which is the belief that the true existence of the world is largely as we perceive it, and that the root of knowledge is therefore sensory evidence. Taken together, these beliefs (popularized by David Hume, and his deep skepticism towards anything outside of the direct evidence of the senses) form a core part of what is often called the "scientific mindset," and have prospered and become all-but-universal as science and technology have taken on an increasingly pervasive presence in our daily lives.

The big weakness of physicalism, however, continues to be the mind/body problem. Although science testifies that the mind is seated somehow in the physical brain, and is impacted by physical changes to it, there is still no adequate physical explanation of consciousness, nor do most people find physicalism satisfying as a root explanation for the more "spiritual" aspects of human existence.

## The Technological Challenge

Ironically, just as the moment that certain advances of science and technology seemed poised to deliver physicalism its final triumph, others have begun to undermine it. On the side of victory, modern neuroscience is tantalizingly close to reducing the mental to the physical. Physical structures in the brain have been shown to encode memories, and stimulation of particular neurons have been mapped to predictable effects on the human consciousness. The physical degradation of the brain has been linked to the mental degradation of the mind, and numerous other body-to-mind correlations have been discovered and documented.

Likewise on the side of victory, the parallel science of artificial intelligence has made comparably broad strides forward. To the extent that we can build an artificial brain, physically, and to the extent that it can convincingly simulate consciousness, it supports Alan Turing's contention that human consciousness is likewise constructed from the physical.

Yet physicalism is in danger of winning the battle, yet losing the war. Technological advances on other fronts have enabled the creation of increasingly sophisticated and convincing simulations of reality. It is easiest to see this, perhaps, in the evolution of videogames. The early videogame, "Pong," was a simulation of a ping-pong game, in which simple squares and rectangles on a screen depicted a low-resolution version of a net, a ball, and two ping-pong paddles. It was neither realistic, nor convincing. Over the last half-century, however, videogames have evolved to create an experience much closer to that of the everyday real world. Characters and settings can be depicted with photorealism, and accurate physics. Meanwhile, virtual reality goggles, and "haptic" devices are being innovated to provide a fully immersive experience.

As the philosopher Nick Bostrom noted, however, the more attainable it becomes to create a fully convincing simulation, the more plausible it becomes that we are already living in such a simulation. In this way, the advance of technology serves to undermine one of the core principles of physical empiricism, the idea that we can and should rely on the direct evidence of our senses. In other words, we are losing the Johnsonian belief that the world is largely as we perceive it, and that we should not allow skepticism to interfere with our common-sense appraisal of that reality. As more-and-more of us interact with wholly simulated, videogame universes, or even create them ourselves, it becomes harder to be convinced by the evidence of kicking the stone.

In addition to undermining empiricism, what we might call "simulationist skepticism" has a corrosive impact on an even-more fundamental assumption of physical monism. After all, if the world might be a simulation, and none of it how we perceive it to be, then what reason is there for believing that the ultimate grounds of the root-level universe are physical? If our world is on a computer, and all of the physics of our world are simulated by that computer, and that computer is in another universe, what convinces us that other universe is physical?

## Existence and Essence

Given that both physical and ideal monism run into difficulties around the mind/body problem, it is worth visiting some wholly alternate ways of conceptualizing the universe. Reaching back to ancient

Greek conceptions, we find a somewhat different dualism than *mind* and *body*. Although Plato would have understood and presumably endorsed the Cartesian idea of an eternal mind housed in corruptible flesh, he might have expressed it rather in terms of the *existence* and the *essence*, where the existence includes all the imperfect, changeable, specific details of an individual's life, including what body a person is in, what gender they are, what race, and how tall; but also less material things such as what vices they have, what depressions may come upon them, what talents they have or lack, and so forth. The essence, on the other hand, is the perfect ideal version of the person (or thing) which, in some conceptions, might include aspects we think of as physical, such as an eternal, perfect body.

Unlike the mind and body, existence and essence operate across all aspects of the universe, not just the human experience of it. A square that I draw on the pavement has existential qualities, accidents of its creation. It is drawn in chalk. It is on the bumpy sidewalk. The lines are crooked. The sides aren't exactly the same length. But the essence of a square exists in a conceptual realm, and all its lines are perfectly straight and equal.

Although Plato and Aristotle disagreed on most things, they both harbored some version of essentialism, the idea that we should pursue making the existing world more like an ideal, essential one (whether that was interpreted metaphysically, as by Plato, or practically, as by Aristotle). This was a view that persisted with little in the way of direct opposition until the twentieth century, when Jean-Paul Sartre formulated the concept of existentialism, which states that the specific accidents of an individual human life are more important than the tyranny of an imagined ideal. From the post-existentialist viewpoint, essentialism is considered the source of racism, sexism, and cultural chauvinism. Rather than divergences from perfection being flaws to be overcome, human individuality and diversity are causes for celebration (a viewpoint that also has roots in Christian theology).

Clearly, existential/essential dualism is not without its own problems. But does it shed light on the mind/body dilemma? One productive way of conceptualizing an union between the two is the "radio analogy" as proposed by neuroscientist David Eagleman, in his book, *Incognito*.

The basic idea is that a person (having never before seen one) discovers an abandoned radio, which plays beautiful music. She discovers all of the following details about it:

a. If you turn one knob, the music gets louder, or softer, or even disappears completely.

b. If you turn another knob, you get a burst of static, and then the music changes.

c. If the radio is damaged, the music quality gets worse.

d. If the radio is destroyed, the music disappears entirely, and does not come back.

e. The radio is entirely physical.

The analogy asks us to compare this with the brain and the mind. We can see that the brain is a physical object. If the brain is destroyed, the mind disappears. If the brain is damaged, the mental quality gets worse. If you stimulate parts of the brain physically, you can introduce confusion, or changes in mental state. Other changes to the physical body, such as hunger or hormones, can create predictable changes in mood.

If we were not familiar with radio technology, we would have no reason to suspect a broadcaster somewhere that was creating the music, and sending it via invisible waves that could pass through solid objects, nor would we credit the suspiciously convenient idea that those waves could only be sensed by this one physical object. We would quite reasonably conclude that the radio was creating the music somehow, and that when the radio was destroyed, the music was destroyed. Similarly, we think of the physical brain as somehow constructing the mind within it, but we cannot (yet) rule out the alternate idea that the brain is a receiver, and that soul might be something broadcast from a distant Source.

In this analogy, the radio is the *body*, and the signal is the *mind*. But we could just as easily label the sounds coming from the radio as the *existence*, and the more perfect rendition of the music present at the source as the *essence*.

## The *Prakriti* **and the** *Purusha*

Outside of Western philosophy, there are other, entirely different ways of conceptualizing reality. As discussed in the preceding podcast, and originating in the Samkhya Yoga school of classical Hinduism, the *purusha* and the *prakriti* are another dualist pair, similar to the essence and the existence. The prakriti, like the existence, encompasses all of the shifting, illusionary, chaotic, multifaceted nature of the phenomenal world, while the purusha, like the essence, is the calm, unchanging deeper reality (also much like the Neo-Platonic idea of the godlike *One*, the unity of all perfections). However, a key difference is that purusha is conceptualized as conscious, or rather, as the seat of all consciousness. The emanations of purusha are witnesses or observers of the world, the still center within each of us that watches as the wheels go round.

This concept is alien to Western philosophy, so another analogy may be in order: Picture a videogame. The purusha is the player, and the prakriti is the game. At some level, the player recognizes that they are playing a game, and that the game is not real. But it is possible to become so caught up in the experience that you begin to think of yourself as the character. You think that you are jumping down pipes, breaking bricks, or ingesting mushrooms. And within the reality of the game, you seem to be bound by the rules and the physics of the universe you inhabit. You think that you are flying one moment, and falling another. You experience an endless cycle of deaths and rebirths/respawns. Ultimately, however, you are a witness of the game. You have extended your consciousness into it, but your consciousness is not contained by it.

This extension of consciousness is a universal-enough feature of the human experience that it does not require as immersive and as sensory an experience as a videogame. A good book can capture a reader in the same way. For the moment, you think you are the character in the book, having her thoughts, and experiencing her emotions. Although you may have read the book a hundred times, you experience it as if it were happening in the moment. You may know there's a happy ending, but you still feel fear at the approach of the villain, still believe there is a chance to make different choices, to freely will yourself down a different path. You are an observer, but you experience yourself as an actor. To escape the trap, however, it is necessary only to remember that the experience—or at least the belief that you are bounded by it—is an illusion.

## The Lonely Dungeon Master

Even with the purusha and the prakriti, however, we are still committed to a fundamentally dualist portrait of the universe. Is it possible to recover a monism that doesn't founder on the shoals of the mind/body dilemma?

Some few readers might be familiar with the "lonely dungeon master" (a thought-experiment introduced in my *Saints and Simulators* series on the *Partially Examined Life* blog). Picture an avid player of tabletop role-playing games who finds themselves trapped in an empty, featureless room, with no exits or escape. They lose all need for food, water, or other bodily functions, and gain both immortality and an infinite intellect. In other words, they become a creature of pure and boundless mind.

Clearly, the major challenge to conquer is boredom. *How will they occupy their time?* One obvious answer is in their previous passion, role-playing games. There is no table, no figurines, no set of multi-sided dice in a little velvet bag. But with an infinite intellect, it is easy enough to recreate all of those things mentally.

Standard campaigns, consuming only finite amounts of time, are barely worth the effort. So one would imagine the dungeon master instead taking on a truly monumental project. The setting is immense, encompassing trillions of stars, and the system is complex, with mental dice being rolled for the interaction of uncountable numbers of subatomic particles. The project, however, is effective. The dungeon-master is drawn into their own creation. At some level they remain aware they are the puppet-master for the characters, having given them their personality quirks, written their dialog, and rolled mental dice for their fates and their interactions. But at another level they experience the lives of each and every character as if they were real.

This is a conception of ideal monism that explains both the existence of the physical world, and the connection between the mind and the body.

*What can we prove about God and the soul?*

## Readings

McGinnis, Jon and D.C. Reisman, editors, *Classical Arabic Philosophy: An Anthology of Sources*, Hackett, 2007.

Adamson, Peter, "From the Necessary Existent to God," *Interpreting Avicenna: Critical Essays*, Cambridge University Press, 2015.

Adamson, Peter and Fedor Benevich, "The Thought Experimental Method: Avicenna's Flying Man Argument," *Journal of the American Philosophical Association, Volume 4, Issue 2*, 2018.

Mayer, Toby, "Ibn Sīnā's 'Bhurhān Al-Siddīqīn," *Journal of Islamic Studies, Volume 12, Issue 1,* January 2001.

# EPISODE 267

*March 21, 2021*

*Halit Sadik*

# PETER ADAMSON ON IBN SINA اِبْن سِينَا

*A*vicenna *(Ibn Sina) historically provided an essential link between Aristotle and Thomas Aquinas. His influence shows up in European "modern" philosophy about God (like that of Descartes), but is even stronger in the Middle East. He wrote his own version of the Aristotelian corpus that had been passed down to him, first in* The Book of Healing *(aka* Shifa *or* The Cure*), then more briefly in* The Book of Deliverance *(*Najat *or* The Salvation*), and then with extreme conciseness in* Pointers and Reminders (Isharat *or* Remarks and Admonitions*). Our sources pulled from all three of these readings and more.*

*- Mark*

# 267 - Adamson on Ibn Sina

**Peter Adamson**

I'm Peter Adamson, who is excited to be on the show, dialing in from Munich, Germany.

**Mark**

Peter, you're the man for this topic. You're saying this was your favorite in all the history of philosophy?

**Peter**

That's what I usually say, if I'm forced to give an answer to the question, just because he's so amazing. And so influential.

**Mark**

The division between primary and secondary sources for Avicenna, at least from an introductory point of view, is tricky, because there are three synoptic works. He wrote about everything in this first thing called *The Healing*, rewrote it shorter as *The Salvation*, and then there's this *Remarks and Admonitions*, a later thing with cryptic little student exercises to remind you of things he's already taught you. But all three of these go through a lot of stuff: Go through physics, go through ethics, go through metaphysics, go through mathematics, *etc.*

**Peter**

You can think of what he's doing as an attempt to rewrite, restructure, and rethink Aristotelian philosophy. He's coming after a couple of hundred years of reflection on Aristotelian and Platonist philosophy, once it's been translated into Arabic. So his goal is to reevaluate all of that, pass judgment on it, and reorganize it as well.

At the same time, he's thought a lot about different ways of writing about philosophy—to help students and readers of different levels.

The three works that you mentioned, in Arabic are called *Al-Shifa'* (الشفاء), *Al-Nijat* (النجاة), and *Al-Isharat wa'l-Tanbihat* (الإشاراتاالإشارات والتنبيهات), which respectively mean, *The Healing, The Salvation,* and *Pointers and Reminders.* But you're right. Sometimes people say *Remarks and Admonitions.*

### Mark

"Reminders" is nicer than "admonitions."

### Peter

*Tanbihat* does mean "to call something to mind," something that you were already supposed to know. That's why it's written in this cryptic, extremely compressed way. The idea would be that you've taken classes with Avicenna. And he's giving you enough to remind you of how the argument goes. Which means that if you weren't there in class—which we weren't, sadly!—then you struggle a bit to see what's going on.

But, surprisingly, the *Al-Isharat wa'l-Tanbihat* is his most commented-upon work. *The Healing* is a massive work, many volumes in the modern printed edition, whereas the *Isharat* is a lot smaller, because it's written in this compressed way. If we bear in mind that we're talking about a culture where everything is written out by hand, that's a big advantage. In addition, it really needs commentary to be understood. And the combination of those two factors led to that being his most widely read, and certainly most commented-upon work.

For listeners who are more familiar with the European philosophical tradition, a good comparison here might be Kant. He's a difficult figure to read, in the sense that there is a challenge to get your head around all of it. I've been working on Avicenna for many years, and I still haven't read everything he wrote. It's just a formidable corpus.

The other respect in which he is comparable to Kant, is that he's similarly important. He's the most influential and important figure in the medieval tradition, between the sixth century and the fifteenth century.

Leaving India and China out of the picture, just for the sake of this conversation, he's the most influential philosopher in that thousand-year period. So he's more influential, for example, than Aquinas. By a lot.

### Dylan

Aquinas is also one of these guys that has gigantic amounts of work, but because of the secular turn, or something like that, Aquinas isn't read the way Kant is anymore.

### Peter

He wasn't as influential as you might expect, in his own time and for a hundred years afterwards. The fetishization of Aquinas, where he becomes the leading thinker of the Catholic Church, really starts to happen in the Renaissance. In his own time, people wouldn't even have thought he was the most important scholastic philosopher in his own generation. They were more excited about Henry of Gantt.

But Aquinas himself is deeply influenced by Avicenna, and quotes him all the time. So the influence of Aquinas is, among other things, a way of spreading the influence of Avicenna. Who also is the dominant figure in subsequent Islamic philosophy. So his influence spans cultural divides in a way that no other medieval thinker does.

### Dylan

You said something earlier, which made me want to get a quick bit of history. You said that Avicenna was bringing together thinking that had been going on for a couple hundred years.

### Peter

I encourage people to think of philosophy in the Islamic world as divided into two parts of unequal sizes. There's the first part, where they're trying to come to grips directly with Greek philosophical texts in translation. The two most famous people from that period are Al-Kindi (الكندي) and Al-Farabi (الفارابي). They live, respectively, in the 9th, and then into the first part of the 10th century, CE. Avicenna is about 100 years after Al-Farabi. People often think there's this sequence of Aristotelian philosophers: Al-Kindi, Al-Farabi, Avicenna, and Averroes, who lives in the 12th century. So you've got one per century, and their works get translated into Latin.

But from the point of view of the Islamic world (which is East Central Asia and the modern-day Middle East) you have a shift where Aristotle stops being the central figure. He's occasionally still read. But mostly what they start doing is responding to Avicenna. You have generation-after-generation of theologian philosophers, criticizing him, defending him and modifying him—the same thing he did to Aristotle.

It's ironic, because people have this myth of intellectual decline in the Islamic world, as if people stopped doing philosophy around the time of Averroes. Which is an understandable misapprehension, because Averroes was the last philosopher to be translated into Latin. But in the Islamic world, they don't care what's in Latin. So not only is there not an intellectual collapse, but you have a continuous and stable intellectual tradition, in contrast to what happened in Europe.

This whole idea that philosophy in the Islamic world marched along impressively for 400 years, and then collapsed and vanished is more like what happened in Europe. Aristotelian philosophy was marching along very nicely through the Middle Ages, and then it collapses in the 17th century. There is no collapse in the Islamic world. But the flip side is, there's no Enlightenment either. What we have is not an Aristotelian tradition, but an Avicennian tradition, that keeps going in Islamic theology and philosophy for a long, long time, and is only disrupted by colonialism.

## Mark

And I'm guessing we're the last generation that will call them "Avicenna" and "Averroes," because it's "Ibn Sina" (إبْن سِينَا) and "Ibn Rushd" (ابن رشد), respectively. Just like now you can't say "Lao Tzu," it's "Laozi," that's the more accurate transliteration. In about half the things we read, we're calling him "Ibn Sina." But it's been "Avicenna" in the western texts for hundreds of years. Whereas Al-Farabi wasn't as big a name, and did not get Latinized in that way.

## Peter

Well, it's actually "Alpharabius" in Latin. But you're right. I'm writing *A Very Short Introduction to Ibn Sina* for Oxford University Press later this year, and that's the title. They were in favor of having

"Ibn Sina," rather than "Avicenna," which surprised me. But I think now we're going to go through a period where people call him "Ibn Sina (Avicenna)." It's sort of like "Confucius," which is obviously not a Chinese name, but it's a familiar name in English.

I actually am less worked up about this than some people, because my main concern is that everyone is reading these people, and knows about them.

### Dylan

You need the search terms.

### Peter

Exactly.

## Let's get into the philosophy

### Mark

His argument for the existence of God seems like one that we've covered before, because we did Aquinas, and he spits out six of them. Here's one of them: *Some things are necessary. Some things are contingent, but if something is contingent, it must have a necessary grounds.* That's going to end up being God.

That doesn't sound a lot different than the cosmological argument: *Everything has a cause. There must be some stopping point, there must be an unmoved mover.* But as we look closely, we see that they're actually quite different. The cosmological one seems to be looking out at the world. It looks like everything in the world has a cause. It's roughly empirical. But if you just are thinking about necessity and contingency, I don't know if we see that in the world in the same way.

### Peter

The core intuition of the cosmological one is something along the lines of *Okay, so what made these things happen?* Whereas the core intuition of Avicenna's argument is *Why is there something rather than nothing?* Because you could think *Gosh, this microphone and computer and these walls and everything around me here could all not exist. So why do they exist?* Avicenna is very strongly into this question, that we also associate with Leibniz. *Everything has to have a sufficient reason.* So he would reject the idea that the existence of things in the world could just be a brute unexplained fact. He would say that that's philosophically unsatisfying.

If we come back at the end to whether this is going to be convincing, one of the easiest ways to avoid Avicenna's argument is to reject the intuition and say, *I don't think that the existence of things—*that may or may not have existed*—needs an explanation.* I'm not saying that's the end of the conversation. But that's a very deep conflict between Avicenna and people who don't want the argument to work, people who think contingent things could just exist without there being any explanation.

### An example might help.

**Peter**

I've got a coffee cup here. By its very nature or essence, it could either exist or not exist. Something has to tip the scales in the direction of existing, rather than not existing.

He admits that you might think that each contingent thing is caused by another contingent thing. So my coffee cup was made by whomever made the coffee cup. And whoever made the coffee cup was made by their parents, and their parents are made by their parents.

So you have these chains of causes of existence, as opposed to chains of causes of motion, which is what you get in the cosmological argument in Aristotle. And the way Avicenna would respond to that is by saying *Sure, you have these chains of causes, which are giving rise to existence. But think about all the contingent things taken together as one aggregate, in other words, the entire universe. Since everything in the entire universe is contingent, the universe is also contingent.* (If it's made of contingent parts, then the whole must also be contingent.) And that will need a cause. Why? Because everything contingent needs a cause.

Here's where someone might object: *No, I think I think the universe is just here. There's no explanation for why it exists. It's just a brute fact.* Then Avicenna would say, *Why is it that the coffee cup needs a cause of its existence, and the universe doesn't? Things don't just suddenly exist for no reason.*

## Let's say we agree there's a *Necessary Being*. Now what? What are Avicenna's arguments on the characteristics of God?

### Mark

A lot of those, as they have to be, are negative theology. In other words, *He's not contingent, so He can't be lacking anything.* So there's a lot of things like *He can't desire anything.* Then it becomes the question of *How could He even know something?* Because the way we know something is by focusing our attention on it. And there's some processes that go on in our brains. But if God is going to be not lacking anything, then He can't learn anything. because then before He learned it, He would have not known it, He would have been lacking something. So He has to be outside time, already knowing everything. And so we have to come up with a new account of God's knowledge, that He knows conceptually—the way that we would understand mathematical things, not the way we would become acquainted with a physical object in front of us.

### Peter

Just to spell it out a little bit more slowly: Why God can't, for example, learn things is a more general phenomenon, which is that God cannot change. When he establishes God's necessary existence, he takes that to mean that everything about God is necessary.

And this becomes a contentious point later on: *Sure, God exists necessarily, but that doesn't mean that there's nothing about God that is contingent, because maybe God has free will.* Maybe God decides, for example, to create the universe when He doesn't have to, whereas Avicenna would say *Everything about God is necessary.* So the universe must come forth from Him necessarily, and God can't change. God can't have any unrealized possibilities, because everything about Him is necessary. So He cannot change, He can't have a body, because if He had a body, He would have parts. And if He had parts, then He would be a whole that is dependent on His parts. So the parts would be a cause for Him, and necessary things don't have causes. That's how he gets *Divine Simplicity.*

**Dylan**

A lot of this turns on what we understand "necessity" to be.

**Peter**

That's absolutely right. That's the core of his philosophical theology in one sentence. But he doesn't think he's done. He needs to extract all of the traditional divine attributes that we expect to belong to God out of this notion of necessity. So... *He's all powerful, because He's necessary in himself, and makes everything else necessary, by reducing it from nearly impossible to definitely existent, by causing it to happen.* So He basically forces things to happen, or forces the universe to exist, makes it inevitable that the universe exists, even though in its own right, it could either exist or not exist.

Similarly, why can't I bring Him to learn that I'm drinking coffee? *If I taught Him that I'm drinking coffee, then I would cause Him to have knowledge and you can't have a cause, because He's necessary.* He ultimately wants to say that you can extract everything there is to be known about God out of the notion of necessity here.

Someone might step in and say, *Hang on a second. What about the Quran? Don't we have this revelation that could teach us a whole bunch of other stuff about God that we didn't know?* In the Christian tradition, we might think of Aquinas here, again. Aquinas would say *Given the natural resources, our own reasoning, we wouldn't,* for example, *be able to know that God is a Trinity, or that God was incarnated as Christ.* But Avicenna thinks there's nothing we can know about God, that we cannot know through reason, and everything we know about God through reason, we know by grasping Him as a necessary existence.

And if you ask him about the Quran, he'd say, *That's what the Quran means. I just told you the inner truth of the Quran, it's the stuff about God being necessarily existent.* So when it says in the Quran that God created everything and is majestic and powerful? That's what that means. *He's a necessary existence. He makes everything exist.*

## Then what about people? What about the human soul?

### Mark

The soul is whatever it is that does these things in our minds, right? It perceives, there's a nutritive part of it, it's whatever makes us alive. And the human soul in particular makes us thinking beings. But we don't know the essence. We don't know the quiddity, we don't know actually what a soul is. So it becomes something very much like how God knows Himself. It's just direct, unmediated. You might think that the only reason that we know we have a mind at all is because consciousness has this intentional structure aimed at something. This is Aristotle's position. *I'm thinking of "dog." I'm thinking of "the number three." What is common to all those things?* There is some "pole" within our experienced mental life. If we didn't have those normal everyday experiences, of perceiving and remembering and imagining things, we would never get this idea of the self as being the thing that is pointed at the outside world.

But Avicenna denies this. He does this with this "flying man" thought experiment: *Imagine yourself instantly created with no memory of your past life. You have full mental faculties, but you've never had an actual experience in the everyday sense. You don't have any sensation of your body.* But he thinks you would still know that you're you, that you exist. In fact, you would know the essence of you. Just in the way God knows his own essence, without having to go walking around in the world, we should have the same idea of our self.

### Peter

For Aristotle, the soul is not merely the mind. In fact, it isn't mostly the mind. And it's not about consciousness or thinking in the first instance. Because for Aristotle, *soul* is supposed to explain everything that living organisms do. So nutrition, digestion, reproduction, sensation and motion. And there are three different kinds of souls: Plant souls, animal souls, and human souls—but human souls have all of the functions that plant and animal souls do.

Humans have a lot in common with animals and plants. We have sensation and the capacity to move—the capacity to pursue prey, the way that predatory animals do. We also have imagination and memory (so do animals, according to Avicenna), and then we also have powers that belong to plants, like the ability to engage in nutrition and digestion. In fact, most of what we can do, through our souls, is something that plants and animals can also do. And that's already what Aristotle says. And then Aristotle says *But there's this one other thing only humans can do, which is to think. And that's something they do without using any bodily organ.*

Now (skipping over 1000 years of philosophy), Avicenna says *I'm not happy about the idea that this thing we're talking about is just a set of functions, most of which are exercised through the body. Because the thing-in-itself is the immaterial thinking (in the case of a human). In the case of a human, this substance we're interested in is primarily a thinking thing, and it can survive without its body. When you die, your powers of nutrition and digestion, reproduction and eyesight, all sensation, locomotion, all that goes, and you're only left as a thinking being.* And that's what the soul is in itself. That's the substance we're interested in.

So this thing, if you want to call it "soul," you're really talking about its relationship to the body. It kind of "projects" into the body when it uses the body as an instrument for exercising a wider range of activities. But in itself, the soul is doing nothing other than thinking. That is its function, that is its activity, it is a thinking substance. So it's a lot more like a Cartesian soul than an Aristotelian soul.

So then he says *This substance, in its own right, is not something that can be observed through observing bodies.* You can look at plants and animals and see that they have souls, because they're engaging in all of these organic processes like nutrition and sensation, but you can't actually empirically observe what the soul is doing in its own right. And then he says, *Fortunately, there's a way that we have access to the soul in itself, which is not through external observation, but it's through grasping oneself.* And then he gives us the flying man argument. *Let's eliminate all sensory input, sort of like the ultimate sensory deprivation tank. And let's also make the person be created just now, to eliminate any memories or anything that they could draw on in terms of imagining anything.* So would this person be a complete blank?

Locke would say this person would have no mental life whatsoever. Whereas Avicenna says, *No, the person would grasp themselves, so they would know that they exist.* He thinks that is a permanent feature of human mental life, which we're often unaware of, but which we can always become aware of whenever we want. You can always introspect and sort of think, *Oh, here I am.* And this act of self-awareness, for him, is our best route into grasping the substance of the soul in-itself. Whereas most of the time, we're distracted by being hungry, or stubbing our toe or seeing a movie, or whatever we're doing. So we're only aware of the activities that the soul is exercising through the body. But if you want to become aware of yourself, of what you really are, then you can always do it just by exercising this self-awareness, which is always available.

*P*eter Adamson is Professor of Late Ancient and Arabic Philosophy at the LMU in Munich. He is the author of Al-Kindi and Al-Razi in the series "Great Medieval Thinkers" from Oxford University Press, and has edited or co-edited many books, including The Cambridge Companion to Arabic Philosophy and Interpreting Avicenna: Critical Essays. He is also the host of the History of Philosophy podcast (www.historyofphilosophy.net), which appears as a series of books with Oxford University Press.

# Commentary on Avicenna

The argument for the existence of God is one of those considered later by Aquinas as "the argument from contingency," and asks the question "why is there something rather than nothing?" We have a strong intuition, says this argument, that anything we experience must have a reason for its existence, must have something that it relies on for its existence. In other words, everything we experience is contingent. The issue is not (as with the cosmological argument) causality over time: We're not asking what temporally prior thing caused the thing we're contemplating, but what right now accounts for the thing. So yes, a house, in a familiar sense, was caused by its builder, but more immediately, its cause is the materials that make it up, arranged in the way they are. And what causes, in this sense, a piece of wood making up the house to provide the support it does? Its makeup: Molecules in a particular type of configuration. And so the chain goes on. If each of the links of this chain is contingent, relying as it does on something else (in other words, if that cause hadn't occurred, neither would the contingent thing; its existence is contingent on the existence of its cause), could it be that the whole chain is contingent? Could it too have an underlying supportive cause? Avicenna says no: That cause would just be part of the whole chain of contingency. The whole chain needs to have some stopping point, or else none of it would exist, and that's the *necessary being*.

So even though we've never experienced anything like this necessary being, reason itself tells us that such a being must exist, based on our experience of contingency in the world. A 2001 article by Toby Mayer says that the argument combines this initial experiential component (like the cosmological argument) with a definitional, *a priori* element (like the ontological argument). It's a sound argument so long as you accept that initial metaphysical intuition that everything we experience is contingent.

Even if this argument works to establish the existence of a necessary being, why would we think that this is God? Avicenna uses the two properties he's proven (i.e. "necessary," and "causes all the other beings") to derive God's other properties. With this picture of instantaneous causality that we've described, God ends up being the immediate cause of everything else: this is His omnipotence. This picture is unlike Plato's *Timaeus* where there was some non-God substance (the *chora* or receptacle) that is the raw material that God uses to build the world. Instead, the world emanates directly from God's nature.

A comparison and contrast with Leibniz may be useful here: Leibniz's *Theodicy* gives us a picture of a God who scans all possible worlds and is compelled by the necessity of His good nature to create the optimal one. So in a sense, God makes a choice, but because He couldn't have made any other choice, this is really no choice at all. For Avicenna, God likewise makes the best possible world for us, but the process does not require scanning other possibilities. In fact, Avicenna's metaphysics entails that everything that is possible actually does happen. Why? Because *possible* is just another word for *contingent*. Considered in itself, the computer in front of me might or might not have been there. Its existence is contingent on many circumstances and compositional factors. But if we then keep going back down the causal chain, we get to the necessary being, whose existence is sufficient to necessitate all the other links in the chain. So really, despite appearances, everything we perceive is really necessary. It's merely contingent when considered in isolation, but since the whole mechanism is necessary, everything that actually happens (that exists) is necessary, and there were no other possible ways that the world could have been. That's merely a human illusion.

God as the underlying ground of everything must, then, exist outside of time. He's not, like a deist might say, someone who was the first cause temporally, hitting the first domino, and then the world rolled into being, with us conscious beings maybe having free will, able to do things that God didn't ultimately determine or know about. Even Leibniz (though not a deist) thought that God creates the plan but then the rest runs like a perfect machine, with part of that machine being us with our free will. God determined that free will would be best for us, and so caused us to have that, but then doesn't cause our choices.

For Avicenna, the relation between God and His creation is much more immediate. This "emanation" means that we're all, in effect, part of God, and His omniscience is explained as His knowledge of Himself. This knowledge is (of course) not like most human knowledge, where at some point we come to learn a fact, because Avicenna's God never changes and so can't come to learn anything, or else before that learning He would have been ignorant of that knowledge. Instead God knows everything abstractly, like the innate knowledge we have according to Plato of the Forms. Essentially, God can reason out everything that has or will happen. Even this doesn't quite capture it, because "reasoning out" sounds like a sequential process, but God's knowledge, just like God's causality, is immediate, or rather atemporal.

Just to give one more example, what would prove God's generosity? This sounds like a human quality that a metaphysical posit like the necessary ground of the universe could not have. But Avicenna said that generosity is defined as giving ("emanating") without need, and God, by definition, doesn't have any needs, and so isn't benefited by creating the world for us. So you keep words like "know," "give," and "love," but you redefine them so they can apply to this very non-human entity. The Scriptures, of course are filled with anthropomorphism, because that's what you need to reach non-philosophical readers, but philosophers who have followed Avicenna's reasoning will know how to read them correctly to get at the literal, hard-to-grasp truths beneath the human-oriented stories.

The second topic was considered is our knowledge of the soul. Avicenna's famed "flying man" experiment asks us to imagine being a person who has just been created with all mental faculties intact, but no memory (because the person has just that moment been created, fully mature), and with no sensation. You're "flying" because your limbs are splayed and you can't feel the earth under you. The word is not quite apt, because you also can't feel air pressure, or gravity, or your own sense of balance. There's no sensation at all, is the point. Yet even then, Avicenna claims that you'd know that you exist.

This is supposed to prove not just *a la* Descartes that "I think, therefore I am" but that what you are essentially, as a soul, is something non-material. Avicenna read Aristotle's definition of the soul as the "perfection" or "form" of the body–in other words something the body does, the state that it's in–and was unsatisfied. This is a characteristic of the soul, i.e. we encounter it in our bodies, but doesn't say what the soul actually is in itself, doesn't capture what *makes* the soul a "soul."

According to Avicenna's epistemology, when we grasp some concept, we necessarily grasp its constitutive attributes, *i.e.* we understand what makes it as it is. Otherwise, we haven't grasped it at all. I might see a passing cow, but if I don't understand what an animal is, then I haven't really seen the cow; I've just seen a shape. Now, I might not explicitly think when I see the cow that it's an animal, and I certainly don't think explicitly about what an animal is such that it's different than a plant or inanimate matter. But all of these logical entailments are right there, implicit in my thought, according to Avicenna.

The flying man argument is supposed to call to mind a self-awareness that we always have, even if we've never explicitly considered it or not. Whenever I have any perception at all, or think any thought, I'm also implicitly aware that it's me having that perception or thought. The explicit content of my perceiving my computer is the computer, but one of the implicit contents (along with things about the computer) is this element "me." While someone like Heidegger or Merleau-Ponty would claim that really, the "me" in that experience is always an embodied me, as in *I am this body physically related to the computer in front of me,* and my merely thinking of (remembering) a computer after the fact is an experienced derived from that perception. The epistemic situation, according to Avicenna, when it comes to knowing yourself is actually more like God's knowledge of Himself: We have this direct knowledge of self that is a prerequisite to our having any of these other experiences. So, I don't learn about the self through having an experience of perception, but instead my prior knowledge of self is required as an ingredient for perception to be possible. I can only perceive myself as being in a body because I already have a prior understanding of myself, and I know from that prior understanding that this self does not include residing in a body as an essential component. I could (in the flying man thought experiment) have a conception of self without having had a conception of body. There's no reason to think that this conception of self was fallacious, that in the flying man situation I really wouldn't be grasping the self at all, so therefore I grasped everything essential about self-hood even in that weird, imagined situation. Therefore it's not essential that a soul be in a body, at least conceptually. In other words, it's possible for a soul to not be in a body.

If you recall my argument that everything that's possible is in fact actual, then you can see how Avicenna uses this to show that the soul not only can but does live on without a body. The soul is experienced as contingent (possible), but in moving to its necessary ground, we don't have to say "the soul wouldn't be there unless the body was." I know as the flying man that there is a soul that is *me*, and that it must be contingent on something, and so I can follow that chain to God, but no other links in that chain are apparent: It seems I was directly caused by God.

You can probably see why I don't agree with this argument. I don't agree with Avicenna's epistemic claim that to be able to grapple with some idea, particularly one we're experiencing, we have to understand its nature. So to me, it's perfectly plausible that the nature of the self may in fact necessarily involve its biological base, and also perfectly plausible that we might not know that even though we can think sensibly about selves. This is the common objection to Avicenna: That it violates the sense-reference distinction, as discussed in our Frege episode. For example, I can be looking at Clark Kent and not know that Clark Kent is Superman. I am in fact looking at Superman, but I don't know that. There would be no justification to say "since I'm sensibly grasping this guy Clark Kent, I have grasped his essence, and can definitively say he's not Superman." In this case, that claim would not only be unjustified, but actually wrong.

*- Mark*

*What is the wisest way to act in the world?*

## Readings

Laozi, *Dao De Jing: A Philosophical Translation*, translated by Roger T. Ames and David L. Hall, Ballantine Books, 2003.

# EPISODE 311

*January 30, 2023*

*Chris Warr*

# THEO BROOKS ON LAOZI 老子

*"Dao" in ancient Chinese means "way," as in a path to follow to get somewhere. It also has a less common meaning of "speech," as in a doctrine about how to best live your life. Like Confucius' Analects and Sunzi's Art of War, this was written, at least in part, as a guide for political leaders, so we start by considering the book's political philosophy against coercion and war. It's also against the creation of a lot of explicit ideals and rules. Instead, the text recommends "wu wei," which can be translated as non-coercive action, or alternately as doing nothing.*

*- Mark*

# 311 - Brooks on Laozi

**Theo Brooks**

This is Theo Brooks, blunting the sharpness, untangling the knots and softening the glare, in Broken Hill, Australia.

**Mark**

You had strong opinions about our translation that we picked, by Roger T. Ames and David L. Hall, called *Dao De Jing: A Philosophical Translation*. They didn't even put Laozi (老子) on the cover, because he wasn't a real person. It just means "old master," it probably was more than one person.

**Theo**

It could literally mean "old child," which is a very Daoist joke.

**Seth**

Are you someone who characteristically has strong opinions?

**Theo**

Well, that would be un-Daoist!

No, Ames was good for me to read, because I tend to read the text as a cynical mirror for princes. He is reading it more sincerely, perhaps making it more usable by Daoist philosophers. He reads it against the grain, as far as I see it.

**Mark**

I'll claim responsibility for picking this translation. But it ended up being much more burdensome to get through. Pretty early on, I was just like, *Let me just pick up my old translation that I read in undergrad.* It's a short thing. But if you read it with all this commentary...

**Seth**

This better not be two hours of us talking about translation choices.

**Wes**

It's only 135 pages excluding the introduction.

**Dylan**

But it felt like 300 pages.

### To Seth's point, let's move on.

**Mark**

It's a very terse text. There are lots of different readings. That's actually one of the interesting things about this, it's been translated so many times, it's been used for so many things. The original Chinese characters are ambiguous, no tenses, no singular versus plural. But there's also multiple source versions of the texts that have differences between them.

And is this even written by the same author? If you assume they're all written by the same author, then you want to make them harmonize. If you think it's a collection of sayings, then you don't care about that. It's hard to get through all that and decide, do I actually like this? Do I actually think this said something wise, that I want to pay attention to?

**Theo**

There's ways to add qualifiers, but the text purposely doesn't. So it is reveling a bit in these ambiguities. The poem itself is playing into the ambiguities of language.

**Dylan**

Especially with the explicit contradictions, right? There's this things-juxtaposed-against-one-another on purpose, for the sake of trying to get at something that is hard to say

**Seth**

It's not unlike the older parts of *The Bible*, in Aramaic, and

Hebrew, which are ambiguous in certain ways. The virtue is not that it's ambiguous, but that it's fecund from the perspective of interpretation. Ambiguity is only seen as a vice from the perspective of trying to come up with a meaning or fixing a referent.

### So, ambiguity is good?

**Seth**

From the perspective of having a living document, that is also a teaching document, a "seeking-finding" document. There's a virtue in having many paths available.

**Mark**

*The Dao* (道) *that you can just state unambiguously what it means is not the real Dao.*

### Wes, you were a little trepidatious getting into this.

**Wes**

I wasn't trepidatious. But I guess I'm probably the least excited about Eastern philosophy, and more generally, anything that's religious, or as seems like it might be a form of mysticism. But each one I've done, I've enjoyed, and this one I enjoyed as well.

It's short and sweet. In a way, it's a self-help book, which I actually like. But we'll have to figure out what we get out of it, other than *Don't force things, man, take it easy.*

**Dylan**

Live in moderation.

**Mark**

It's easy to compare this to the Stoics. And the Epicureans. Also, some of it came out during the Warring States period, and at least a few of the chapters seem explicitly about conducting yourself in war. A large number of them are aimed at leaders, just like *The Analects.* So possibly this whole thing was intended to be a guide for leaders. But certainly, you don't have to read it that way (just like people read Sunzi that are not at war).

This is very open-ended. *How can I live in accord with nature?*

Or *What is wisdom?* The kind of thing that Socrates asks. *What is the wisest way to understand act in the world?* In other words, this is a wisdom tradition. It's always interesting to approach things with no Greek preconceptions, and see a whole fresh conceptual scheme.

**Wes**

As you mentioned, you could think of it as a virtue ethics. Although the word that's often translated as the word "virtue," *de* (德), is translated in our text as "character."

I like the points where there's smackdowns of Confucianism. That makes it interesting, the tension between those two.

### Let's get into the text.

> With the most excellent rulers, their subjects only know
>     that they are there.
> The next best are the rulers they love and praise.
> Next are the rulers they hold in awe.
> And the worst are the rulers they disparage.
> Where there is lack of credibility,
> There is a lack of trust.
> Vigilant, they are careful in what they say.
> With all things accomplished, and the work complete.
> The common people say, "We are spontaneously like
>     this." (17)

**Wes**

That word "spontaneity." That's why I was talking about emergence, the whole idea of *wu wei*, which is commonly translated as...

**Theo**

"Non-action."

**Mark**

"Non-coercive action?"

**Wes**

It's about not forcing it. It's a matter of how action is done, whether it's forced, whether it's top down, or more spontaneous.

**Theo**

*Wu wei* (無為) is problematic because it does literally mean "non-action," but no one wants to read it like that (unless you have acquired *de* as a spiritual force and therefore, you don't need action.) But I think of it as doing very small things that aren't noticed. "Minute things" is kind of the essence of this passage. And you also have this "slow to speak" idea. We have the sage speaking, but very carefully. The Daoist is not attached to language, but uses it in a strategic sense.

If anyone has seen *Yes, Minister!* you have the civil servants, who always have to get the Minister to think that every idea is his own idea. It's that kind of political strategy, getting others to think that acting a certain way was their own idea. That's a bit cynical, perhaps.

**Seth**

It's not cynical, it's called "people management." That's how you operate in any sufficiently large organization—church, government, business. You will encounter people with whom you can only have a productive relationship if they're convinced that they're the ones making the decisions, or having the ideas. One strategy is to fight that, and point out they're wrong, and create strife. And the other is to get them convinced they have the idea that you want them to have.

**Wes**

Are we supposed to get the idea that the people are being manipulated? That they're being flattered? I don't think so. The common people say "We are spontaneously like this." It's not a top-down order where someone says, *Here, I set the laws*. This reminds me of Hart's internalization, where people accept the norms. They're internal, we accept the norms as having a certain kind of authority.

But this even seems to go deeper than that. It's almost like *This is just the way we are naturally. We don't steal because who does that?* It's not to say there aren't laws, they just don't feel grafted on and discordant with people's natural impulses. The impulses and habits line up with the legal apparatus.

### Dylan

It's a kind of a taxonomy of rulers. Where the first one is the highest kind of rulers, those below them simply don't know that they exist. There's leading happening, but you don't know that you're being led. And then, all the way down to the bottom kind of rulers. Everybody ridicules them, they know they're just full of crap. They don't pay any attention to them.

The key here is when trust is insufficient, there'll be no trust in return. So there's a kind of exchange going on between the leadership that is the foundation of this natural activity. The condition of the well-balanced state is that things are happening naturally. You get your intuitive sense of what to do. You're not fighting against the leadership.

### Wes

This idea of credibility reminded me of ethos in *The Poetics,* where there's moral authority involved. It's not just about reasoning with someone, and saying, *Here's my deduction, this is why you've got to do X, Y and Z.* It's something about your character, which is evident and which is persuasive. So the most excellent rulers might be just ruling with the spectacle of their character. Leading by example.

### Theo

The tension I have in this is whether people are being led by example—being allowed to harmonize their own self-beings with each other—or actually being led somewhere. They say *This is how we are,* but the sage has led them.

### Let's get into that fight with Confucius.

It is when grand way-making is abandoned
That authoritative conduct and appropriateness appear.
It is when wisdom and erudition arise
That great duplicity appears.
It is when the six family relationships are disharmonious
That filiality and parental affection appear.

It is when the state has fallen into troubled times
That upright ministers appear. (18)

**Wes**

Love it. All those things have positive connotations for Confucianism, but here, they have negative associations.

**Mark**

I take it as about the *yin-yang* (陰陽), it's about the *Book of Changes* (易經), it's the interpenetration of opposites. Whenever there's day, there must be night. You can't just try to clutch to the one and neglect the other. They come as a package.

I do like your anti-Confucian interpretation. When there's ren (仁), "virtue," there's no real virtue. There's just this nominalist nodding-respectfully to virtue, but not actually feeling it with your heart. I like that interpretation.

**Wes**

This is the way Ames takes it, as an anti-Confucian polemic. The idea is that all these things that Confucians value—authoritative conduct, appropriateness, even things like upright ministers—seem good on the surface, but they're indicative of a rot underneath. You wouldn't need them if things were happening spontaneously, if things were happening according to nature, according to the Great Way. You don't need upright ministers unless there are troubled times. You shouldn't be celebrating what a great minister they are. You should be thinking *Why would we need that? What's not functioning correctly that we need this top-down management?*

**Seth**

This is one of those "opposites" things. Righteousness only emerges when the opposite of righteousness is present. Yes, it might be a slam on Confucianism, but it's part of *You can only be soft when there's hard, you can only be weak when there's strong.* In order to have somebody act righteous, there must be some sense of inequity, or falling-from-the-path. In *The Bible* when do prophets appear? When people have fallen off the way of the path of God. You build a golden calf and then suddenly you get Moses.

In the Western tradition, prophets are explicitly called just to say,

*Hey, you told us to do this, but you're doing the opposite.* Prophets only arise when times are bad. There's a tight synergy here with the *Dao De Jing* (道德經) where it's saying, *If you're in a place where prophets arise, things must be bad.* The equilibrium is out of whack. If you take the prophet as something other than a sign of disorder, you're missing the point.

### Wes

The prophet is a good analogy, except it's really more about spontaneous natural feeling versus external rules of conduct. All of these things—upright ministers, authoritative conduct, and appropriateness—represent externalities of behavior, top-down forces of control, that only need to arise when people's natural propensities have become corrupt.

### Theo

We can take them as symptoms. Once people start talking about righteousness, and benevolence, that's the problem. But if we didn't talk about them, then it may be we are naturally humane. Or it could be that the ideas don't match the pure, natural Way.

When you have good ministers, it doesn't just signify that something's gone wrong, they're actively making it worse. They're a kind of accelerant to the confusion. They see the problem, and try to fix it. The Daoists are saying, *Every time you try to fix something, you make more distinctions. You befuddle people more, you make more crooks, you make more war, because you insist upon the good.*

### Wes

*We need less government, not more.*

### Dylan

The criticism doesn't sound like *Do nothing!* It's more of a criticism of the kind of intervention they're talking about. The veneration of certain kinds of distinctions, socially, leads to the very problems that they're trying to solve. That criticism (I guess it's a criticism of Confucianism) is that the mode of solving those problems is to further venerate the things that are the source of the problem itself.

It's not an indictment of problem-solving, it's an indictment of the particular kind of problem-solving. The indictment is we need to be more in line with the way the world is. That's the *Great Way*. And it's when we're fighting against it, and we're trying to prescribe to it—which is this cultivation of knowledge and wisdom—then we run into problems.

**Wes**

> Cut off authoritative conduct
> and get rid of appropriateness
> And the common people will return to filiality,
> and parental affection. (19)

I thought that was worth mentioning, because it substitutes something more formal and impersonal for something familial and personal. I'm not sure I like that idea. The whole point of our justice system is based on the idea of impersonal relationships between people. It's not like the *mafia*, where you're in the family, or you're out of the family, and we do things because we love you, or because you've betrayed us, and things like that. That contrast between the Confucian conception and this Daoist conception is important. There's something about these "more natural" affections.

**Dylan**

There may be a sanguiness about the Daoist criticism, right? *We just need to be more in tune with the way things are, and not try to be messing things up so much.*

### What about the metaphysics?

**Wes**

We get all these associations between emptiness and potency.

**Mark**

I don't know if it's Hegel, but we've definitely run across the idea of a formless chaos. And then distinct things come out of it through the process of conceptualization, or the process of recognition, or perception, concepts that we impose. There's just the stuff out there, whatever it may be, the *numina* and we create objects using the little cookie cutters that are our senses. Our language makes little pieces of it, but then we have to realize what a contingent activity that is.

Metaphysically, things arise into individuality and they fade back, they recede. When it initially manifests itself, it's at its maximum potency, and from then on, it's just downhill. Something is born and it's when it's a baby, it's the most supple. It's flexible, it's the most awesome, in a certain way. And then it rigidifies, goes into its adult form, and goes toward death.

### Theo

*The Way* is always described as generating things. I can't think of a chapter where it draws people back to death. Maybe it's just the nature of being away from the Dao, people kind of fall into death by not being in tune with the Dao. But the Dao is generative, that's what it does. There is a cycle, but the Dao is always generative.

*After successfully surviving childhood in the land of the Antipodeans, Theo bumbled amateurishly through university, receiving a bachelor with honors in philosophy at the University of New South Wales and a lingering fatigue from a forlorn attempt at a PhD. Later gaining a Masters in Classics from the University of New England (though not the New England most readers are probably thinking of), he became a dyslexic with an interest in languages and is currently torturing himself by means of the Japanese Language. His working life is eminently uninteresting.*

*What is it to live the artistic life?*

## READINGS

Kierkegaard, Søren, *Either/Or: A Fragment of Life*, edited by Victor Ermita, translated by Alasdair Hannay, Penguin Classics, 1992.

# EPISODE 330

*November 11, 2023*

*Chris Warr*

## KIERKEGAARD

*W*hat is it to live your life as if it were a work of art? Kierkegaard here explores this "aesthetic" way of being in the world from the inside, as a character known only in the text as "A," who sees the absurd in everyone else's pretensions and tries to live per the Romantic philosophy of Kierkegaard's time. The introductory set of aphorisms to this volume climaxes in a section called "Either/Or: An Ecstatic Discourse," where whatever a person chooses will inevitably cause regret. True freedom comes in the moment before any choice at all is made, when the world is limitless possibility.

*- Mark*

# 330 - Kierkegaard

**Mark**

Here we have a whole book, written in the guise of characters that are going to have views that are different from Kierkegaard. And they're not purely critical. If you have the background assumptions that these characters do, here's the kind of things that you might say, here's the kind of troubles that you might be pulled into. Knowing Kierkegaard's view that religion is going to be the answer, we can say, *Oh, I see. Okay, so this person was driven to despair, and to boredom and all this stuff, because they have no fundamental values.* But there's nothing in this book that actually spells out what those alternatives are.

The "Either" half is from the point of view of somebody who is in the aesthetic frame of mind, who does not have the ethical or the religious to serve as a bedrock. And so we get someone that looks a lot like Camus. He's definitely critiquing the romantics.

This Louis Mackey article we were reading says he's critiquing the average person of his day. This is like, *Kids today!* Except he's criticizing his peers, not his students.

**Wes**

It's worth pointing out that "the aesthetic way of life" is something we should take very broadly. It's not just people living a bohemian, artistic life. It has two possible meanings. One is "the aesthetic," in the sense of having to do with sense experience. And one is "the aesthetic," as in having to do with art. And for Kierkegaard, it means both. So you could talk about the aesthetic person as someone who lives for their desires, lives in their own direct, immediate experience, lives in the world of sensation and feeling. And it's not all that reflective. Or you could think about the artist's solution to the kind of dialectical problems that arise with respect to that position. According to Mackey, his aesthetic position reflects both those things.

The structure of it (as Mark was pointing out) is Kierkegaard—instead of giving us a straightforward treatise, his position on these things—writing a book in true ironic style, where he's going to have different characters argue from inside their positions.

This first half gives a glimpse into the mind of someone in this aesthetic position. The second half will give us the opposing ethical point of view. And then, of course, hovering all over this is the third position, that of religious faith and the embrace of the absurdity of religious faith.

But in this first part, we get a rumination of someone trying to work out on how to live, but from within this limited position.

### Seth

*The aesthetic, the ethical and the religious*: Is this a framework that was imposed by later readers onto the Kierkegaardian texts? Because it doesn't present itself that way. It's not obvious, without context, that in the first part of *Either/Or* we're in the "aesthetic persona."

I'm not trying to make anything of this, I'm just curious. Is it something that it took people time to work out, or did he somehow put this framework forward while he was alive?

### Mark

The preface is by another character, Victor Eremita, who is the "editor." He is someone who stumbled across these manuscripts, and he doesn't know who wrote them. That's why he just calls them *A* and *B*, and doesn't present them as B is responding to A. He wants to just put them side-by-side. It's not necessarily that the editor is presenting B as the next dialectical step, which in turn must be overcome to get to the religious.

But yeah, it's universal, this interpretation. I think it's totally uncontroversial.

**Let's get into it.**

### Mark

So, there are many essays making up this book. What we looked at primarily was the first one, which is not an essay. It's a set of aphorisms, refrains. He calls them by the Greek word *Diapsalmata*. It's sort of a warm up.

The most famous part is this "Diary of the Seducer" at the end. We only ended up reading the introduction to that, by A, talking about stealing this manuscript. He knows the seducer. He knows the person Cordelia who he seduced. And he's sort of shocked by the whole thing, which is very strange. Given that in one of the earlier essays, he's praising Don Juan, it seems like this should be the kind of thing that he'd be into.

But this maybe is telling us that living the romantic life is more about thought than action. The romantic is ruled by his whims, and won't commit to anything. Actually putting yourself all-in to seduce somebody might not be the core of this kind of romantic figure.

### Wes

Part of the aesthetic persona, particularly in the "Diapsalmata," is being moody and depressed. It's not just someone who's living for pleasure. We don't even know that this person is an artist, or that we could conceive of them as making their own life a work of art.

To sum up the "Diapsalmata," there's a section on aspiration, and the paradoxical nature of aspiration. There's one on sorrow, as the flip side of laughter. And there's reflections on the "perils of the ethical," and the way in which reflection actually makes us less free.

These are in the context of Hegel and Kant, because part of what Kierkegaard is objecting to is the reduction of religion to morality. And part of that is the conception of the ethical as purely rational and reflective, when in fact, there are costs to that position.

So, he talks about feeling like a chess piece that can't be moved, which is a great image of the way in which rationality can be something binding, rather than a grounds for autonomy. Now, granted, this is from the perspective of the aesthetic person, this objection to too-much rationality. But I also do think it's part of Kierkegaard's position.

## Seth

Mackey's thesis is that Kierkegaard's aesthetic person is not aesthetic in the sense of appreciation of art or beauty, but that, etymologically, it's associated with the idea of immediacy. So he connects the notion of the aesthetic man with sense perception, the idea that you're something pre-reflective. The aesthetic man is at the same level as animals. But you can't actually get there. We can't unburden ourselves of consciousness to become these pre-reflective, purely sensory beings. So there's this weird irony of taking on the immediacy of experience without reflecting on it.

## Wes

We can't experience being in nature, our prelapsarian origin as he calls it, we can't experience being an animal again, purely unreflectively. And when we think about that position, we are always doing it from the standpoint of reflection. We are alienated from immediacy, but we still go after it. (These are all very Hegelian themes.) Not in the sense of I'm just going to eat pizza all day and sit on the couch. That's how I'm gonna get back in touch with my animal naturalness. We try to get back through art.

So one version of the aesthetic merges into the other one. Dialectically, you get a higher level of the aesthetic out of the more basic one. So it does lead to aesthetics in the broadly artistic sense.

## Seth

But there's a price to pay to maintain ironic distance.

## Wes

The aesthete becomes preoccupied with fantasy. It's not realistic to be a Don Juan—the whole idea of 1003 lovers. The kind of immediacy we're after can't be experienced in life. So we try to experience it in fantasy, which is what A does in admiration of Don Juan. He's actually disenchanted with the pleasure-seeking way of life, what he wants us to admire is the fantasy.

## Mark

The climax of the "Diapsalmata" is a little section called "Either/Or: An Ecstatic Discourse" which is about the choices that you have all being equally meaningless. Or all equally things that you will regret. Nothing ends up being satisfactory. The solution, therefore, is going to be some sort of detachment. You do want to throw yourself into things. But always be ready to jump out, so there's a certain kind of safety.

**Wes**

It's really funny:

> If you marry, you will regret it; if you do not marry, you will also regret it; if you marry or if you do not marry, you will regret both. Laugh at the world's follies and you will regret it; weep over them, you will also regret it; if you laugh at the world's follies or if you weep over them, you will regret both; whether you laugh at the world's follies or you weep over them, you will regret both. (54)

**Mark**

Why is this fourth one in there? That's just a slight wording variation. Is this a satire of syllogistic talk?

**Wes**

Maybe. It looks like a synthesis. It's laying out the premises and then coming to a conclusion. But I think rhetorically, there's something to be said for the repetition. It's almost like a prayer, or catechism.

## But what does it all mean?

**Wes**

Let's say the choice is marrying or not marrying. What's the significance of those two positions? One of them represents freedom from responsibility, and from social ties and demands. And the other one, marriage, represents getting into that and becoming a social creature and having responsibilities. So it's about ethical responsibility versus complete freedom, and you can't win either way.

**Seth**

The point is that the aesthete can't have any encumbrances—

relationships, friends, jobs, spouses, children—because it's an impingement on their freedom to do or not do all these things, to make the choice between A and B, to make the choice of regret. If you're not free to choose one path or the other, then you're not able to live this life of an aesthete. This is the "Oscar Wilde" position in this text.

### Wes

The aesthete can't really ever be fully satisfied with where they are. There's an element of nihilism. He tries to work out the position, but it seems to always come back to melancholy, and depression, and death, things which you might not immediately associate with the aesthetic position.

### Seth

Absolutely.

I don't like where philosophers take on personas. He's taking it to the nth degree, trying for shock value, but also to draw upon your sympathies, to get you to say *This is the natural conclusion. If you're going to take this position, if you're going to be this kind of person, if you're going to hold to these kinds of values, this is what you're committed to.* That's okay. But understanding that this is not ultimately what he's arguing for is extremely helpful. Otherwise, it's very confusing.

### Mark

If this was a straw man, it'd be really hard to write his dramas for 700 pages. But he's living in this character, he's recognizing that this was him as a slightly younger person. This is something that he has sympathy for, that this is a character that can be self-reflective, and critique some of the aspects of romantic views. It's not merely a one dimensional character.

### Wes

Probably these are a bunch of separate pieces that he wrote—that's my impression of it. *Let's scrape my hard drive for a bunch of stuff that I wrote when I was younger.* None of it is the perfect fit. Some of this is obviously diary entries, or an essay he wrote here or there. It doesn't perfectly fit this persona.

He asked "What is a poet?" If you're a philosopher, that's where you rub your hands together: *We're gonna get into the nitty gritty now! Tell me what a poet is.* Then it turns out to be a bit of a parody. One of the comparisons he makes is to this bronze bull, in which people were put and slowly tortured over a fire. But the apertures of the bull were fashioned in such a way that their screams would be turned into beautiful music. And that's what it's like to be a poet. You're anguished, you're tortured. And then when you cry, just the shape of your lips makes it so that all it comes out beautiful.

This is a parody of sublimation, of one conception of what it means to be an artist. At the end of that, he says directly that this is a misunderstanding of the poet. The critic he's attributing this theory to is like a poet in every way, except that he not only does not have the anguish and the personal pain, he doesn't have the music either. He is neither of those things. Otherwise, exactly like a poet!

> I would rather be a swineherd... and be understood by the swine than a poet and misunderstood by people. (43)

Pretty brilliant.

### He has some interesting things to say on children

**Wes**

What does baby want? The baby wants morality, it wants to be given rules for life. A is suggesting that we inherently want punishment. And we want moral prohibitions. When we cry out, our infantile urges are actually seeking out the moral realm, they're searching for conscience. And that's a fascinating idea. It's not just something that a strawman aesthete would say.

> I prefer talking with children, with them one can still hope they may become rational beings; but those who have become that—Lord save us! (43)

You look at a child, and you have hope for them, *One day they're going to be rational*, but then you look at adult human beings, and rationality is a big turn off. A really rational person is a nerd, and they're robotic, or they're obsessional. And you say, *Good Lord!* So rationality is something we desire, prospectively. It's an ideal.

This is where the "free speech" thing comes in. Free speech is another idea we desired in the abstract, we desired as an ideal, but when it touches reality, when it touches the concrete, it leeches the vitality out of it. We don't like it, it seems to cancel out the concrete immediacy part of things, the thing that the aesthete is trying to hold onto, or in search of. So we mourn the loss of that. We look at a child misbehaving and being irrational, and we're like *Okay, I hope they grow up and mature.* But then, as adults, that vitality of the child is no longer there.

*From left: Wes, Seth, Mark & Dylan, Live at Brown University, October 27, 2016*

*Why can't you just grow up?*

## Readings

Hornby, Nick, *High Fidelity*, Riverhead Books, 1995.

Kierkegaard, Søren, *Either/Or: A Fragment of Life*, edited by Victor Ermita, translated by Alasdair Hannay, Penguin Classics, 1992.

Kierkegaard, Søren, *Fear and Trembling; Repetition*, edited by Howard V. and Edna H. Hong, Princeton University Press, 1983.

Percy, Walker, *The Moviegoer*, Vintage Books, 1961.

# Kierkegaard's Narrative

*2004, revised 2015 and 2024*

*Genevieve Arnold*

## Christopher Sunami

*Love him or not, Kierkegaard was a great writer—one of the true poet-philosophers. Given that, it's not such a surprise to discover his omnipresent influence on modern literature.*

*This essay first appeared, in somewhat different form, on my websites* Kitoba.com, Yes and Other Answers *and the* Pop Culture Philosopher.

*- Kitoba*

# Kierkegaard's Narrative

"Kierkegaard's Narrative" is an existential-humanist plot outline named after the Danish philosopher Søren Kierkegaard. In general, it runs as follows: An aimless young man drifts through life, obsessed with aesthetics, and seeking sexual fulfillment with a series of women, yet never making substantive choices or real commitments. The climax of the story is the protagonist's decision to commit to a single woman, and to enter into marriage.

The raw source material for this plotline is found in Kierkegaard's books *Either/Or* (1843), *Fear and Trembling* (1843), and *Repetition* (1843) in which he takes on the persona of various first-person narrators, and describes their experiences. Among the characters described are:

1. "The Aesthete," who is obsessed with art and aesthetic experience,

2. "The Seducer," who falls deeply in love with a woman and pursues her heatedly until he gets her, and then discards her for a new conquest, and

3. "The Repeater," who is caught up in past experiences, and the doomed hope of recreating them.

These characters are contrasted to a fourth, the "Married Man," who lives an existence that seems ordinary and mundane from the outside, but that is rich and fully lived on the inside.

American author Walker Percy was perhaps the first to weave these distinct personas together into a single coherent plotline. In his book *The Moviegoer* (1961), he traces the evolution of Binx Bolling, a protagonist who spends most of the book as an aesthete, obsessed with movies; a seducer, having carried on a series of affairs with his secretaries; and a "repeater," in constant search of his own past; but who finishes by taking a leap of faith into the life of a married man.

Percy also introduced an additional element for narrative interest, the death of a person close to the protagonist as a counterpoint to the protagonist's desire to fully embrace life. The book was widely admired, and the plotline passed into popular culture, where it became the foundation of a number of well-regarded books and movies.

The reason for the appeal of this narrative is that it speaks directly to the unique challenges of modern times. In a world of weakened traditions and societal demands, where individuality is elevated, and where culture and religion are matters of personal choice, many people have found themselves adrift in a sea of overwhelming options.

Traditional cultures may have been often oppressive and suffocating, but they provided a pre-established context, larger than the self, in relationship to which a life of significance and meaning could be built. In the absence of such a context, many people in real life take on the same series of attempts of establishing self-referenced meaning as described by Kierkegaard and Percy: They lose themselves in the pursuit of sexual and sensual pleasures, they dedicate their lives to the cultivation and appreciation of aesthetics, or they pursue a doomed attempt to recover an imagined idyllic past.

The transition from the arrested development of such pursuits into the mature life of the pair-bonded individual is particularly fraught with modern tensions, because in context of the weakening of the social pressures towards marriage, it represents an entirely voluntary surrender of a significant measure of personal freedom, individuality and identity.

The "Married Man" (or woman) can no longer be wholly selfish or self-indulgent. His new relationship takes on the position of centrality and preeminence in his life formerly held by devotion to his aesthetic or sensual passions. He is forced to embrace not only new responsibilities, but also the reality of his own mortality. To cross that threshold— in a world where you have the choice to not do so—requires what Kierkegaard termed a "leap of faith." *Kierkegaard's Narrative* promises us that what awaits us on the other side of that leap is the door to a new world, not to a prison, a world larger on the inside than on the outside.

It never made it into Percy's book, but Kierkegaard's writings do outline a further phase of personal development, in which one enters into relationship, not with another human being, but with God; a phase as much deeper, richer and more endlessly novel than the life of the married individual as the life of the married individual is deeper, richer and more novel than the life of the aesthete, seducer or repeater.

Even without the religious and spiritual dimension that was the ultimate foundation of Kierkegaard's work, the narrative he inspired continues to garner resonance and popularity among a wide audience wrestling with his characteristic existential themes. The book (and movie) of recent times that perhaps best exemplifies Kierkegaard's Narrative is Nick Hornby's "lad lit" classic, *High Fidelity* (1995, the title is a pun that juxtaposes good audio quality against sexual faithfulness). The story of a young, but not-as-young-as-he-once-was record-store owner, it was hugely popular among an audience of twenty- and thirty-something Generation Xers who could deeply identify with the protagonist.

Like Percy's "Binx," and Kierkegaard's "Aesthete," Hornby's main character Rob is deeply, passionately and compulsively dedicated to an aesthetic pursuit, which, in this case, is the collection, appreciation and occasional sale of classic vinyl records. His aesthetic orientation is so strong, he even claims that "what really matters is what you like, not what you are like," or in other words, that your aesthetic choices are your most important characteristics.

When he is dumped by his girlfriend Laura, who is transitioning into a mature adult, and who is frustrated by Rob's refusal to do the same, he attempts what amounts to a combination of Kierkegaard's concepts of repetitions and seduction, by pursuing a renewed connection with each one of his former girlfriends. Following the death of Laura's father, however, Rob realizes that what he most wants is not an exciting new sexual partner, the repetition of an old relationship, nor even a perfect collection of records, but rather the chance to marry Laura, and move forward with his life.

Few other books or movies embody the model to such a perfect extent, but echoes of the narrative abound in popular culture. The title character in the *40 Year Old Virgin* (2005) is a male, forty-year old virgin whose aesthetic obsession is action-figures. "Don Jon," from the movie of the same title (2013), is a young man whose aesthetic preoccupation is pornography. In the seventies cult classic, *Harold and Maude* (1971), Harold is a callow, but troubled youth obsessed with the aesthetics of suicide, and in the Northern California romp *Sideways* (2004), the protagonist Miles has an aesthetic fixation on wine that is indistinguishable from alcoholism. In the critically acclaimed *Silver Linings Playbook* (2012), the protagonist is trapped, not by aesthetics but by a repetition, the desire to reconnect with his ex-wife. In the Oscar-winning *American Beauty* (1999), Kierkegaard's three obsessions are combined uniquely into one, as the main character's attempts to repeat and recapture his lost youth are symbolized by a series of aesthetically striking fantasies about the seduction of a young girl. In each case, the main character has to make an existential choice to move beyond self-absorption and the tyranny of freedom in order to achieve genuine connection with another human being.

*Keels Photography*

# The Partially Examined Credo

 $W$ hat you see before you, *i.e.* me, is, admittedly, very awesomely partially examined, but I was not always this way.

I used to try to stretch myself to conform to codes of conduct and ideals of being foreign to my nature, like I tried not to swear at all for a bit when I was about 12... until I became very embarrassed about my saying "Gosh!" really loudly when punched in gym class.

I used to use my girlfriends in college exclusively as a sounding board for my hideous self-reflections, externalizing every little notion to cross my brain in an attempt to make myself an external clump, for the world to pick at like a carrion-hungry buzzard.

Why, one time I was caught midway between a watering hole and a big, juicy steak, and being unable to decide between them, just stood there contemplating the choice until I starved to death.

So I can confidently say that while the unexamined life may not be worth living, the constantly, strenuously, annoyingly examined life sucks!

But now—but now!—I can read and watch things that are dumb and not feel bad about it. I can put myself out there without being so self-conscious about how I can't actually fit all the caveats I would ideally like to into everything I say. I can, much like the Ramones, create explosive idiotic songs that are not meant to expose the entirety of my psyche, but only to repeat and elaborate a trope in a way that will resonate with, and hence extend, a mere tiny slice of my emotional life.

For I am *partially examined*, dammit, with enough reflection for me to know the foolishness that is me, without so much reflection so as to be unduly bothered by that.

But you, you sad sack sitting out there with *Being and Nothingness* under your pillow. You object of a voyeuristic God that not only sees right through your soul but commands that you do the same. You, that constantly needs to talk talk talk talk talk through all of your problems. I know you don't like it. I know it's hard. But there is hope.

I stand before you today as living proof that if you fail to try hard enough, you might just succeed. You too can have a partially examined life, with only some of your experiences spoiled by excessive reflection and omnipresent irony, with relationships that are only partially built on a narcissistic desire to expand your echo chamber, with some expectations undefined and some options not considered.

When you hear about someone living under a bridge, you don't have to imagine yourself what it would be like to live under such a bridge, and decide for a second that it would be cool, but then decide, no, of course it would not be. When you hear a new band that your friend likes, you don't have to go and listen to everything that band has ever recorded and wade into the music up to your eyeballs until you have an "insider's view," and only THEN dismiss them as actually pretty shitty. When you read a book, you can just read it, without stopping to write down your own philosophical musings, inspired by the sentence you were just reading, but in fact only tangentially related to it. When someone calls you untalented, you can just say "screw off!" instead of asking follow-up questions about WHY the person thinks you're untalented and, when you don't get clear enough answers, making up a lot of answers yourself and then dwelling on them for months afterward.

*No*, I say, *there is hope.* By just mostly giving up and not worrying about it, you can, like me, slowly become a more nearly tolerable person to be around, who doesn't drive himself absolutely batshit for no reason. With just a touch of philosophy (and just a touch, now!) and some good old fashioned elbow-grease or some other meaningless cliché that you don't think about enough to edit out of your inspirational speech, you too can, like me, have the Partially Examined Life.

*- Mark, 2010*

# Epilogue

*Continued from* Episode 64:

**Mark:**

I don't want to be mean to him because he's not famous. This guy is basically one of us, in that he is not a former academic but yet he's a smart guy, went to Cambridge, got a book deal and did all this research.

**Wes:**

It annoyed the shit out of me. It has a lot of the flaws that you see in the types of books published today. There's a lot of free-floating speculation and he told a lot of stories. That's a popular thing to do today, but it's not one that interests me—people who load up their books with anecdotes, whether it's from Homer's *Odyssey* and *Iliad,* or whatever. It doesn't make it better, just because your anecdotes come from the classics.

**Mark:**

My general take on these kinds of attempts to make the culture accessible is "Great." I'm all for people trying to think about things. This is so much better to be reading something like this and to be writing something like this than to be reading the latest trashy romance novel or whatever the alternative is.

But I know you've come down as the opposite, that actually maybe these things are harming real scholarship. It's like watching *Xena* to learn about Greek history.

**Wes:**

They're trying to obtain unwarranted celebrity from these types of books so I think that's where they go wrong.

## Oh, the irony...

**Mark:**

So, aren't we guilty of the same thing? We're not producing dynamite original work.

**Wes:**

But I think we're trying to be precise. We're doing the best we can to be accurate and precise.

**Mark:**

I'm sure Payne was doing the same thing. He was doing the best he could.

**Seth:**

Lucy, this is a hot button topic for us right now because we're trying to pull a book together. So, how do we go about doing that without selling ourselves out?

**Wes:**

I'm all for selling out.

**Mark:**

There you go.

Christopher "Kitoba" Sunami (he/his) is a philosopher, programmer, composer and organizer from Columbus, Ohio. He is the author of the socially progressive Christian devotional *Hero For Christ,* and the critically acclaimed picture book *How the Fisherman Tricked the Genie.* He is descended maternally from mixed-race Revolutionary War soldier Bazabeel Norman (and from Tuskegee Airman Major Henry A. Norman), and paternally from pioneering art-photographer Soichi Sunami. He is married to artist April Sunami. He is a graduate of Columbus Alternative High School, Swarthmore College and *The* Ohio State University.

角南祈祷場

*Keels Photography*

*I would like to thank God, as well as the amazing* Partially Examined Life *podcasters. Special thanks to Wes, who brought me into the family, and to Mark, who built not only the house but much of the furniture. Thanks also to Seth and Dylan, whose brilliance and humanity shines through their words. Thanks to the* PEL *listeners, the best fanbase in philosophy—there's no way any of this could have happened without you. Thanks to our advance readers, especially Tammy Gottschling for volunteer proof-reading.*

*Thanks to my parents, who were my first philosophy teachers, and to Professor Schuldenfrei, my own personal Socrates. Shout-outs as well to Professors Mitchell, Petrik, Hoy, Errante, Erlich and Zucker for their mind-expanding teaching and kind mentorship.*

*Thanks to my wife April, who once described life with me as "a philosophy meetup every day of the week." She's an amazing artist, so check out her work on instagram @ajsunami. Dedicated to my children River and Ella, who I am fully convinced will be world-changing philosophers some day.*

*One final shoutout, to my "co-author" Lucy Lawless, in honor of the year of my life where* Xena: Warrior Princess *was the only thing that got me through.*

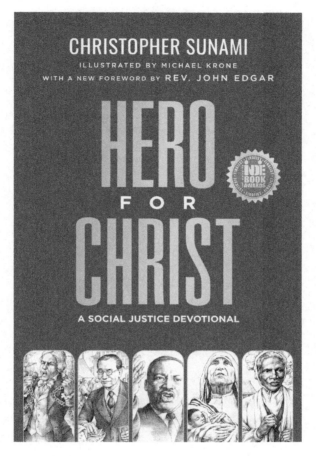

*Finalist, best religious non-fiction, the Indie Book Awards*

"*Hero For Christ* provides profound inspiration and practical spiritual guidance for Christians who want to put into practice creation-care."

*Rev. Jim Ball,* The Evangelical Environmental Network

"*Hero For Christ* speaks to issues of importance to Christians of all races, and is a great resource for devotional and reflective reading."

*Rev. Luis Cortés, Jr.* Esperanza USA

*kitobabooks.com*

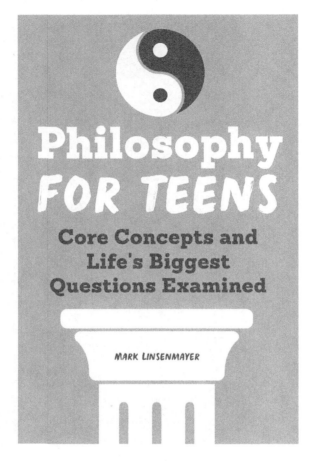

*Rockridge Press, 2022*

"Linsenmayer arms children with deeper understanding and a highly accessible survey of the historic sweep of philosophy."

*- Drew Pinsky, MD*

"Especially notable and admirable for its inclusion of many non-Western thinkers."

*- Peter Adamson, author*

*You can also find Mark's 10+ albums of music at* marklint.com

Printed in Great Britain
by Amazon

42944867R00195